Corporate Law in the Netherlands

Dutch Business Law

The series Dutch Business Law is a continuous publication in loose-leaf form under the editorial supervision of Steven R. Schuit, a former partner of Allen & Overy and professor of law at Utrecht University and at Nyenrode Business Universiteit.

This current publication is a bound edition of the series previously published in loose-leaf form.

The purpose of Dutch Business Law is to provide a good understanding of the practical implications of the relevant areas in Dutch law under consideration. The authors are seasoned practitioners, experienced in representing international clients in the Dutch legal arena.

This series makes no pretence at being a survey of the entire Dutch business law – either in scope or in substance. It contains generalisations and simplifications and cannot be regarded as presenting complete and in depth advice in the areas covered.

Corporate Law in the Netherlands

Revised and updated by

Maarten H. Muller (Ed.)

Partner at Allen & Overy Amsterdam

Wolters Kluwer
Law & Business

Published by:
Kluwer Law International
P.O. Box 85889
2508 CN The Hague
The Netherlands
E-mail: sales@kluwerlaw.com
Website: http://www.kluwerlaw.com

Sold and distributed in North, Central and South America by:
Aspen Publishers, Inc.
7201 McKinney Circle
Frederick, MD 21704
USA
E-mail: customer.service@aspenpublishers.com

Sold and distributed in all other countries by:
Extenza-Turpin Distribution Services
Stratton Business Park
Pegasus Drive
Biggleswade
Bedfordshire SG18 8TQ
United Kingdom
E-mail: kluwerlaw@turpin-distribution.com

Printed on acid-free paper.

ISBN 978-90-411-2864-5

Printed and Bound by CPI Group (UK) Ltd, Croydon, CR0 4YY

Foreword

Corporate Law in the Netherlands provides a practical and comprehensive guide for all foreign lawyers, businesses and individuals involved in dealing with Dutch corporate entities. Its aim is also to be a resource for Dutch lawyers who wish to advise their English-speaking clients on Dutch corporate law.

Corporate law in general brings together the principal players in the business world. However, the differences in the law per country can be significant, including within Europe. Even more important are the variations in the practice of dealing with corporate law issues, often a reflection of the relevant national and corporate cultures. Dutch corporate culture can be characterised by an open mind for new business and legal requirements, which also stems from the experience of other countries, as is demonstrated by the many references that Dutch courts make to developments elsewhere. It is also characterised by a strong regard for fairness, not only by way of statutory provisions, but also with respect to the interpretation and enforcement of corporate resolutions or contracts and by the legally required orientation of the boards on the interests of all stakeholders, sometimes to the detriment of shareholders' interests.

This book was first written in 1978. The last update was in 2002, some time ago. Maarten Muller undertook the current complete revision. This book covers both public companies (NVs) and private companies (BVs). Due to recent legislation, the law for private companies has changed substantially. This new updated version will accommodate the many users of earlier editions.

Steven R. Schuit
(steven.schuit@allenovery.com)

Selected Websites

Netherlands Authority for the Financial Markets

www.afm.nl
Information and legislation regarding the financial market sector; databases for licenses and notifications

Confederation of Netherlands Industry and Employers (VNO-NCW)

www.vno-ncw.nl

Corporate Governance

www.commissiecorporategovernance.nl
Dutch Corporate Governance Code Monitoring Committee
www.ecgi.org/codes/index.php
All European corporate governance codes and principles

De Nederlandsche Bank

www.dnb.nl
Dutch Central Bank; supervision and policies

European Union

www.ec.europa.eu/internal_market/company/index_en.htm
Directives, regulations and other official acts, consultation documents, links regarding company law

Netherlands Foreign Investment Agency

www.nfia.nl
First port of call for foreign companies wishing to establish their business in the Netherlands

NL Agency (Ministry of Economic Affairs)

www.agentschapnl.nl/en
Contact point for businesses for advice, financing, networking and regulatory matters

NYSE Euronext (Stock Exchange)

https://europeanequities.nyx.com
Indices; market and listing rules

Socio-Economic Council (SER)

www.ser.nl
Tasks; labour market advice, including explanation of 'Dutch Polder Model'

Table of Contents

Chapter 2
Legal Business Forms 13

Preface

This book was originally written by Steven R. Schuit, a former partner of Allen & Overy, to provide business executives, bankers, accountants and lawyers from other jurisdictions with an understanding of the intricacies of Netherlands corporate law.

Various chapters of the book have been revised and updated with the help of colleagues at Allen & Overy Amsterdam: Gerbrand Visser (Chapters 3 and 12); Joyce Leemrijse (Chapter 5), Günther Rensen (Chapters 2, 4, 9 and 11) and Richard de Haan (Chapter 10). Chapter 13 (Works Councils) has been written by Leonard Verburg.

I would like to thank Joanna Jonker Roelants, Caroline Obenhuijsen and Liselotte Heijckmann for their overall drafting assistance.

This book incorporates the recent changes brought about by the modernisation of BV law (introducing the so-called '*Flex BV*'). It also incorporates the new provisions on management and supervision of companies ('*Wet Bestuur en Toezicht*') which, among others, introduce the one-tier board and provide new rules for conflicts of interest of board members. These provisions came into force on 1 January 2013. The same is true for recent changes to the enquiry proceedings.

This book inevitably contains generalisations and should not be considered a substitute for legal advice in any particular circumstances.

This book states the law as of 1 January 2013.

Maarten H. Muller
(maarten.muller@allenovery.com)

Chapter 1
Introduction

1.1 General

During the last four decades Netherlands law concerning businesses and companies has changed dramatically, sometimes developing characteristics unknown in other countries.

The emphasis in legislative drafting during the first three decades of this period was on fostering the interests of both employees and creditors. This higher degree of protection was achieved by reducing the power of shareholders (see Chapter 8), improving disclosure to creditors and to the public in general (see Chapter 12), adopting strict rules concerning capitalisation (see Chapter 4) and imposing liability on founders and directors in cases of corporate abuse (see Chapter 9). In the last decade there has been more emphasis on the rights of shareholders, which has led to certain changes in the law (see Chapters 7 and 8).

Although these developments are most noticeable in the context of companies, they have also left their mark on unincorporated businesses and branch offices of foreign companies.[1]

This book describes the laws concerning incorporated and unincorporated businesses. Banks, securities and investment operations as well as insurance companies are covered by special legislation that is not discussed here. Matters concerning accounting and financial reporting are only briefly described.

The principal source of legislation concerning legal entities is Book 2 of the Dutch Civil Code. This is mandatory law it cannot be deviated from, save otherwise provided by law.

Particular rules may apply to any specific business that a company may carry on.[2] For listed Dutch companies special rules will apply.[3]

---

1. Most notably with respect to provisions in the WOR, the Wfbv, and the HrW 2007, that apply to these entities.
2. Reference is made to the contribution of Jennen on banking regulation in: Jennen & Van de Vijver 2010.
3. Reference is made to the contribution of Van de Vijver on securities regulation in: Jennen & Van de Vijver 2010.

1.2 Corporate Governance

One of the distinct characteristics of Dutch corporate law has always been a two-tier management structure comprising a management board and a supervisory board (see § 8.1.1). As from 1 January 2013 it will, however, also be possible for companies to have a one-tier board.[4] This also applies to companies which qualify as 'large' companies. A 'large' company is required to have a supervisory board or may in the future have a one-tier board containing one or more non-executive directors. To these 'large' companies a special set of mandatory rules, the 'large company rules', apply. These rules will apply to a company which has made the required registration to that effect and subsequently, for a consecutive period of three years, meets the test criteria of equity in excess of EUR 16 million, establishment of a works council as imposed by law and with 100 or more employees in the Netherlands.[5] Under this mandatory two-tier structure the supervisory board has (or as from 1 January 2013 the non-executives will have) far-reaching powers, superseding to some extent those of the shareholders and the management board (see § 8.2). Companies which do not qualify as 'large' companies have an option: their articles of association may or may not provide that the company has a supervisory board.

A works council is a representative body of employees which is mandatory for companies with 50 or more employees in the Netherlands (see § 13.1). On the basis of its statutory powers, a works council may exercise considerable influence on management decisions in such areas as mergers, acquisitions and joint ventures, investments, split-ups and divestitures.[6]

These characteristics emanate from a social and economic environment that has accepted the notion that the management board is, in principle, not subordinate to the shareholders,[7] and may under certain circumstances even be allowed to take positions that are not in the best interests of shareholders.[8] The management board must protect the 'interests of the company',[9] which may include the interests of shareholders, employees, the group (see § 3.1.2)[10] and,

4. See Act on Management and Supervision (*Wet Bestuur en toezicht*), Stb. 2011, 275.
5. See § 8.1.2 for a more detailed description regarding 'large' companies.
6. See Chapter 13.
7. Supreme Court 21 Jan. 1955, NJ 1959, 43 (*Forumbank*).
8. Asser/Maeijer, Van Solinge & Nieuwe Weme 2-II* 2009/413.
9. See Art. 2:129(5)/239(5) BW. The 'interests' of the company are often defined in terms of its continued existence and growth, and thus its profitability. See Asser/Maeijer, Van Solinge & Nieuwe Weme 2-II* 2009/394.
10. Enterprise Court 13 Mar. 2003, NJ 2003, 248 (*Corus*); Enterprise Court 11 Mar. 1982, NJ 1983, 30.

according to certain legal commentators, the company's business relations, as well as certain basic societal interests.[11]

If a company qualifies as a 'large' company, this may result in reduced power for the shareholders, which is particularly noticeable in relation to the appointment of managing directors. The managing directors of companies which do not qualify as 'large' companies are appointed by the shareholders' meeting; while for 'large' companies the management board is appointed by the supervisory board.[12] The latter, however, does not apply to companies which are majority owned by a company of which the majority of the employees is employed outside the Netherlands.[13] Members of the supervisory board are appointed by the shareholders' meeting upon nomination by the supervisory board. The shareholders' meeting may refuse such appointment by a simple majority vote, representing at least one third of the issued share capital. Shareholders and the works council can make recommendations for such appointments. For one third of the number of members of the supervisory board/the group of non-executive directors, the supervisory board/the group of non-executive directors should follow the recommendation of the works council in its nomination to the shareholders' meeting. If the supervisory board/the group of non-executive directors wants to reject a recommendation made by the works council, if it is of the opinion that the candidate is not suitable for appointment as a member of the supervisory board/the group of non-executive directors or that the appointment would cause the supervisory board not to be 'properly constituted', it needs to file a request to the Enterprise Court to validate its objections (see § 8.3.3.2).

As from 1 January 2004 a *Corporate Governance Code* (Dutch Corporate Governance Code) (CGC) has been in force, which is applicable for all companies whose registered office is in the Netherlands and whose shares are listed on a regulated stock exchange and to all large companies (with a total balance of more than EUR 500 million) whose shares are traded on a multilateral trading facility.

As in most countries, the CGC is based on the principle 'comply or explain'. The listed companies are by law obliged to report on their compliance with the CGC in their annual report and if necessary to explain why any of the provisions have not been complied with.

The CGC contains provisions on the role, constitution and remuneration of the management board and the supervisory board. The CGC furthermore contains provisions in relation to conflict of interests, the role of committees of the supervisory board, the relationship with shareholders and the external

11. Asser/Maeijer, Van Solinge & Nieuwe Weme 2-II* 2009/394.
12. Art. 2:162/272 BW.
13. Art. 2:155/265 BW.

accountant. The last revision to the CGC was made in December 2008 by the Monitoring Committee Corporate Governance Code. The main adjustments were in the areas of risk management, executive pay, shareholder responsibility, diversity in the composition of the supervisory board and corporate social responsibility. The role of the supervisory board has been strengthened, for example in relation to takeover bids. A response time has also been introduced to give the management board the opportunity to give due consideration to all interests when confronted with a shareholder proposing a different strategy.

Although the CGC, strictly speaking, applies to listed companies, it influences the best practice of other companies and the relationships between the various corporate bodies.[14]

1.3 EU Harmonisation of Company Law

Many changes in corporate law can be attributed to the European Union. The TFEU provides for the progressive harmonisation of the economic policies of member states in order to promote the proper functioning of the internal market.[15] This includes the harmonisation of company law. Furthermore, the TFEU aims to abolish obstacles to the free movement of goods, persons, services and capital between member states.[16]

An important principle embodied in the TFEU is the right of establishment. Under this principle, nationals of member states have the freedom to establish themselves in the territory of other member states under the same conditions that apply to the nationals of the host country.[17] This includes the right to pursue activities as self-employed persons, set up branch offices, incorporate companies and carry on business according to the host country's law.[18] Member states are bound to eliminate any existing restrictions and refrain from introducing new restrictions on the freedom of services or the right of establishment.[19]

Companies may prefer to establish themselves in the member state with the most favourable company law. The divergence of company laws in different member states is acknowledged by the TFEU, which provides the legal

14. As from 1 January 2010 the Banking Code came into effect, and as from 1 January 2011 the Governance Principles for the insurance industry came into effect. Both codes provide specific governance principles for the relevant industries.
15. Art. 26(1) TFEU.
16. Art. 26(2) TFEU, Part Three Title II, IV TFEU.
17. Art. 49 TFEU, CJEU 9 Mar. 1999, JOR 1999, 117.
18. Arts 49, 54 TFEU (the term 'companies' shall mean companies under civil or commercial law, including co-operative companies, and other legal persons under public or private law, with the exception of non-profit-making companies).
19. Arts 49, 56 TFEU.

basis for the harmonisation of company law. European Union institutions are responsible for the harmonisation of company law 'by co-ordinating to the necessary extent the safeguards which, for the protection of the interests of members and others, are required by member states of companies or firms with a view to making such safeguards equivalent throughout the Union'.[20] Furthermore, certain regulations are based on Arts 114 and 115 of the TFEU which call for directives on the harmonisation of statutory and administrative law provisions in the member states that have direct influence on the establishment and operation of the internal market.

Harmonisation is realised by way of directives, treaties and regulations which approximate the company laws of the member states and try to mitigate important differences between them.

A directive must be implemented by national legislation by all member states, by way of introduction or adoption of national statutes within a prescribed period.[21] Individuals may rely on the directive to have incompatible national legislation overruled, if a member state fails to implement a directive on time or does so incorrectly.[22]

Regulations constitute a truly uniform European company law and represent a new European legal regime.[23] Rather than requiring implementation by national legislatures, a regulation has direct effect, i.e. it gives rise to rights which private parties may enforce before national courts.[24]

The first directive on corporate law was established in 1968. Various directives on corporate law have followed since then. The directives are primarily aimed at public companies (*naamloze vennootschappen*), but some are partially or wholly applicable to private companies (*besloten vennootschappen*).

1.3.1 The First Directive

The First Directive[25] provides that certain information on the internal governance of companies must be made available to the public through public registers and national gazettes. The information includes the articles of association, names of the board members and the corporate agents, subscribed capital and,

20. Art. 50(2)(g) TFEU.
21. Art. 288 TFEU: 'A directive shall be binding, as to the result to be achieved, upon each member state to which it is addressed, but shall leave to the national authorities the choice of form and methods'.
22. CJEU 19 Jan. 1982, C-8/81, ECR 1982, 53 (*Becker*).
23. Art. 288 TFEU 'A regulation shall have general application. It shall be binding in its entirety and directly applicable in all member states'.
24. A regulation can be considered as 'self-executing'. See CJEU 5 Feb. 1963, C-26/62, ECR 1963, 3 (*Van Gend en Loos*).
25. Directive No. 2009/101, O.J. EUR. COMM. (No. L258) 11 (2009), as amended.

in the case of public companies, the annual financial results. This directive has been implemented in Netherlands law.

1.3.2 The Second Directive

The Second Directive[26] provides that companies must disclose some elementary corporate information of the various bodies of the company and provides safeguards for the maintenance of capital (such as minimum share capital and financial assistance). The Netherlands has implemented this directive.

1.3.3 The Third Directive

The Third Directive[27] deals with statutory mergers of public limited liability companies within a member state. This directive provides for the protection of the interests of shareholders, creditors and employees. In a statutory merger the assets and liabilities of the acquired company (the so-called 'disappearing' company) are transferred to the acquiring company (the so-called 'surviving' company) by operation of law (see § 11.3.1). The shareholders of both the acquiring and the acquired company receive a proportional interest in the merged company. This directive has been implemented in the Netherlands. The directive helped to pave the way for cross-border mergers, provided for in the Tenth Directive (see § 1.3.10).

1.3.4 The Fourth Directive

The Fourth Directive[28] contains detailed requirements for the preparation of balance sheets, profit and loss statements and annual reports. This directive applies to both private and public companies. Special accounting rules apply to banks and insurance companies.[29] Certain small and medium-sized companies specified in national legislation are exempt from the most stringent publication requirements. This directive has been implemented in the Netherlands.

26. Directive No. 2012/30, O.J. EUR. COMM. (No. L315) 74 (2012).
27. Directive No. 2011/35, O.J. EUR. COMM. (No. L110) 1 (2011).
28. Fourth Council Directive No. 78/660, O.J. EUR. COMM. (No. L222) 11 (1978), as amended.
29. For the rules concerning accounts of banks and other financial institutions, see Directive No. 86/635, O.J. EUR. COMM. (No. L372) 1 (1986), as amended. For the rules concerning accounts of insurance companies, see Directive No. 91/674, O.J. EUR. COMM. (No. L374) 7 (1991), as amended. These directives have been implemented into Netherlands law.

1.3.5 The Proposal for a Fifth Directive

The proposal for a Fifth Directive deals with the structure and administration of public companies and the powers and obligations of their corporate bodies. If the directive were to be enacted in its current form, it would have a significant impact on Netherlands corporate law.[30] However, there has been Europe-wide opposition to this proposal since it was first drafted in 1972.

1.3.6 The Sixth Directive

The Sixth Directive[31] covers the divisions of public companies in which all assets and liabilities are transferred by operation of law to two or more companies in exchange for shares in the recipient companies. This directive has been implemented in the Netherlands. The statute will be applicable to all legal persons. By implementing this directive, a mirror of the statutory merger (see § 11.3) has been introduced, offering a relatively straightforward procedure for the restructuring of businesses and for structuring joint ventures.

1.3.7 The Seventh Directive

The Seventh Directive[32] deals with consolidated annual accounts for groups of companies. This directive complements the Fourth Directive concerning individual company accounts. Since 1 January 1990, all groups of companies established within the European Union must prepare consolidated annual accounts. This directive has been implemented in the Netherlands.

1.3.8 The Eighth Directive

The Eight Directive 2006/43[33] contains minimum requirements for the educational and professional qualifications of auditors and requires member states to ensure the independence of such auditors. Netherlands law is in conformity with this directive.

---

30. The proposal O.J. EUR. COMM. (No. C131) 49 (1972) as amended, in its current form limits the issuance of protective preference shares (see § 5.2.2) to 50 % of the issued capital and prohibits, *inter alia*, limitations on voting rights with respect to ordinary shares (see § 7.3), and qualified majorities for ballots to appoint or remove managing directors or supervisory directors (the latter prohibition would only apply to public limited companies where these rights accrue to the shareholders, i.e. not to 'large' NVs (see § 8.3.3.5).
31. Sixth Council Directive No. 82/891, O.J. EUR. COMM. (No. L378) 47 (1982), as amended.
32. Seventh Council Directive No. 83/349, O.J. EUR. COMM. (No. L193) 1 (1983), as amended.
33. Directive No. 2006/43, O.J. EUR. COMM. (No. L157) 87 (2006), as amended.

1.3.9 The Draft Proposal for a Ninth Directive

The draft proposal for a Ninth Directive[34] aims to create a legal structure for the unified management of a public limited liability company which is controlled by another company. Such group could be formed by a 'control contract' or by a 'unilateral declaration of control'. This directive would protect creditors of a company that is subordinate to its parent by introducing liability of the parent for the debts of its subsidiaries. In 2003 the Commission expressed that there is no need to revive the draft Ninth Directive on group relations.[35]

1.3.10 The Tenth Directive

The Tenth Directive[36] aims to remove difficulties in realising a cross-border merger of companies established in member states and tries to avoid 'forum-shopping', i.e. cross-border mergers in one member state in order to avoid certain mandatory laws in another member state.[37] This directive has been implemented in the Netherlands.

1.3.11 The Eleventh Directive

The Eleventh Directive[38] limits the information to be disclosed by branches of companies. A branch only needs to disclose basic information, such as its name, address and activities, as well as the name of its parent company. This directive permits a branch to submit consolidated annual accounts and annual reports rather than its own accounts, as long as they are prepared in accordance with the Fourth and Seventh Directives (see §§ 1.3.4 and 1.3.7). Netherlands law is in conformity with this directive.

---

34. A preliminary draft for a proposal was circulated informally to the member states in December 1984 for consultation. The consultation showed that there was very little support for such a comprehensive framework on group law.
35. See the Communication from the Commission to the Council and the European Parliament on Modernising Company Law and Enhancing Corporate Governance in the European Union – A Plan to Move Forward, COM (2003) 284.
36. Directive No. 2005/56, O.J. EUR. COMM. (No. L310) 1 (2005), as amended.
37. The Tenth Directive provides, *inter alia*, for minimum requirements with respect to employee participation, provisions with respect to the supervision of mergers and publication requirements.
38. Eleventh Council Directive No. 89/666, O.J. EUR. COMM. (No. L395) 36 (1989), as amended.

1.3.12 The Twelfth Directive

The Twelfth Directive[39] ensures the legal recognition of single-member private limited liability companies throughout the European Union. This directive is intended both to protect third parties dealing with such companies and to encourage sole proprietors to incorporate. Netherlands law is in conformity with this directive.

1.3.13 The Thirteenth Directive

The Thirteenth Directive[40] contains provisions relating to public bids. This directive applies to companies which are wholly or partly listed on an official stock exchange in the European Union. Member states are obliged to designate a supervisory authority which would be empowered to supervise compliance with the takeover rules. This directive has been implemented in the Netherlands.

1.3.14 The Regulation concerning the European Company

The Regulation concerning the European Company[41] provides a statute for a public limited liability European company ('*Societas Europaea*' or SE) (together with a complementary directive on the role of its employees[42]). This regulation intends to offer companies in the European Union the opportunity to form a new corporate entity for cross-border co-operation. The SE will in many respects be governed by national legislation. It will be possible to transfer its seat from one member state to another.

The purpose of the SE is to enable companies established in various member states to merge cross-border or to establish a cross-border joint venture company. For that purpose, an SE may be established as a newly incorporated SE or an existing NV may be converted into an SE. This regulation has been implemented in the Netherlands.

1.3.15 The European Co-operative Company

The Regulation concerning the creation of the European Co-operative Company (SCE)[43] has been implemented into Netherlands law by a separate statute

39. Directive No. 2009/102, O.J. EUR. COMM. (No. L258) 20 (2009).
40. Directive No. 2004/25, O.J. EUR. COMM. (No. L142) 12 (2004), as amended.
41. Council Regulation No. 2157/2001, O.J. EUR. COMM. (No. L294) 1 (2001), as amended.
42. Directive No. 2001/86. O.J. EUR. COMM. (No. L294) 22 (2001).
43. Council Regulation No. 1435/2003, O.J. EUR. COMM. (No. L207) 1 (2003).

which came into force on 13 October 2006.[44] The position of employees of an SCE is governed by a separate EU Directive that is implemented into Netherlands law by an act that also came into force on 13 October 2006.[45]

The legal framework regarding SCEs is based on that of SEs and thus very similar. This also means that an SCE is governed by European law as well as the law of the state where it has its registered office (*statutaire zetel*).

The purpose of the SCE is to enable co-operatives established in various member states to merge cross-border or to jointly establish a cross-border co-operative. For that purpose, an SCE may be established as a newly incorporated SCE or an existing co-operative may be converted into an SCE. See further § 2.5.5.

1.3.16 The Regulation on the European Economic Interest Grouping

The Regulation on the European Economic Interest Grouping (EEIG)[46] took effect on 1 July 1989, and provides for a new separate legal person capable of cross-border co-operation in different member states. An EEIG (*'Europees Economisch Samenwerkingsverband'*) may be formed by two or more companies based in the European Union and is analogous to a joint venture in the way it is managed by its members. An EEIG is formed through the execution of a contract or notarial deed that is then registered in the member state in which it maintains its head office. The EEIG's purpose must be to facilitate and develop its members' economic activities, rather than to pursue its own separate activities. This directive has been implemented in the Netherlands (see § 2.5.3).

1.3.17 The Directive for the European Works Council

The Directive for the European Works Council[47] applies to companies or groups of companies in the member states (which for the purpose of this directive is defined to include Norway, Iceland and Liechtenstein) with 1,000 or more employees of whom 150 or more are employed in two different member states. This directive encourages such company or group of companies to

44. *Uitvoeringswet verordening Europese coöperatieve vennootschap*, Act of 14 September 2006, Stb. 2006, 425.
45. *Wet houdende wijziging van de Wet rol werknemers bij de Europese vennootschap in verband met de uitvoering van richtlijn nr. 2003/72/EG van de Raad van de Europese Unie van 22 juli 2003 tot aanvulling van het statuut van een Europese coöperatieve vennootschap met betrekking tot de rol van werknemers (Wet wijziging uitvoeringswet rol werknemers Europese coöperatieve vennootschap)*, Act of 5 July 2006, Stb. 2006, 361.
46. Council Regulation No. 2137/85, O.J. EUR. COMM. (No. L199) 1 (1985), as amended.
47. Directive No. 2009/38, O.J. EUR. COMM. (No. L122) 28 (2009).

negotiate with the employees' representatives as to how its information and consultation obligations should be fulfilled. This directive has been implemented in the Netherlands (see § 13.3).

1.3.18 Other Relevant Directives

Other relevant directives are the Transparency Directive,[48] which regulates the information that must be published on a yearly, half-yearly and quarterly basis by listed companies and provides for an obligation to disclose holdings in listed companies, and the Directive on certain rights for shareholders in listed companies, which contains rules or procedures for convening general meetings of shareholders.[49]

48. Council Directive No. 2004/109, O.J. EUR. COMM. (No. L390) 38 (2004), as amended.
49. Council Directive No. 2007/36, O.J. EUR. COMM. (No. L184) 17 (2007).

Chapter 2
Legal Business Forms

2.1 General

2.1.1 Foreign or Dutch Corporate Law

Any individual, partnership or company, whether Dutch or foreign, resident or non-resident, can conduct business in the Netherlands without being required to adopt a particular legal form. However, a foreign legal entity may be required to comply with certain rules of Dutch company law if it qualifies as a formal foreign entity (see § 2.2.1). The foreign owner must therefore first determine whether it wants the business in the Netherlands to be conducted through a Dutch legal entity, a partnership or a branch (*filiaal*) of the foreign business.

2.1.2 Representative Office

Many foreign business organisations are represented in the Netherlands by an agent. If that agent is operating from within that foreign organisation, it may keep its representative offices in the form of a Dutch branch of that foreign organisation (see § 2.2) or adopt a Dutch corporate form, usually a BV (see § 3.2.1). The choice is highly dependent on the nature of the business, the agent's tax position and the tax status that the foreign organisation is willing to accept in the Netherlands.

2.1.3 Legal Entities

In order to qualify as a Dutch legal entity, a legal entity must be incorporated under the laws of the Netherlands (see § 3.3.2) and must have its statutory seat in the Netherlands. It is not required to have its head office or any business in the Netherlands. This is because the Netherlands applies the incorporation principle, and not the 'real seat theory' which prevails in certain other European countries.

The law stipulates which private legal forms have legal personality, i.e. can be called a 'legal entity': associations (*verenigingen*), co-operatives (*coöperaties*), mutual insurance associations (*onderlinge waarborgmaatschappijen*), foundations (*stichtingen*) and companies (*NVs* and *BVs*).[50] Next to these legal entities the following European business forms can also have their statutory seat in the Netherlands and are legal entities: European Economic Interest Groupings,[51] European Companies (SE)[52] and European Co-operative Companies (SCE).[53] A Dutch legal entity has its domicile at its statutory seat, i.e. the seat of the entity as provided for in its articles.[54] Apart from the association with limited legal capacity (see § 2.5.1.1), the SE and the SCE, a legal entity is established by a deed executed by a Dutch civil law notary. General and limited partnerships created under the laws of the Netherlands have no legal personality.[55] A legal entity is (in respect of the laws of property, contract, tort and succession) equivalent to a natural person, unless the law stipulates otherwise.[56] A legal entity formed under the laws of the Netherlands can have its principal place of business outside the Netherlands. Netherlands law recognises the existence of foreign legal entities which are governed by foreign law.[57] In this book, certain aspects of legal entities are described in the context of Netherlands corporate law only.

The company-type legal forms, the NV and the BV, are described in Chapter 3 and the other legal business forms are described in this chapter.

2.2 Branch Office of a Foreign Company

2.2.1 General

If a foreign individual or legal entity or its Dutch business has not adopted a Dutch legal form, the Dutch business will be treated as part of the foreign owner's assets and liabilities. These liabilities include all responsibilities and obligations of that business which may arise under Netherlands law.

If the Dutch business is wholly owned by a non-resident foreign legal entity, it is considered a branch office (*filiaal* or *nevenvestiging*). In the event that a foreign legal entity with capital divided into shares operates its business entirely or almost entirely in the Netherlands, while this business has no real

50. Art. 2:3 BW.
51. Art. 1(3) European Council Regulation Nr. 2137/1985 in conjunction with Art. 3(1) *Uitvoeringswet EESV Verordening*, Act of 28 June 1989, Stb. 1989, 245.
52. Art. 1(3) European Council Regulation Nr. 2157/2001.
53. Art. 1(5) European Council Regulation Nr. 1435/2003.
54. Art. 1:10 BW.
55. See §§ 2.4.2.1 and 2.4.3.1.
56. Art. 2:5 BW.
57. Art. 10:118 BW.

connection with the state under which laws it is incorporated, this entity qualifies as a formal foreign entity as defined in the Wfbv.[58]

If a foreign entity qualifies as a formal foreign entity, its managing directors must file with the Dutch commercial register:

(a) an official copy of the deed of incorporation and the articles;
(b) the registration details of its place of incorporation;
(c) if the shares are held by one person or entity, information about this single shareholder; and
(d) each year, a proof of registration with its original commercial register.

The qualifying formal foreign entity is under the same obligation as Dutch companies with respect to orderly bookkeeping and has to comply with the mandatory provisions regarding the preparation and form of annual accounts and reports. The management board of the qualifying foreign entity must prepare the annual accounts within five months following the end of a financial year, and shall file these accounts with the commercial register within 13 months following the end of the financial year.

Case law of the CJEU regarding the freedom of establishment, led to a change of the Wfbv in 2005,[59] which limited its original scope. It was amended in such a way that only one provision of the Wfbv (Art. 6, regarding liability of directors) applies to companies incorporated within a member state of the EU or within the European Economic Area. The Wfbv fully applies to companies incorporated outside the European Union or European Economic Area.

Managing directors of qualifying foreign entities may be held liable in the same way as Dutch managing directors in the event of improper filings and publication of misleading financial figures (see Chapter 9). Branch managers of qualifying legal entities may be held equally liable as managing directors.

A business in the Netherlands can also be jointly owned by two or more legal entities or individuals and be established under foreign law. These joint ventures frequently take the form of a general or limited partnership (see § 2.4). The directors of the foreign legal entity and the persons in charge of the business operations in the Netherlands may also be liable for 'apparent negligence' in the event of a bankruptcy in the Netherlands (see §§ 9.2 and 9.4)[60] if the legal entity is subject to Dutch corporate income tax.

58. In force as per 1 January 1998, Stb. 1997, 697.
59. Act of 28 April 2005, Stb. 2005, 230.
60. Art. 10:121(1) BW; Asser/Maeijer,Van Solinge & Nieuwe Weme 2-II* 2009/457.

2.2.2 Power to Represent the Branch Office

The power to represent a foreign company is subject to the laws of the country of incorporation. The HrW 2007 and the implementing HrB 2008, however, require the branch office of a foreign company, whether or not it qualifies as a formal foreign entity under the Wfbv, to register with the Dutch commercial register (see Chapter 12). The information registered is binding upon the foreign company, even if the registered data is in conflict with the charter or by-laws of that foreign company or the laws under which that foreign company was formed. Third parties may therefore rely on the registration with the commercial register in all respects. The HrW 2007 requires the designation of one or more persons who can legally represent and bind the company. It is prudent to be fully aware of the limitations on this authority.[61] Registration is often made by the branch manager. If he registered that he has unlimited power to represent the branch, he may, as a practical matter, by operation of the HrW 2007, have a much wider authority to represent the foreign company than even the chief executive officer of that foreign company. In other words, third parties may rely on the representative authority as it appears in the commercial register.

A branch office of a foreign company may enter into a wide variety of agreements, thereby binding the foreign company. Certain agreements will by their nature be governed by Netherlands law. To the extent that enforcement of agreements that purport to be governed by foreign law is sought in the Netherlands, Dutch conflict of law rules apply.

2.2.3 Name

A branch office may operate under the name of its head office, its owners, or almost any other name, provided that the name does not confuse the public or infringe the name[62] or trade mark rights[63] of third parties (see § 3.3.3.2). Regardless of the name used in the Netherlands, third parties can ascertain the name and business of the foreign owner from the commercial register (see Chapter 12).

2.2.4 Equal Treatment of Foreign and Dutch Enterprises

A foreign enterprise (legal entity, partnership or sole proprietorship) is treated on an equal basis with Dutch enterprises. Netherlands law is essentially

61. For the applicable theory concerning agents and their authority, see § 8.2.5.3.
62. Arts 5, 5a, 5b HnW.
63. Art. 2.20 BVIE.

non-discriminatory towards foreigners, but there are exceptions with regard to the legal form by which the business must be conducted, as well as the formalities to be complied with, e.g. in sectors as securities trading, banking, insurance and energy.

2.2.5 Mandatory Rules

A business enterprise in the Netherlands, regardless of its legal form, must comply with certain requirements of Netherlands law, including registration with the commercial register, establishment of a works council if it has 50 or more employees (see § 13.1), compliance with the Merger Code if it is involved in takeovers or mergers[64] and compliance with rules governing registration for various taxes.

2.3 Choice between Branch and Subsidiary

Apart from tax aspects, which are generally decisive, the choice between setting up a branch office of a foreign legal entity or a subsidiary established under Netherlands law involves a number of considerations. The financial background and reputation of the head office determine the creditworthiness of the branch. A subsidiary will, from a legal point of view, be judged on its own financial standing. A subsidiary in the form of a legal entity possesses the attribute of limited liability, thereby limiting the legal responsibility of the head office, i.e. the parent of such subsidiary. A branch, being a part of the foreign company, acts directly on behalf of the head office. To mitigate the liability of the head office for the debts of the branch, the head office may consider establishing a subsidiary in its country of residence which acts as a special purpose vehicle for its branch in the Netherlands. In that case, the liability will be limited to the amount of share capital of the special purpose vehicle.

Under Netherlands law the management of a subsidiary in the Netherlands has its own responsibilities and is entitled to a certain degree of independence from the parent company (see § 8.2.1.1). The management of a branch is completely subject to the control of the head office. If a subsidiary is a Dutch legal entity, it is subject to certain auditing and public filing requirements.

With the exception of registration with the commercial register and disclosure required by the HrW 2007 (see § 12.2), no Dutch auditing or publication requirements exist for branches (except for those engaged in banking and insurance) provided they do not qualify under the Wfbv (see § 2.2.1).

64. See § 11.3.1.3.

In the absence of contractual restrictions, shares in a subsidiary company can be sold or otherwise disposed of by their owner. If the subsidiary is set up in the form of an NV or a BV, the transfer of shares may be subject to a certain transfer restriction in the articles of association (see § 5.3.4). However, if the subsidiary is wholly owned by one parent company, the practical effect of such restriction is nil. A branch is not a legal entity separate from the head office, and can therefore be sold only by way of an asset transaction. Obviously, where a special purpose vehicle is used to establish the branch, the shares of this special purpose company can be sold in order to sell the branch.

A Dutch subsidiary gives a certain substance to the local presence. From a practical point of view it can be important to have the appearance of being Dutch, for instance, with regard to customer relations, marketing and labour relations.

Branches sometimes suffer from 'red tape' requirements imposed by government agencies or contractual parties to prove their authority to enter into agreements or to make certain filings. On the other hand, branches have a fairly unrestricted legal structure.

It takes little time to establish a branch. As such a branch would operate a business enterprise, it should be registered with the commercial register and the appropriate tax filings must be made. The formation of a Dutch company will usually take more time but can be effected in one or two weeks (in the case of an NV) or even in one day (in the case of a BV) (see § 3.3.2).

Costs for setting up a branch are minimal. For the costs of establishing a Dutch legal entity, see § 3.3.4.

2.4 General Partnership and Limited Partnership

2.4.1 Introduction

For the establishment of a business venture under Netherlands law (other than bank or insurance companies), the basic choices are a sole proprietorship (*eenmanszaak*), a general partnership (*vennootschap onder firma*), a limited partnership (*commanditaire vennootschap*), an NV or a BV, a European Economic Interest Grouping (*Europees Economisch Samenwerkingsverband*), a European Company (*Europese vennootschap*) or a European co-operative company (*Europese coöperatieve vennootschap*).

A private partnership (*maatschap*) is used in order to exercise a profession rather than a commercial business and is often used by professionals such as lawyers, accountants, tax consultants and architects, although under Netherlands law it can be the business form for all business enterprises. However, if the private partnership conducts business that is not the business of professionals, but other business for profit, and conducts this business under a common business name, the rules of a general partnership apply by operation of law. The main characteristics of the general and limited partnership forms available under Netherlands law are described below. A sole proprietorship is similar to a general partnership, except that there is only one owner, and consequently no need for a partnership agreement. This implies that, contrary to the general partnership, a sole proprietorship has – from a legal point of view – no equity that is separated from that of its sole owner.

2.4.2 General Partnership

2.4.2.1 General

A general partnership (*vennootschap onder firma*) established under Netherlands law is based on an agreement between two or more partners, which may be individuals or legal entities. It is not a legal entity separate from its owners.

None of the partners need to be Dutch or resident in the Netherlands. A partnership can hold property,[65] sue and be sued, and contract in its own name (through its partners). Third parties may hold the partners jointly and severally liable for the partnership's debts (see § 2.4.2.4). The purpose of the partnership must be mutual co-operation in order to make a profit. By law, the partners must contribute either cash, property, labour or goodwill. A contribution of business relations with third parties or know-how is also acceptable.[66]

2.4.2.2 Commercial Register

General partnerships must be registered with the commercial register.[67] Registration requires the disclosure of, *inter alia*, the names and addresses of the partners, their nationality and signatures, and a description of the partnership's business.[68]

2.4.2.3 Partnership Agreement

A written partnership agreement is recommended, although not mandatory.[69] It should cover the partnership's name, the partnership's purposes or objects,

---

65. In the form of a joint ownership by the partners.
66. Asser/Maeijer & Van Olffen 7-VII* 2010/37.
67. Art. 23 WvK; Art. 5(a) HrW 2007.
68. Art. 10(3) HrW 2007 and Arts 17, 19 HrB 2008.
69. The existence of a general partnership may be demonstrated by all possible means. Supreme Court 28 Nov. 1997, NJ 1998, 167 (*D/S*).

the authority of the partners to bind the partnership (the scope of authority is determined by the partners), the manner in which profits and losses are to be distributed among the partners, the (capital) contribution of each partner, the consequences of the resignation and expulsion of a partner, and the dissolution of the partnership.

The partnership will not necessarily be dissolved if one of the partners resigns, unless only one partner remains. The remaining partners may continue the business and keep the assets if this is provided for in the partnership agreement. The agreement should be drafted taking into account its tax consequences.

2.4.2.4 *Liability of the Partners*

Details of the partnership's purposes and the authority of the individual partners to represent the partnership should be disclosed in the commercial register.[70] In the absence of proper registration, third parties may hold all partners jointly and severally liable for any action performed by any partner on behalf of the partnership, whether or not this action falls within the partnership's objects.[71] A proper entry in the commercial register ensures that the unlimited personal liability of each of the partners can only be invoked to the extent the liability is incurred by a partner acting within the scope of his authority as disclosed.[72]

As the equity of the partnership forms a joint ownership, creditors of the partnership may choose to recover their claims *vis-à-vis* the partnership either on the equity of the partnership or from the partners individually. A private creditor of a partner may not recover private debts of that partner on the equity of the partnership (see § 2.4.2.8).

2.4.2.5 *Annual Accounts*

The annual accounts of the partnership need not be disclosed to the public or filed with any register or agency. If a general partnership has only foreign partners which are foreign companies with capital divided into shares, the general partnership[73] is subject to the Dutch rules concerning annual accounts and the annual report (see § 7.1.2).

---

70. Art. 19 HrB 2008.
71. Art. 29 WvK.
72. Arts 17 and 18 WvK; Art. 19 HrB 2008.
73. Art. 2:360(2) BW.

2.4.2.6 *Distribution of Profits and Losses*

Profits can be distributed according to the partnership agreement. If the profits are retained, they must be included in the income statement submitted by each partner for tax assessment. Netherlands law does not permit the establishment of a partnership in which a partner is liable for all losses or specific losses, without having a share in the profits.[74]

2.4.2.7 *Capacity to Sue*

Although it is not a separate legal entity separated from its owners, the partnership can sue or be sued.[75]

2.4.2.8 *Position of Creditors*

In the event of bankruptcy of the partnership, which also implies the bankruptcy of the partners, the claims of the business creditors of the partnership have priority over those of the creditors of the individual partners, with respect to the assets of the partnership.[76]

2.4.2.9 *Partnership Interests*

The partnership agreement may provide for the transfer of partnership interests. Interests in the partnership may even be in the name of a bearer of a share certificate. The use of this legal device may, however, have far-reaching negative tax implications.

2.4.3 Limited Partnership

2.4.3.1 *General*

A limited partnership *(commanditaire vennootschap)* is similar to a general partnership, but has one or more limited partners, referred to in Dutch as 'silent' partners (*stille vennoten*), whose liability is limited to the amount of their (capital) contributions.[77] A limited partnership is not a legal entity.[78]

---

74. Asser/Maeijer & Van Olffen 7-VII* 2010/71.
75. Art. 4(4) Rv and Art. 7A:1682 BW.
76. Supreme Court 26 Nov. 1897, W7074.
77. Art. 20(3) WvK.
78. The equity of the partnership forms a joint ownership.

2.4.3.2 The Managing Partners

A limited partnership has one or more managing partners whose liability for debts of the partnership is that of a general partner, i.e. unlimited. To avoid the adverse effects of unlimited liability, the managing partner may be an NV or a BV, the shares of which may be held by the limited partners.

2.4.3.3 Management by Limited Partners

If a limited partner is involved in management (directly or by proxy) or if his name is disclosed in matters related to the partnership, his liability will become unlimited (even if third parties know of his status as a limited partner).[79] The partnership agreement may (and often does) provide for a list of resolutions of the managing partners that require prior approval of the limited partners; such approval right does not create liability of the limited partners.

2.4.3.4 No Shares

A limited partnership with a capital divided into shares is not permitted under Dutch law.[80]

2.4.3.5 Annual Accounts

The strict rules for the auditing, format, adoption and publication of annual accounts and the annual report that apply to a company (see § 7.1.2)[81] apply to limited partnerships only if all general partners liable for the partnerships' debts are foreign companies with their capital divided into shares.[82]

---

79. Art. 21 WvK.
80. Act of 28 May 1975, Stb. 1975, 277.
81. Arts 2:300, 2:360(3) BW.
82. Art. 2:360(2) BW.

2.5 Other Legal Forms of Conducting Business[83]

2.5.1 The Association and its Qualified Forms

2.5.1.1 General

An association (*vereniging*) in its general form is prohibited from having as its purpose the making of profits for distribution to its members.[84] For this reason, an association in its general form is not a desirable form for doing business. There are, however, sub-categories of the legal form of an association that may be used for specific business purposes and that can distribute profits to its members: the co-operative and the mutual insurance association (see §§ 2.5.1.2 and 2.5.1.3).[85] For the conversion of any association to an NV or a BV, see § 11.5.

In fact, two types of association exist in the Netherlands: (i) an association with articles of association drawn up in a notarial deed; and (ii) an association of which the articles are not drawn up in notarial form but which nevertheless qualifies as an association given its structure and organisation. The latter association has limited legal capacity, which means e.g. that it cannot own real estate, and its managing directors are jointly and severally liable for the debts of the association.[86] An association with articles drawn up by a notarial deed must register with the commercial register (see Chapter 12).[87]

2.5.1.2 The Co-operative

A co-operative (*coöperatie*)[88] was originally a popular organisational form for agricultural businesses. Today, several co-operatives in the Netherlands own considerable business operations. One of the largest banks, *Rabobank*, originally largely geared to the agricultural business, is a co-operative. Nowadays, co-operatives can also be found in the energy distribution sector and sometimes in the healthcare sector. Over the last five years the co-operative has also often been used as a holding entity in tax-driven structures of companies.

---

83. For a more detailed description of the other legal forms referred to in this paragraph, see: Asser/Rensen 2-III* 2012.
84. Art. 2:26(3) BW.
85. Art. 2:53a BW.
86. Art. 2:30 BW. The management board may register such association with the commercial register, with the effect that the board members will be liable for the debts of the association only to the extent that the third party may prove that the association will not meet its obligations; Art. 2:30(4) BW.
87. Art. 2:29(1) BW and Art. 5(a) HrW 2007.
88. Art. 2:53(1) BW.

In these structures the activity of the co-operative consists of holding shares in a Dutch BV. Profits distributed by such BV through the co-operative to the members of the co-operative are, in particular circumstances, not subject to Dutch dividend withholding tax.

2.5.1.3 The Mutual Insurance Association[89]

The legal form of a mutual insurance association (a mutual) (*onderlinge waarborgmaatschappij*) may only be used in the insurance industry, in which case the insurance policy holders are the members of the mutual insurance association.

2.5.1.4 Limitation of Liability

The co-operative and the mutual are basically subject to the same rules. The initials W.A., B.A. or U.A. are usually part of the name, and indicate the extent of the members' liability towards the co-operative or mutual at the moment of dissolution of the said entity. U.A. stands for *uitgesloten aansprakelijkheid*, i.e. an absolute exclusion of the liability of the members and former members for the deficit (if any) at the moment of dissolution of the co-operative or the mutual.[90] The articles should state this exclusion of liability explicitly. B.A. stands for *beperkte aansprakelijkheid*, i.e. the restricted liability of the members, as determined in the articles and disclosed in the commercial register. W.A. stands for *wettelijke aansprakelijkheid*, i.e. the personal liability of the members, each unlimited and – in principle – for an equal part.

If the articles do not provide for a U.A. or B.A. regime as described above, the W.A. liability regime applies to the co-operative and mutual.

2.5.1.5 Commercial Register

Both the co-operative and the mutual must file registrations with the commercial register similar to the registrations required for companies (see Chapter 12).

2.5.1.6 Executive Powers

The co-operative and the mutual must each have a management board, and may have a supervisory board.[91] If the co-operative or the mutual qualifies

89. Art. 2:53(2) BW.
90. Art. 2:56(1) BW.
91. Art. 2:57 BW.

as 'large' for more than three consecutive years, it must have a supervisory board.[92] The test for this qualification is similar to the test for a company to qualify as a 'large' company (see § 8.1.2.2). Many decisions of the management board of a 'large' co-operative or mutual require prior approval by the supervisory board.[93]

The duties of board members and the rules concerning the personal liability of managing directors of companies (see § 9.2) apply similarly to managing directors of co-operatives and mutuals, as do the rules concerning the powers of the managing directors of an NV and a BV (see § 8.2).[94]

2.5.1.7 Annual Accounts

Strict rules concerning auditing, the prescribed format, adoption and publication of annual accounts and the annual report apply to co-operatives and mutuals (see § 7.1.2).[95]

Associations in their general form that conduct a business enterprise having a net turnover of at least EUR 4.4 million, must also comply with these rules.[96]

2.5.2 The Foundation

A foundation (*stichting*[97]) has certain similarities to a foundation in the United States. Unlike its US counterpart, however, a foundation is not necessarily limited to charitable purposes. To the extent that the legal concept of a trust is recognised under Netherlands law, a foundation functions in much the same way as a common law trust. It has no members, and cannot make distributions to its managing directors or its founders. Any distributions to third parties must have a charitable or non-commercial purpose.[98] The purposes of a foundation may, however, include commercial activities. For conversion of a foundation to an NV or a BV, see § 11.5. There are several foundations with large business enterprises.

The legal form of a foundation is often used for the issuance of depository receipts by an NV or a BV and for the exercise of control by the management

92. Arts 2:63f, 2:63c BW.
93. Art. 2:63j BW.
94. Arts 2:53a, 2:44, 2:45 BW.
95. Art. 2:58 BW.
96. Arts 2:49, 2:360(3) BW. The minimum turnover threshold may be altered by Royal Decree, to conform to EU legislation (Art. 2:398(4)) BW).
97. Art. 2:285(1) BW.
98. Art. 2:285(3) BW.

board over the shareholders by use of priority shares and preference shares (see §§ 5.2.2 and 5.2.3).

A foundation can be formed only by a notarial deed.[99] It is a legal entity, separate from its founders or managing directors. It can own property, contract in its own name, and sue or be sued. The foundation must register with the commercial register (see Chapter 12).[100] Foundations that conduct a business enterprise having a net turnover of at least EUR 4.4 million must comply with the strict rules for the auditing, format, adoption and publication of annual accounts and the annual report[101] that apply to companies.

The Dutch Civil Code does not contain many provisions regarding the governance of a foundation, which means that, e.g. the appointment and dismissal of the directors of a foundation can be construed as the incorporator of the foundation intends.

2.5.3 The European Economic Interest Grouping (EEIG)

The Council Regulation concerning the creation of the EEIG (see § 1.3.15)[102] has been implemented into Netherlands law by a separate act.[103] However, many material aspects are still directly governed by this EU Regulation, and it should be noted that the interpretation of this Regulation and its implementation into Netherlands law are subject to the jurisdiction of the CJEU. Nevertheless, each member state has been given certain choices in its implementation of the EU Regulation, and consequently each country has its own EEIG. In the Netherlands, the EEIG (*Europees Economisch Samenwerkingsverband*, or EESV) is a legal entity, but in many other respects shows great similarity to the general partnership (see § 2.4.2). The most notable differences are that:

(a) the EEIG must serve the interests of its members (entrepreneurs or professionals, companies or individuals) and not have corporate purposes of its own;
(b) its members must be domiciled or resident in one of the member states;
(c) the EEIG must have at least two members from two or more different member states;

99. Art. 2:286(1) BW.
100. Art. 2:289 BW.
101. Arts 2:300, 2:360(3) BW.
102. Council Regulation (EEC) No. 2137/85 on the European Economic Interest Grouping (EEIG), O.J. EUR. COMM. (No. L199) 1 (1985).
103. Act of 28 June 1989, Stb. 1989, 245.

(d) while the activities of the EEIG must be of support to its members, the EEIG itself should not be an independent profit centre. However, the making of profit by the EEIG in itself is not prohibited;
(e) the EEIG cannot hold shares in the capital of its members;
(f) it cannot have more than 500 employees;
(g) membership is personal. The transfer by a member of its participation in the EEIG requires the approval of all other members;
(h) the provisions concerning the liability of board members in the event of bankruptcy (see § 9.2) and enquiry proceedings (see § 10.2) also apply to the EEIG;
(i) the EEIG must have its annual accounts audited by an independent auditor; and
(j) the members of the EEIG shall compensate the EEIG in equal parts for the amount for which the losses exceed the profits (unless a different allocation of compensation has been agreed upon in the formation agreement).[104]

An EEIG is not considered an independent taxpayer. Like a general partnership, it serves for tax purposes as a transparent vehicle in which profits and losses are attributed to its members.

Since its introduction in 1989, there have not been many EEIGs established in the Netherlands.

2.5.4 The European Company (SE)

The EU Regulation on the Statute for a European Company[105] has been implemented into Netherlands law by a separate act which came into force on 1 April 2005.[106] The position of employees of an SE is governed by a separate EU Directive which is implemented into Netherlands law by a statute which also came into force on 1 April 2005.[107]

An SE is governed by European law as well as the law of the state where it has its registered office (*statutaire zetel*). For example, an SE with its registered office in Amsterdam, the Netherlands, is governed by the rules of the EU Regulation and with regard to subjects not, or not entirely, covered by this Regulation the rules of Dutch corporate law regarding NVs apply. This creates

104. Art. 21(2) Council Regulation (EEC) No. 2137/85 on the European Economic Interest Grouping (EEIG).
105. Council Regulation No. 2157/2001 on the Statute for a European Company (SE), O.J. EUR. COMM. (No. L294) 1 (2001).
106. *Uitvoeringswet verordening Europese vennootschap*, Act of 17 March 2005, Stb. 2005, 150.
107. *Wet rol werknemers bij de Europese vennootschap,* Act of 17 March 2005, Stb. 2005, 166.

a non-transparent system of applicable laws and it is deemed to be one of the reasons why the use of SEs has not been very popular in Europe. One cannot speak of 'the' SE, because in fact there exist as many types of SEs as there are EU member states. Advantages of an SE are the possibilities for cross-border movement, such as cross-border mergers and change of registered office to another EU member state. An SE can only be established by a merger of at least two companies from two or more different member states or by incorporation by a parent SE or through conversion of an NV into an SE.

Currently, approximately 25 SEs are established in the Netherlands.

2.5.5 The European Co-operative Company (SCE)

The Council Regulation concerning the creation of the European Co-operative Company[108] has been implemented into Netherlands law by a separate act which came into force on 13 October 2006.[109] The position of employees of an SCE is governed by a separate EU Directive that is implemented into Netherlands law by an act that also came into force on 13 October 2006.[110]

The legal framework regarding SCEs is based on that of SEs and thus very similar. This also means that an SCE is governed by European law as well as the law of the state where it has its registered office (*statutaire zetel*). The SCE is, unlike the Dutch co-operative, a legal entity with its capital divided into shares. Advantages of an SCE are the possibilities for cross-border movement, such as cross-border mergers and change of registered office to another EU member state. An SCE can be established by incorporation by at least five individuals or companies from two or more different member states, by merger of at least two co-operatives from two or more different member states or through conversion of a co-operative into an SCE.

There have only been a few SCEs established in the Netherlands since its introduction in 2006.

---

108. Council Regulation (EC) No. 1435/2003 on the Statute for a European Cooperative Society (SCE), O.J. EUR. COMM. (No. L207) 1 (2003).
109. *Uitvoeringswet verordening Europese coöperatieve vennootschap*, Act of 14 September 2006, Stb. 2006, 425.
110. *Wet wijziging uitvoeringswet rol werknemers Europese vennootschap*, Act of 5 July 2006, Stb. 2006, 361.

Chapter 3
Types and Formation of Companies

3.1 Introduction

3.1.1 General

Any company incorporated under foreign law can validly carry on business in the Netherlands. From a Dutch legal perspective, however, foreign companies continue to be governed by the corporate laws of the jurisdiction of their incorporation and this law will be recognised by Dutch courts, unless it conflicts under Netherlands law with Dutch public order, even if the main centre of activities of the company (*siège réel*) is in the Netherlands rather than in the country or state of incorporation. An attempt by a foreign company to transfer its corporate seat to the Netherlands will not be recognised and a Dutch court may declare the company as void or non-existent for existing Dutch legal purposes. However, in the event of conflict, the situation shall be determined pursuant to the provisions of Book 10 of the Dutch Civil Code (private international law). For a transfer of the seat of a Dutch company, see § 11.7.

Most Netherlands law concerning companies is statutory law, contained in Book 2 of the Dutch Civil Code. Book 2 contains mandatory provisions, only to be deviated from in the articles of association (*statuten*) if the relevant statutory provision expressly so provides. Netherlands law recognises two different types of company: the NV (*naamloze vennootschap*) and the BV (*besloten vennootschap met beperkte aansprakelijkheid*). Both the NV and the BV are separate legal entities, separate from their shareholders, with a capital divided into shares.[111] The NV and the BV can be used for the same business purposes, can own and transfer property, lend money, buy and sell securities, engage employees, contract and borrow in their own name, participate in other ventures and sue or be sued. As a general rule, the transferability of BV shares is restricted, which makes the BV a privately held or closed company, while unless the articles of association provide for a restriction on the transferability of its shares, which is optional for an NV, the free transferability of NV shares makes the latter a public company (see §§ 3.2 and 5.3.4).

---

111. Art. 2:64(1)/175(1) BW.

3.1.2 The Concept of the Group

Netherlands law recognises that companies often do not operate on a stand-alone basis. A significant number of business organisations consists of a holding company, several sub-holding companies and a considerable number of subsidiary companies. Larger groups may also have, within the group, a management company and a finance company. There is no standard pattern for any group structure. Every group has its own history, tax parameters, organisational requirements, production and service locations, sales outlets, financing arrangements, captive insurance plans, etc.

The diversity of these group arrangements has created a need for legislative reform and clarification, especially with respect to such matters as annual accounts and disclosure requirements, the rules concerning 'large' companies (see Chapter 8) and the requirements of the WOR.

Netherlands law defines a 'subsidiary' (*dochtermaatschappij*) as a legal entity in which a parent company: (i) can exercise more than one half of all eligible voting rights at a shareholders' meeting; or (ii) can appoint or remove more than one half of the management or supervisory boards (assuming all votes are cast).[112] The parent company's rights may be derived from its majority as a shareholder or from a shareholders' agreement (see § 7.4) and may be held either by the company alone or jointly with any of its other subsidiaries. A general or limited partnership in which one or more companies or any of their subsidiaries is fully liable to creditors is deemed to be a 'subsidiary' of such company. A company may also be a subsidiary of more than one shareholder. This situation may occur, *inter alia*, if one of its shareholders, pursuant to the articles or a shareholders' agreement, is entitled to appoint the majority of the managing directors and another shareholder is entitled to appoint the majority of the supervisory directors.[113]

Netherlands law defines a 'group' (*groep*) as an economic structure in which legal entities, partnerships, or both, are united in one organisation (i.e. centralised management).[114] If a party has majority control over a company that qualifies as 'centralised management', that other company will be a group company of the first party.[115] Equity interests are not conclusive evidence for the qualification of a company as a group company. A minority participation or a participation of 50% may suffice, provided ancillary provisions granting decision-making powers exist. Consequently, a company may be a group company in more than one group.

112. Art. 2:24a BW.
113. Asser/Maeijer, Van Solinge & Nieuwe Weme 2-II* 2009/821.
114. Art. 2:24b BW.
115. Asser/Maeijer, Van Solinge & Nieuwe Weme 2-II* 2009/817.

A 'participation' (*deelneming*) exists when a legal entity or partnership, for its own account, either directly or through one or more subsidiaries, has an equity interest in another company, with the objective of having a long-term association with that other company for the furtherance of its own business purposes. Contributing one fifth or more of the issued capital creates a rebuttable assumption of a 'participation'.[116] A company participates in a partnership if it or its subsidiary as a partner: (i) is fully liable towards its creditors; or (ii) has as its objective a long-term association with that partnership for the furtherance of its own business purposes.

For the statutory definition of a 'dependent company' (*afhankelijke maatschappij*), see § 8.1.2.2.

Netherlands law has to some extent adopted a consistent theory concerning groups of affiliated companies. The reality of the group as a business concept has had an effect on the development of theories concerning the responsibility of a parent for the actions of its subsidiary and *vis-à-vis* the creditors of the subsidiary (see § 3.5), the availability of subsidiary assets as collateral for loans made to the parent or to sister companies (see § 4.7), and the extent and nature of the instructions that a parent may give to the management board of a subsidiary (see § 8.2.1.1).

3.1.3 Investment Company with Variable Capital

Investment companies, both open-end and closed-end, that meet the requirements stated below are exempt from certain strict rules concerning the capital of the company. These exemptions relate to the power of the management board to decide on the issuance of new shares and the pre-emptive rights of shareholders (see § 4.4), the repurchase of shares (see § 4.3.6), and the redemption of shares (see § 4.6.2). Investment companies qualify for these exemptions only if they meet the following requirements:[117]

(a) the investment company must be an NV;
(b) the investment company must have the exclusive purpose to invest its assets with spread risk, with the objective of sharing the benefits with its shareholders;
(c) the articles must empower the management board to issue, acquire and dispose of shares in the capital of the investment company;
(d) a licence for placing of its shares, as referred to in the Wft is granted to a manager;

116. Art. 2:24c BW.
117. Art. 2:76a(1) BW.

(e) the articles must state that the NV is an investment company with variable capital; and
(f) the issued capital of the investment company in excess of the shares acquired and held by it must equal at least 10% of the authorised capital (see § 4.1.1) stated in the articles.[118]

3.1.4 Corporate Formalities

Netherlands corporate law is relatively complex and generally strict, while maintaining flexibility in certain areas. Since the modernisation of the BV law, as per 1 October 2012, the law offers more flexibility for BVs to establish a bespoke governance structure. Also, certain formalities have become less stringent (e.g. decision-making by shareholders outside meetings) or have been abolished (e.g. regarding preservation of capital).

Great emphasis is placed on the articles (see § 3.3.3), capitalisation and subscription (see Chapter 4), the annual accounts, disclosure requirements at the commercial register (see Chapter 12) and the representation of labour in management decisions (see Chapter 13). The management board must keep a record of all shareholders' resolutions available for inspection by shareholders and the holders of depository receipts[119] (see § 5.5). Subject to any special requirements stated in the articles, resolutions of the management board or the supervisory board can be adopted in any manner, without any formalities being required. Shareholders' resolutions require special attention (see § 7.2).

3.1.5 No By-laws

A company is formed by the execution of a deed of incorporation, which contains the articles. By-laws of the type commonly drawn up in the United States are unknown in the Netherlands. The articles are considerably less detailed than most by-laws, but have a similar practical function. However, the articles can only be amended by a shareholders' resolution (see § 11.2). The articles are effectively amended by the execution of a Dutch notarial deed, an official copy of which must be filed with the commercial register for public inspection (see Chapter 12). Internal rules governing the distribution of powers and the decision-making process of the management board and the supervisory board may be adopted in the form of a regulation or manual (see § 8.2.1.1).

118. Art. 2:98(8) BW.
119. Art. 2:120(4)/230(4) BW.

3.2 Public and Private Companies

3.2.1 Differences between an NV and a BV

Netherlands law provides for two types of company, the NV and the BV. NV shares can be either in bearer form, which makes them freely negotiable, or in registered form.[120] The transfer of registered NV shares may (but need not) be restricted in any way; the shareholders are free to set out transfer restrictions in the articles[121] (see § 5.3.4.1). BV shares must be registered shares[122] and, as a general rule, cannot be freely transferred. However, since the modernisation of BV law, which came into effect on 1 October 2012, a restriction on the transfer of BV shares is no longer imposed by law. If the articles do not provide otherwise, the transferor must offer the shares on offer to his co-shareholders (see § 5.3.4.2). The management board of an NV may decide to give loans for the acquisition of its shares with due observance to strict rules and after approval of the general meeting of shareholders; however, with the exception of loans for employees' shares (see § 4.3.7).[123] The amount of treasury shares permitted is limited to 50% for the listed NV[124] as opposed to the position of the non-listed NV and the BV, where there is no limitation other than that at least one share must be held by a third party[125] (see § 4.3.6). For the NV a minimum capital requirement of EUR 45,000 is applicable. For the BV there is no minimum capital requirement. There are other differences, but these are usually of minor significance for business matters. Both the BV and the NV can be a statutory 'large' company (see § 8.1.2). Many substantial companies in the Netherlands have adopted the BV form (in contrast to the situation in certain other Member States, such as the United Kingdom, where the closed company form is available only to small or medium-sized companies). The specific audit and disclosure requirements are almost identical for NVs and BVs, irrespective of whether they are 'large' companies.

3.2.2 Modification of Corporate Form

An NV may convert to a BV[126] and a BV may convert to an NV.[127] This conversion of form does not affect the company's existence or identity (which

120. Art. 2:82(1) BW.
121. Art. 2:87(1) BW.
122. Art. 2:194(1) BW.
123. Art. 2:98c(1), (2), (8) BW.
124. Art. 2:98(2) BW.
125. Art. 2:64(1)/175(1) BW.
126. Arts 2:18, 2:183(1) BW.
127. Arts 2:18, 2:72(1) BW.

would have disastrous tax consequences).[128] A decision by the shareholders to convert the corporate form is executed in the same way as other amendments to the articles (see § 11.2).[129] If a BV converts into an NV additional requirements relate to the equity of the company.[130] An auditor must declare that, at a certain moment in a period less than five months prior to the conversion, the equity of the BV was equal to at least the issued and paid up capital of the NV as stated in the notarial deed of conversion. For the conversion of an association, a co-operative, a mutual insurance association and a *stichting* to an NV or a BV and *vice versa,* see § 11.5.

3.3 Formation

3.3.1 General

The formation of a Dutch company is subject to a number of formalities. The company can be formed either by an individual acting in his or her own capacity, on behalf of a legal entity, or on the strength of a power of attorney.[131] One or more parties, known as the founders, must appear before a Dutch civil law notary, or be represented pursuant to a power of attorney, and confirm their desire to form the company with articles as read to them, in full or in summary form.

The initial management board is appointed in the deed of incorporation.[132] Each of its members is, in addition to the company, jointly and severally liable for each transaction for which the company is bound until the moment that the company has made the application for registration with the commercial register and the minimum capitalisation requirements have been met.[133]

3.3.2 Incorporation

3.3.2.1 The Deed of Incorporation

A company comes into existence upon the execution before a Dutch civil law notary of the deed of incorporation (*akte van oprichting*), which contains three parts. In the first part, each of the parties is identified and declares the desire to incorporate a company. The second part states the articles.[134] In the third part

128. Art. 2:18(8) BW.
129. Arts 2:183(1), 2:72(1) BW.
130. Art. 2:72(1) BW.
131. Arts 2:4(1), 2:64(2)/175(2) BW.
132. Art. 2:132/242 BW.
133. Art. 2:69(2)/180(2) BW.
134. Art. 2:66(1)/177(1) BW.

the parties confirm their participation for a certain number of shares, stating how those shares are or will be paid up and appointing the initial managing directors and the members of the supervisory board, if applicable. The articles are subject to and must be consistent with the law. By-laws of the US type are unknown. A filing with the commercial register must be made within one week after its incorporation. This filing is not in any way a prerequisite for the incorporation or completion of existence.

3.3.2.2 Procedure

The draft deed of incorporation is prepared by a Dutch civil law notary or an attorney who specialises in corporate matters. The notarial deed must be in the Dutch language.[135] The civil law notary is required by law to retain the original of the deed. Certified copies may be issued to the founders and the management board.[136]

3.3.2.3 The Founders

The deed of incorporation must be signed by the civil law notary and by the founders or their duly authorised representatives. Both companies and individuals may be founders. Persons, not being founders, who subscribe for shares at incorporation must also sign the deed of incorporation.[137] The aggregate contribution to the issued capital of the NV is required by law to be at least one fifth of the authorised capital (see § 4.1.2).[138] Issued capital is the sum of the nominal value of all shares issued, commonly referred to in US corporate law as 'stated capital'.[139] The authorised capital is the maximum capital as stated in the articles of the NV up to which shares may be issued without amendment to the articles being required. Any issue of shares in excess of the authorised capital is null and void. The articles of the BV may include authorised capital, but there is no minimum capital requirement.

All of the shares may be held by a single individual or company.[140] For the disclosure and recording requirements of a company with a single shareholder,

135. Art. 2:65/176 BW.
136. Art. 49 Wna.
137. Art. 2:64(2)/175(2) BW.
138. Art. 2:67(4) BW. Different rules apply to investment companies with variable capital (see § 3.1.3).
139. Please note that the stated capital under US State law may be calculated as the shares issued and outstanding, which shares have been paid in full. Under Netherlands law, the shares may under certain circumstances (see § 4.1.2) be partly paid up and treasury stock will still remain to be considered as 'outstanding'.
140. Art. 2:64(2)/175(2) BW.

see § 5.1.4. The founders may be of any nationality and may be domiciled anywhere.

A founder can be represented only by a written power of attorney,[141] which must conform to the requirements of the law applicable to the founder. A duly signed power of attorney transmitted by fax, by e-mail or by any other means of electronic communication is acceptable to most civil law notaries, provided the power of attorney is legible and reproducible, and possibly, for a foreign founder, is notarized. Once incorporated, the company does not automatically cease to exist should the power turn out to be invalid. The courts may, however, dissolve such a company (see § 11.6.2.2).[142]

3.3.2.4 Personal Liability of Managing Directors

The management board of the NV, or the civil law notary on its behalf, must register the company's data and deposit a certified copy of the deed of incorporation of the NV and, depending on the nature of the contribution of the shares in cash or in kind, respectively, a certified copy of the bank statement or the auditors' statement (depending on the contribution in respect of the shares, respectively, in cash and in kind) with the commercial register of the Chamber of Commerce (see Chapter 12).[143] The management board of the NV must also ensure that, at the date of incorporation, at least 25% of the nominal value per issued share of the NV is paid up, and that the total nominal value paid up equals at least EUR 45,000 (see § 4.3.3). Until both of these mandatory requirements are complied with, the managing directors of the NV are jointly and severally liable for the transaction by which the NV is bound, in addition to the company's liability for such obligations[144] (see also Chapter 9).

The management board of the BV, or the civil law notary on its behalf, must register the company's data and deposit a certified copy of the deed of incorporation with the commercial register.[145] If in breach of this requirement, the managing directors of the BV are jointly and severally liable for the transaction by which the company is bound, in addition to the company's liability for such obligations.[146]

141. Art. 2:65/176 BW.
142. Arts 2:4(2), 2:21(1)(a) BW.
143. Art. 2:69(1) BW.
144. Art. 2:69(2) BW.
145. Art. 2:180(1) BW.
146. Art. 2:180(2) BW.

3.3.2.5 Defective Incorporation

A company that was formed without complying with all the formalities as stated under § 3.3.2.4 above, or otherwise was not formed in conformity with the law or has articles that violate the requirements of the law, is subject to an action by the public prosecutor or other interested party to have it dissolved by the court.[147] The court will allow for an action by the founders to redress the defects.[148]

However, when business is conducted in the name of a company whose deed of incorporation was not signed by a Dutch civil law notary, then it would be found that the company had never come into existence.[149] In this case, the estate is liable for all of its obligations, jointly and severally, with its present managing directors or those who were acting as such, in the absence of whom the persons who created these obligations in the name of the company are liable.[150] This *de facto* company[151] should be clearly distinguished from the company 'to be formed' (see § 3.4.2).

Netherlands law does not recognise the concept of companies by estoppel as such exist in the United States.

3.3.3 Articles of Association

3.3.3.1 General Introduction

The rules governing a company's conduct are set out in the law and in the articles. Netherlands corporate law does not recognise or require by-laws that are separate and distinct from the articles.

The articles must not be in conflict with mandatory provisions of the law.[152] The law requires that the following subjects are dealt with in the articles:[153]

(a) the name of the company (see § 3.3.3.2);
(b) the official seat (see § 3.3.3.3);
(c) the objectives of the company (see § 3.3.3.4);

147. Art. 2:21(1) BW.
148. Art. 2:21(2) BW.
149. Art. 2:4(1) BW.
150. Art. 2:4(3), (4) BW.
151. Dutch courts will not recognise a *de facto* company.
152. Art. 2:21(1)(b) BW.
153. Arts 2:66(1)/177(1), 2:67(1)/178(1), 2:134(4)/244(4) BW.

(d) the authorised share capital specified by type of shares[154] (the issued share capital must be stated in the deed of incorporation) (see § 3.3.2.1, but it is not part of the articles); and
(e) a provision for the event that a member of the management board and (in the case of a BV) the supervisory board fails in or is prevented from performing his or her duties.

In order to give management, shareholders and others a more complete and balanced picture of the company's structure, practice has demonstrated the value of stating in the articles various additional legal provisions that apply mandatorily to the company.

3.3.3.2 The Name

The name must contain an indication of the corporate form, either the abbreviation NV[155] or BV.[156] It cannot contain any such indication in a foreign language.

Any name is acceptable as long as it is not too general or too vague (e.g. city names are prohibited), does not imply that the company has powers or purposes that it does not have, is not confusing or deceptive to the public and does not violate the trade name or trade mark rights of others.[157] Names referring to a certain business activity may only be used if the company is actually engaged in that business; the words 'bank'[158] or 'insurance company' can be used only if the company meets the statutory requirements applicable to banks or insurance companies. An investment company with variable capital (see § 3.1.3) must refer to this status whenever its name is used.[159]

The full name (including the NV or BV abbreviation), the official seat and the registration number must appear on the company's stationery and on all other papers (except advertising announcements) emanating from the company (see § 12.1.3).[160]

If the business is carried out under a trade name which is different from the company name, the trade name must also be filed with the commercial register.[161]

154. For the BV authorised capital is not a mandatory requirement (Art. 2:178(1) BW.
155. Art. 2:66(2) BW.
156. Art. 2:177(2) BW.
157. Art. 5, 5a, 5b HnW; Art. 2.20 BVIE.
158. Art. 3:7 Wft.
159. Art. 2:76a(2) BW.
160. Art. 2:75(1)/186(1) BW, Art. 27(1) HrW 2007.
161. Arts 9, 18(1) HrW 2007.

3.3.3.3 The Seat

The official or statutory seat is normally the principal office of the company. It can be in any municipality in the Netherlands.[162] The official seat must be stated in the articles. Frequently, it will be the municipality in which the company's principal office is situated, but this need not be so.

Under the HrW 2007, a company must register with the commercial register. An application form can be filed at any Chamber of Commerce. The registration itself will be performed by the Chamber of Commerce in the district in the Netherlands in which the company has its principal place of business, or in the event that it has no business in the Netherlands, at its official seat.[163]

Netherlands law does not recognise the concept of a registered office or registered agent. A company can be sued by the serving of process on a member of its management board or on its head office.[164] In order to establish the seat of the competent court with regard to claims against the company, the determining factor is the location of the official seat.[165] For a transfer of the seat, see § 11.7.

3.3.3.4 The Corporate Purposes or Objectives

The objectives may consist of a short general description of the company's major activities. The purposes clause can be changed only by an amendment of the articles. It can be very general, normally specifying the principal business or activity of the company, coupled with such language as 'and to engage in any other similar business'. Investment companies with variable capital (see § 3.1.3) must include in the purposes clause a reference to defined activities.[166] The corporate purposes provision can limit the power of the company. Unless the articles state otherwise, a company has the power to engage in any lawful business, to own property, to buy or sell securities, to lend money, to enter into contracts, to sue, to borrow money, to issue notes or bonds, to grant mortgages on its property as security, to fix the compensation of employees and managing directors, to participate in ventures as a partner or a manager, to own shares in another company, and to act as a founder of another Dutch or foreign company. While it may be argued that in theory the powers of a

162. Art. 2:66(3)/177(3) BW.
163. Art. 18(6) HrW 2007.
164. Art. 50 Rv.
165. Art. 1:10(2) BW. It will be this District Court which will be competent to decide in proceedings regarding corporate matters. Enquiry proceedings are solely conducted by the Enterprise Court (see § 10.2).
166. Art. 2:76a(1)(d) BW.

company cannot extend beyond promoting its own individual interests,[167] it is nevertheless useful for subsidiaries to include in their purposes clauses a statement that the interests of the company include the interests of the parent and other companies of the group and that its assets can serve as collateral on behalf of other companies of the group.[168] As part of the articles, the purposes provision is available for public inspection. If the company acts in a way that exceeds the scope of its express or inherent powers, the doctrine of *ultra vires* (see § 3.5) may operate to nullify the transaction, within three years, if it can be shown that the other party knew, or was supposed to have known, on the basis of *prima facie* information, that the transaction was beyond the scope of the company's purposes.[169] These other parties to the transaction cannot, however, invoke this doctrine, even if they can prove that the company knew that the act exceeded its purposes. Therefore, they are bound by the transaction whether or not it is within the scope of the company's purposes. Managing directors who act beyond the company's purposes may be personally liable for damages incurred by the company.[170]

3.3.3.5 *Infinite Term*

The articles may not contain any limitations on the duration of a company's existence,[171] i.e. a company is incorporated for an indefinite period of time.

3.3.4 Costs of Formation

The costs of corporate formation consist of fees for consultants such as notaries, attorneys, tax specialists and auditors which reflect the work involved.

The annual levy of the commercial register (see § 12.4) is calculated on the basis of a schedule that takes into account the number of employees of the company.

3.4 Pre-Incorporation Transactions

3.4.1 General

The initial steps in forming a company are undertaken by a company or an individual who arranges the necessary funding for the new company, recruits

167. For a different view, see § 3.1.2.
168. See § 3.5.
169. Art. 2:7 BW. This provision does not impose a duty to make inquiries.
170. Art. 2:9 BW.
171. Art. 2:17 BW.

the management and outlines the corporate structure. This individual is not always the founder. Certain individuals may wish to enter into business transactions for the account of the new company prior to its inception, assign existing business to the new company or encumber the new company with certain commitments made prior to the date of incorporation.

3.4.2 The Company to be Formed

Netherlands law recognises the concept of actions on behalf of a company prior to its incorporation. Consequently, any person or entity can act on behalf of the company to be incorporated and, in such capacity, can enter into contracts.[172] There are, however, significant limitations.

All transactions must be ratified,[173] expressly or implicitly, by the company after its incorporation, i.e. by the management board, in order for it to be construed that the rights and obligations arising from such a transaction will actually be conferred upon the company. Ratification of a contract that is detrimental to the company can constitute an act of mismanagement (see § 9.2). Until ratification occurs, the persons acting on behalf of the company 'to be formed' are personally bound and liable unless it is otherwise expressly stipulated.[174] Upon ratification, the company is bound, with retroactive effect until the incorporation. If the company then cannot honour the contract, and the persons who acted on behalf of the company to be incorporated knew or could reasonably be expected to have known of the company's future inability to perform, they will be personally liable for damages suffered by the third party as a result thereof. Bankruptcy within one year after the date of incorporation creates a rebuttable statutory presumption of this knowledge of the person who acted on behalf of the company when it was in formation (see § 9.2.2).[175] However, a third party may, under certain circumstances, also hold the management board liable on the basis of tort in the event that the management board when ratifying the transaction knew, or reasonably could have known, that the company would not honour its obligations arising from the transaction so ratified.[176] In the event that the company did become bankrupt, the management board may be held liable for the deficit of the bankrupt estate (see § 9.2.2).[177] Internally, the members of the management board may be held liable on the basis of the principle of proper care (see §§ 9.1.2 and 9.2.1)[178] for

172. Art. 2:93(1)/203(1) BW.
173. Art. 2:93(1)/203(1) BW.
174. Art. 2:93(2)/203(2) BW.
175. Art. 2:93(3)/203(3) BW.
176. Supreme Court 28 Mar. 1997, NJ 1997, 582 (*Kabeh Jewels*).
177. Art. 2:138/248 BW.
178. Art. 2:138/248 BW.

damages incurred to the company. If the contract is not ratified, it is not enforceable against the company. If a transaction with a company to be formed entails the transfer of title to property prior to incorporation, the title may only legally be deemed to accrue to the parties acting on behalf of such company if this is specifically stated in the deed of transfer. If not, the title to the property remains with the transferor until the ratification. Upon ratification, the title will transfer to the newly formed company by operation of law without any additional taxes being incurred.

These rules regarding actions on behalf of the company in formation do not apply to the following actions by the founders, provided these actions will be incorporated in the deed of incorporation: (a) the issue of shares; (b) the acceptance of contributions to those shares; (c) the appointment of managing and supervisory directors; and (d) potentially onerous transactions as listed in § 3.4.3.[179] In these cases the incorporator(s) will bind the company directly in the deed of incorporation. For potential liabilities with respect to these actions, see § 3.4.4.

In order to work with the concept of actions on behalf of a company to be formed, there must be made some first steps towards incorporation. This is necessary in order to establish the identity of the company to be formed and the company that has actually been formed. If no such identity exists, the company after its incorporation cannot ratify the transactions which were entered into on its behalf prior to its incorporation.[180] In order to establish this identity, as a minimum, the name of the company to be formed, the persons or entities involved and the proposed capital (in view of the transaction) should be established.

In the event that, prior to its incorporation, an enterprise is started on behalf of the company to be formed, such enterprise must be registered with the commercial register.

To avoid confusion regarding the actual existence of the company or the intention to contract on behalf of the company to be formed, it is customary to indicate that the company is in the course of incorporation by adding the abbreviation '*i.o.*' (*in oprichting*) after the name of the company.

3.4.3 Potentially Onerous Agreements

In order to be relieved from personal liability, as far as possible, the founders or other parties acting on behalf of the company 'to be formed' may wish to ensure that the company will honour certain obligations from its inception,

179. Art. 2:94/204 BW.
180. Supreme Court 8 Jul. 1992, NJ 1993, 116 (*Clara Candy*).

without any need for ratification by the management board. A mere agreement to this effect with the other founders or parties acting on behalf of the company 'to be formed' will not suffice. This result can only be achieved by setting out the obligations in the deed of incorporation or by reference to the obligations in an attachment to the deed of incorporation. This is, however, limited under Netherlands law to the following types of transaction:[181]

(a) subscriptions for shares that impose special obligations on the company;
(b) acquisitions of shares on conditions other than those available to the general public (applies to NVs only);
(c) transactions that confer a benefit on a founder or third party incorporator; and
(d) capital contributions other than in cash.

After incorporation, these types of transaction may be entered into only with the prior approval of the shareholders, except if and to the extent that the management board is so expressly authorised in the articles.[182] If the articles do not provide for this authorisation of the management board or no approval has been given by the shareholders, the company will not be bound to this transaction.[183] The notes to the annual accounts for the year in which any such transaction is entered into must disclose this transaction.[184]

3.4.4 Liability of the Founders

A founder may incur liability[185] if he does not exercise sufficient care in placing the initial shares, accepting contributions to the shares, or appointing the initial management board (and supervisory board, if there is one), or by entering into any of the types of transaction set out in § 3.4.3. This cause of action is similar to a mismanagement claim (see §§ 9.2.1 and 9.2.2).

3.4.5 Organisational Expenses

The company is responsible for the payment of all reasonable expenses relating to its formation. The management board of the NV must disclose the total

181. Art. 2:94(1)/204(1) BW.
182. Art. 2:94(2)/204(2) BW.
183. Asser/Maeijer, Van Solinge & Nieuwe Weme 2-II* 2009/109 for the opinion that even without this approval, the company may nevertheless be bound to the transaction involved.
184. Art. 2:378(3) BW.
185. Arts 2:93(4)/203(4), 2:9, 2:138 BW.

amount of these expenses, or an estimate thereof, in the commercial register. There is no such obligation for the management board of the BV.[186]

3.5 Ultra Vires

This doctrine focuses on the purposes or objects clause in the articles of association (see § 3.3.3.4). The purposes of a company can merely give guidance to the interpretation of the interest that a company may have in a certain transaction.[187] If a company acts in gross violation of its own interests, it may be acting *ultra vires*. Courts will interfere only when the challenged action could not possibly be in the 'interests of the company'. The interests of a subsidiary prevail over the interests of its parent (see also § 8.2.1.1). Consequently, a subsidiary may act *ultra vires* by providing collateral for a third party loan to its parent company, thereby incurring a serious risk to its own future financial security (see also § 4.7). A company may only void a transaction that could not conceivably be within the scope of its purposes, when the other party knew the corporate purposes and should have known that this transaction was *ultra vires*. The other party is not required to make inquiries.[188] The mere availability at the commercial register of the articles containing the purposes provision does not create a presumption of the requisite knowledge. The other party cannot invoke the nullity, but can require the company to decide within a reasonable period of time whether or not it intends to proceed with the transaction.[189]

186. Art. 2:69(1) BW.
187. Supreme Court 7 Feb. 1992, NJ 1992, 438 (*Astro*); Supreme Court 16 Oct. 1992, NJ 1993, 98 (*Nagtegaal Westland/Utrecht Hypohteekbank*).
188. Art. 2:7 BW.
189. Art. 3:55(2) BW.

Chapter 4
Corporate Finance and Funding

4.1 Equity and Debt

4.1.1 General

Although for corporate finance and accounting purposes a conceptual delineation is made between equity and debt, this distinction may be blurred in practice. Certain financing and tax schemes have spurred the development of various 'hybrid' financing instruments that possess attributes that complicate a classification as either equity or debt on the basis of the conventional criteria (fixed return versus sharing of business risks etc.).[190] Examples thereof include profit participation rights (*winstrechten*) issued in the form of profit participation certificates (*winstbewijzen*) (see § 5.2.7) and profit participating loans or subordinated loans. Although the holder of a profit participation certificate does not have any voting rights, he is entitled to share in the company's profits and, depending on the articles, may have certain specified additional rights. This instrument bears some resemblance to a non-voting share, which currently only exists in the Netherlands with respect to BVs. In the example of subordinated loans, the rights of a subordinated creditor with respect to interest payments and for the liquidation proceeds rank below the rights of other creditors, which may provide the company with debt that can be considered 'near-equity'.

4.1.2 Equity

Under Netherlands law various notions of capital are in existence. When using the word capital in relation to shares, the following distinctions should be made. The authorised capital (*maatschappelijk kapitaal*) is the maximum share capital provided for in the articles of association. An NV must include an amount of authorised capital in its articles, while the articles of a BV (since the modernisation of BV law, which came into effect on 1 October 2012) may

190. For convertible debt securities and cumulative preferred profit-sharing-shares, see §§ 5.1.3 and 5.1.5.

include authorised capital. The authorised capital may be issued without an amendment of the company's articles being required. The authorised capital is divided into a certain number of shares with a nominal value, which is the amount expressed in Euros. The nominal value of BV shares may be expressed in another currency than Euros. The number of shares actually issued multiplied by the nominal value of each of the shares of any type will result in the issued capital (*geplaatst kapitaal*), which must in respect of an NV be at least one fifth of the authorised capital. Shares must be fully paid up when subscribed for, unless these shares are registered shares for which the articles specifically allow and the company and the initial holders of these shares have agreed to contribute less than the nominal value. In that case the paid up capital (*gestort kapitaal*) shall be less than the issued capital, but should in the case of an NV be at least 25% of the issued capital.[191] Bearer shares must be fully paid up upon issuance.[192] With respect to BV shares, it is allowed to postpone the payment of the nominal value in whole or partially, if this is agreed upon between the BV and the shareholder concerned. The difference between the nominal value and the lesser amount actually contributed to the shares (*obligo*) will only be due and payable by the holders of these shares if the corporate body empowered by the articles to do so calls for payment. Upon that moment the unpaid but called for part of the capital shall be shown on the balance sheet as the called up capital (*opgevraagd kapitaal*) and the asset side of the balance sheet will show a receivable. The unpaid portion may function as a cushion which supports the equity. However, until the moment the company actually calls for further payment of the unpaid part of the nominal value, the unpaid part is not due by the shareholders and is not as such a part of the equity of the company. Therefore, the company may not put this future claim on its balance sheet. It is also possible for a shareholder to pay more than the nominal value on a share to be issued, in which case there will be a capital surplus (share premium) (*agio*). Equity refers to shareholders' funds. It includes the amount actually contributed to capital, called up capital, capital surplus, reserves and retained earnings.[193]

Netherlands law recognises in principle three types of reserves: (i) statutory reserves (*wettelijke reserves*), which are reserves which the company must maintain pursuant to a statutory obligation, such as a participation reserve[194] and a revaluation reserve,[195] (ii) reserves required to be maintained

---

191. The paid-up capital should amount to at least the minimum capital, i.e. EUR 45,000 for an NV. Since 1 October 2012 a minimum capital is no longer prescribed by law for a BV.
192. Art. 2:82(3) BW.
193. Art. 2:373(1) BW.
194. Art. 2:389 BW.
195. Art. 2:390 BW.

by the articles of association (*statutaire reserves*) and (iii) freely distributable reserves (*vrije reserves*), such as the share premium reserve and the general reserve. Both the statutory reserves and the reserves required by the articles are not freely distributable. The total nominal value of the issued shares (i.e. the issued capital) has particular significance in Dutch corporate law, but bears no direct relationship to shareholders' equity, the value of the shares, the value of the assets or the cash position of the company. As stated, in respect of an NV, the issued capital must at all times be at least one fifth of the authorised capital stated in the articles.[196] If the articles of association of a BV provide for authorised capital, no such threshold applies. For the various types and classes of shares, see § 5.2.

There are no statutory rules on debt-equity ratios for companies other than banks and insurance companies and with the exception of certain tax rules. However, it should be noted that if the total equity of an NV is less than one half of its issued and called up capital, the management board must convene a shareholders' meeting within three months[197] after this situation becomes clear to the management board in order to discuss any possible measures to be taken. This provision does not apply to BVs.

4.2 Rules regarding Preservation of Equity

There is a wide variety of diverse statutory provisions aimed at defending the company, as far as possible, against a deterioration of its equity. The following rules must be seen in this context:

(a) rules for the preservation of equity (see § 4.3) and for any reduction of issued capital (see § 4.6);
(b) rules concerning the payments in respect of shares for the amounts that may exceed the nominal value (i.e. share premium contributions, see § 4.4.1);
(c) restriction on the use of corporate assets for the benefit of persons other than the company (see §§ 4.3.5 and 4.3.7). This includes empowering the company to void a transaction that violates the corporate purposes (see § 3.5);
(d) rules for the presentation of annual accounts, and disclosure thereof for audits and for the accounting profession;
(e) rules for the accounting of the financial results of subsidiaries, group companies and affiliates; and

196. Art. 2:67(4)/178(4) BW.
197. Art. 2:108a BW.

(f) subjecting members of the management board and the supervisory board to liability for mismanagement and other malfeasance in cases of non-compliance with certain statutory requirements (see § 9.2).

Until recently the rules regarding preservation of equity that applied to NVs and BVs were the same or very similar. As per 1 October 2012, the date when the modernisation of the BV law came into force, this is no longer the case.[198] With the new BV law it is intended to establish a system which is more efficient in its aim to protect creditors of the company. Most important in this respect is the introduction of new rules regarding all kinds of distributions to shareholders (i.e. distribution of dividend, buy back of shares, capital reduction), in which the management board has to review whether the company will be able to keep up with its debts payments after the distribution has been made.

4.3 Preservation of Equity

4.3.1 Objective

The rules concerning capital to a large extent reflect the implementation of the Second and Fourth EC Company Law Directives (see §§ 1.3.2 and 1.3.4). These rules focus on the concept of the nominal value per share and of the issued and paid in share capital. Their prime objective is to prevent the dilution of the issued capital, which might leave creditors and shareholders with a mere 'shell'. With respect to the BV certain rules that have been established with the modernisation of the BV law as per 1 October 2012, no longer reflect the Second Directive referred to above.

Although a potential creditor of a company might check the commercial register for the amount of the issued and paid in capital (see § 12.2) and may rely on the published annual accounts of the company, in a large number of cases the amount of the issued capital will be only a small fraction of eventual claims. Nevertheless, the rules concerning the preservation of capital must be strictly observed. If the rules have not been strictly observed, the transaction may be void and the managing directors may be personally liable.

198. See Stb. 2012, 299, Stb. 2012, 300 and Stb. 2012, 301.

4.3.2 Nominal Value

Shares must have a nominal value.[199] The nominal value is a fixed amount per type of share. It is an arbitrary figure stated in the articles. The articles may provide for shares with different nominal values.[200] Shares without a nominal value are not permitted.[201] The share capital and the nominal value of each share must be expressed in Euro,[202] although the nominal value of BV shares may be expressed in (one type of) foreign currency. Shares may, of course, be issued at a price above their nominal value. The consideration in excess of the nominal value is called share premium or capital surplus (*agio*).

4.3.3 Minimum Capital

In order to ensure that the capital will not fall below an absolute minimum level that will remain available to the company to the extent not deteriorated by losses, the law requires for an NV a minimum capital of EUR 45,000.[203] The statutory amount of the minimum capital may be increased. Increases are pegged to mandatory increases prescribed by EU legislation.[204] There are specific rules applicable for the minimum capital of banks and insurance companies.

The minimum capital may be an amount that is very small in relation to the nature of the business of the company and the risks it may incur in its ordinary course of business. This is one of the reasons that in relation to the modernisation of the BV law that came into force on 1 October 2012, the minimum capital requirements have been abolished for BVs. The minimum capital for a BV was EUR 18,000. Nowadays, a BV can be incorporated with a capital of e.g. one eurocent. Additional related requirements, such as the bank statement of incorporation, have also been abolished.

The paid in capital (see § 4.1.2) is that part of the issued capital for which contributions have actually been made. In the case of an NV it must amount to at least 25% of the issued capital, but in any event be no less than the minimum capital of EUR 45,000.[205]

---

199. Arts. 2:67(1)/178(1), 2:79(1)/190 BW.
200. Art. 2:67(1)/178(1) BW.
201. Art. 2:67/178 BW.
202. Art. 67(1) BW.
203. Art. 2:67(2) BW.
204. Second Company Law Directive, see § 1.3.2.
205. Art. 2:67(3), 2:80(1) BW.

A shareholder is liable for the unpaid balance on his shares, but not in excess of their nominal value.[206] He is also liable for the amount of the agreed subscription price in excess of the nominal value.[207]

Even after selling shares that are not fully paid up, all previous shareholders remain liable for the unpaid balance until a previous shareholder is released from such obligation by a notarial deed or a registered non-notarial deed by the management board and, where applicable, the supervisory board.[208] This liability only concerns the unpaid part of the nominal value. In spite of the release, however, the released former shareholder remains liable with respect to payments which are called up within one year after the day on which the notarial deed of release was executed or the non-notarial deed was registered at the tax authorities. The company's share register is not open to the public, except with regard to shares that are not fully paid up.[209] The fact that shares are not fully paid up must be registered with the commercial register.[210] If shares are subscribed for under the agreement, that share premium will be paid at a time in the future (only possible for BVs); the obligation to pay such a surplus remains with the original subscribing shareholder.

4.3.4 Shareholders and Creditors

The issued share capital is sometimes considered as some sort of guarantee for the company's liabilities. As indicated above, such liabilities can of course extend widely beyond the issued share capital. Upon dissolution of the company, the claims of shareholders are subordinate to claims of debenture holders and other creditors.[211] A shareholder may not, without the company's consent, set off the company's claims against the amount due for payment on his or her shares.[212] The trustee in bankruptcy (*curator*) may contest any such consent granted prior to bankruptcy.

4.3.5 Contributions to Capital

The required contribution to the issued shares must, in principle, be made at the time of issuance of the shares (see § 4.4). There are two forms of capi-

206. Art. 2:81/192 BW.
207. Art. 2:80(1) BW.
208. Art. 2:90(1)/199(1) BW.
209. Art. 2:85(4)/194(4) BW.
210. Art. 22(1d) HrB 2008. See Chapter 12.
211. Art. 2:23b(1) BW.
212. Art. 2:80(4)/191(3) BW, this also includes the former shareholder for payment on shares which are not fully paid up (see § 4.3.3.).

tal contributions: contribution in cash[213] and contribution in kind (non-cash contribution).[214]

Cash contributions can be made either in Euro or in a foreign currency. At the time of formation of an NV, the civil law notary involved must obtain a statement from a Dutch bank (or another bank within the European Economic Area that is under governmental supervision[215]) that upon formation the amount is indeed available to the company immediately after its incorporation, or that the bank has received the required amount of cash in an account in the name of the company 'to be formed' (see § 3.4.2). This bank statement must be issued not more than five months prior to the date of incorporation of the NV. The deed of incorporation may state that the company accepts this contribution, even though the amount of cash available at the date of formation may differ from the amount originally paid into the bank account.[216] If payment is made in foreign currency, the bank statement must state the amount in Euro into which the amount in foreign currency may be freely exchanged on any given day during the one-month period prior to incorporation. If the bank statement relates to a moment prior to that month, a new statement must be obtained, stating the exchange rate on the day of incorporation.[217] An official copy of the statement by the bank is deposited with the commercial register (see § 12.1.1) for public inspection. When shares are issued after incorporation of the NV, a statement from a bank is required only when foreign currency is contributed;[218] the statement is limited to the exchange rate only.

An NV may allow a shareholder to contribute only partially to the nominal value of his shares and to agree that the remainder, up to a maximum of 75%, must be contributed when called for by the company (see § 4.1.2).[219] The obligation to contribute the nominal value of shares in a BV may be postponed in whole or in part.[220] The issuance of shares at a discount to their nominal value is allowed only in cases of issuance by an NV to a professional underwriter, and the discount may not exceed 6% of the nominal value. The underwriter is not entitled to contribute in kind but must pay in cash.[221] These shares are thereafter regarded as having been issued at nominal value.

213. Art. 2:80a(1)/191a(1) BW.
214. Art. 2:80b(1)/191b(1) BW.
215. Art. 2:93a(3) BW.
216. Art. 2:93a(1) BW.
217. Art. 2:93a(2) BW.
218. Art. 2:93a(6) BW.
219. Art. 2:80(1) BW.
220. Art. 2:191(1) BW.
221. Art. 2:80(2) BW.

In order to make valid contributions in kind, both at the time of incorporation[222] of the company and thereafter,[223] certain formalities must be observed, which are different for BVs and NVs.[224] Several provisions counter the issue of 'dilution', i.e. nominal value shares are issued for a non-cash contribution that has a value below the aggregate nominal value of the issued shares. In addition, as a complement to these rules, and only for NVs, Netherlands law contains certain statutory provisions that subject certain transactions between a founder and the company, which differ in their form from contributions to shares, but judged on their substance are equivalent, to similar control rules. The German 'buzz word' for these statutory provisions, *Nachgründung*, has become the Dutch term as well.[225]

Contributions in kind in respect of shares are restricted to assets that can be objectively appraised and can be actually transferred. Promises to perform work or services cannot serve as capital contributions.[226] In addition thereto, the contributor, i.e. the future shareholder, must have the objective to actually transfer the asset and to put it at the disposal of the company. If this is not the case, it may be argued later that the shares have actually not been paid up.[227] This may result in an additional obligation for the shareholder to make a contribution in cash or in kind and may under certain circumstances also result in a liability for each member of the management board of an NV for actions performed by the company during that period (see § 9.2.4.5).[228]

At the formation of the company, the contributed assets must be described and valued in writing by the incorporators. In the event of an issue of shares after incorporation, this description must be prepared by the management board. If it concerns an NV, in both cases the description must be accompanied by an auditors' statement stating that the value of the contribution in kind equals at least the aggregate amount to be paid up on the shares to be issued (see § 4.4).[229] The auditor's statement and the description of the assets, must, in the case of an NV, be deposited with the commercial register for public inspection.[230] With respect to a BV, the description must be deposited at its office for inspection by its shareholders and others holding meeting rights.[231] Exemptions apply, inter alia, to contribution in kind on shares of group com-

---

222. Art. 2:94a/204a BW.
223. Art. 2:94b/204b BW.
224. Certain exceptions may be applicable for NVs; see Arts 94a(3) and 94b(3) BW.
225. Art. 2:94c BW.
226. Art. 2:80b(1)/191b(1) BW.
227. Supreme Court 24 March 2000, NJ 2000, 354 (*WTN*).
228. Art. 2:69(2) BW.
229. Arts. 2:94a(2) and 2:94b(2) BW.
230. Arts. 2:94a(1)(2) and 2:94b(2) BW. A violation of these provisions is a criminal offence, see Art. 1(4) WED.
231. Art. 2:204a(1)/2:204b(1) BW.

panies (see § 3.1.2) for which another group company has assumed liability pursuant to a statutory procedure.[232]

If a contribution in kind is proposed at incorporation of the company, it must be stated in the deed of incorporation or in an attachment thereto (see § 3.4.3). Thereafter, approval of the general meeting of shareholders is required for contributions in kind, unless the management board is expressly authorised in the articles of association to accept this contribution.[233] Any contribution in kind must be made forthwith after the shares have been subscribed for.

In some cases the contribution in kind is structured in such a way that the future shareholder contributes assets under the obligation that the company assumes certain liabilities. In order to fulfil the payment obligation on the shares issued, the balance of the value of the assets minus the value of the liabilities to be assumed must equal at least the amount expressed in Euros to be paid on such shares. This structure is used, *inter alia*, for the contribution of an enterprise as payment on shares.

During the two-year period following its first registration with the commercial register, an NV must observe certain formalities when entering into any transaction involving the acquisition of assets that were personally owned by any founder at any time during the one-year period preceding the formation date.[234] The acquisition of assets as well as any preparatory action serving to acquire assets in the future, such as an option agreement, falls under the scope of these *Nachgründung* rules.[235] The prohibition does not apply to acquisitions: (i) made at a public auction or stock exchange; (ii) completed within the normal course of business of the company; (iii) for which an accountant's statement has already been issued; or (iv) resulting from a statutory merger (see § 11.3) or statutory division (see § 11.4).[236] The risk of non-compliance with the *Nachgründung* rules is that a transaction may be voided by the NV[237] during the three-year period following such transaction.[238] The directors may be liable for breach of their fiduciary duties (see § 9.1.1) towards the NV when they neglect to seek the nullity of such transaction. The formalities required to comply with the *Nachgründung* rules (and thus to avoid nullification of the transaction) are: (i) a description to be prepared by the management board relating to the assets to be acquired by the company stating the acquisition

232. See for applicable exemptions: Art. 2:94a(3(6) BW and Art. 2:94b(3)(6) BW.
233. Art. 2:94(2)/204(2) BW.
234. Art. 2:94c(1) BW.
235. Various schemes have been developed in practice to set aside the *Nachgründung* rules. See M.L. Lennarts and J.M. Schutte-Veenstra, Versoepeling van het BV kapitaalbeschermingsrecht, Kluwer, Deventer 2004, p. 30.
236. Art. 2:94c(7) BW.
237. Or the trustee (*curator*), in the case of bankruptcy of the NV.
238. Art. 3:52 lid 1, sub d BW.

price; (ii) an auditors' statement confirming that the price to be paid equals at least the value of the assets; and (iii) a resolution of the shareholders' meeting, authorising the acquisition.

Until 1 October 2012 the *Nachgründung* rules described above were also applicable for BVs, but in the context of the modernisation of the BV law the rules have been abolished because of their lack of effectiveness.

4.3.6 Treasury Shares

Netherlands law allows a company to acquire its own shares, often referred to as treasury shares (*eigen aandelen*).[239] There are, however, significant limitations:

(a) a company cannot subscribe for shares that it will issue at incorporation or at any time thereafter;[240]
(b) the nominal value of the shares held in treasury must be fully paid;[241]
(c) a listed NV may not, directly or indirectly through its subsidiaries, acquire or hold in ownership or hold as a pledgee more than 50% of its own stock. For a BV and a non-listed NV, a maximum of 100% minus one (voting) share applies;[242]
(d) an NV may not repurchase shares in an amount that (pursuant to the latest adopted annual accounts and at all times subject to the restrictions stated under (f) below) would bring its equity below the aggregate of the amount contributed to the issued capital, any amounts called up and statutory reserves and reserves required by the articles of association.[243] The purchase price paid by a BV to repurchase its shares, may not bring its equity below the amount of statutory reserves and reserves required by its articles – if any;[244]
(e) a repurchase by an NV must be approved by the general meeting of shareholders prior to the actual repurchase.[245] A general authorisation cannot exceed an 18-month period for a listed NV and five years for

239. For this purpose the term 'shares' encompasses depository receipts issued therefore (Art. 2:98(9)/207(6) BW). Different rules apply to investment companies with variable capital (see § 3.1.3 and Art. 2:98(8) BW).
240. Art. 2:95(1)/205 BW.
241. Art. 2:98(1)/207(1) BW.
242. Art. 2:98(2) BW and Art. 2:175(1) final sentence BW.
243. Art. 2:98(2) BW. This means that the purchase price to be paid by the NV may not exceed the free distributable resources.
244. Art. 2:207(2) BW.
245. This authorisation is not required for an acquisition for the purpose of transferring such shares to employees of such NV or a group company (see § 3.1.2), provided the articles so permit and the shares are listed on an exchange (Art. 2:98(5) BW).

a non-listed NV.[246] Without a (valid) authorisation, the management board is not authorised to repurchase the shares.[247] Since 1 October 2012, such restrictions no longer apply to a BV, unless the articles of association restrict the repurchase of shares;

(f) a repurchase by an NV is prohibited during the last six months of the company's financial year if the annual accounts for the preceding financial year were not adopted and approved, where applicable, during the first six months;[248]

(g) parties who purchase shares in their own name for the account of the company are, in the case of a BV, deemed to have purchased for their own account[249] or, in the case of an NV, under a statutory obligation to transfer the acquired shares to the company;[250]

(h) the possibility of subsidiaries to hold shares in a parent is restricted. A subsidiary of an NV or a BV, whether or not this subsidiary is a foreign company, may not subscribe for shares issued by the parent. It may, however, purchase shares of its parent and repurchase its own shares held by its parent company only to the extent this parent company may do so (NV) or with consent of the management board of the parent company (BV);[251] and

(i) voting rights cannot be exercised on treasury shares.[252] Unless the articles provide otherwise, treasury shares of an NV are entitled to distribution rights. For a BV, a reverse rule is in place: treasury shares are not entitled to distributions, unless the articles provide otherwise.

Repurchased shares remain part of the issued capital until redeemed (*ingetrokken*) (see § 4.6.2). Redemption has the effect of reducing issued capital by the amount of the total nominal value of the repurchased and redeemed shares. Treasury shares may not be shown in the annual accounts as assets.[253] Equity must be reduced by the price of the repurchased shares. The value attributed to an investment in a subsidiary is reduced by the price at which the subsidiary purchases shares of the parent company.

A repurchase of shares in an NV within two years after the first registration with the commercial register upon its incorporation may fall under the rules of *Nachgründung* (see § 4.3.5). This means that in such a case those

246. Art. 2:98(4) BW.
247. An unauthorised repurchase may be invoked against the selling shareholder.
248. Art. 2:98(3) BW.
249. Art. 2:207b BW.
250. Art. 2:98b BW.
251. Art. 2:98d(1)/207d(1) BW.
252. Art. 2:118(7)/228(6) BW.
253. Art. 2:385(5) BW.

shares to be repurchased should be appraised and described in writing, an auditor's opinion should be obtained and shareholders' approval should be given before this transaction is entered into.

If a company intends to sell the treasury shares which are registered shares where the articles provide that the transfer is restricted (see § 5.3.4), the company must observe these provisions.

4.3.7 Financial Assistance Rules

Netherlands law generally prohibits NVs from giving financial assistance to third parties (whether shareholders or others) if this assistance is 'for the purpose of' the subscription or acquisition by third parties of its shares or depository receipts issued therefore. These financial assistance rules were incorporated into Netherlands law to implement the Second EC Company Law Directive (see § 1.3.2). These rules purport to preserve corporate equity and to protect creditors.

Implementation of this directive in the Netherlands has created statutory provisions which differ in their treatment of NVs[254] and BVs[255] (an NV may, however, convert to a BV, see § 11.5). In respect of the modernisation of BV law, the statutory provisions regarding financial assistance have been abolished for BVs as per 1 October 2012.

For NVs, the financial assistance rules prohibit the company from providing collateral, guaranteeing payment of a certain acquisition price or otherwise guaranteeing or binding itself with or for third parties 'for the purpose of the subscription or acquisition by third parties of its shares or depository receipts issued therefore'.[256] In the past the granting of a loan by an NV for this purpose was prohibited. Since 2008, the NV has been allowed to grant a loan for the purpose of subscription or acquisition by third parties of shares in the company under the following conditions: (i) the loan is on fair market terms (this also relates to interest and security); (ii) the net assets, less the amount of the loan, shall not be less than the sum of the paid and called up part of the capital increased by the statutory reserves; (iii) the creditworthiness of the third party or parties has been carefully examined; and (iv) in the event of an issuance of new shares or a sale of shares by the company, the price of the shares should be fair.[257] For the amount of the loan the NV must maintain a non-distributable reserve. A decision by the management board to grant such a loan requires approval by the shareholders' meeting. If less than one half of

254. Art. 2:98c BW.
255. Art. 2:207c BW (deleted as per 1 October 2012).
256. Art. 2:98c(1) BW.
257. Art. 2:98c(2)(d) BW.

the issued share capital is represented at the meeting, the resolution for approval must be adopted with a majority of at least two thirds of the votes cast. For a listed NV the majority is 95% under all circumstances.[258] The respective prohibitions also extend to subsidiaries (see § 3.1.2).

Finally, the financial assistance prohibitions do not apply to NV-shares acquired by or for the account of employees of the company or its group companies (see § 3.1.2).[259]

The imprecise language of the law may complicate various forms of leveraged acquisition that are common in other countries. Several alternative means of financing a leveraged acquisition have developed in practice. However, in the absence of case law which provides a conclusive interpretation of the financial assistance prohibitions, care should be exercised.

The assessment of whether or not to provide financial support falls within the competence of the management board. Although the statutory rules regarding financial assistance have been abolished for BVs, managing directors of a BV should take care in providing financial assistance as the general rules regarding directors' liability (see Chapter 9) apply.

4.4 New Issuance of Shares

4.4.1 General

A new issuance of shares increases the issued capital, which must at all times remain within the limits of the authorised capital of an NV and – only if included in the articles of association – of a BV.[260] The authorised capital can only be increased by an amendment of the articles (see § 11.2).

With respect to the payment on the shares, the following distinction should be made, which applies both to shares to be issued at the incorporation and thereafter.

With respect to the NV, the law provides[261] that the payment obligation on a share to be issued consists of:

(a) the nominal value of the share (unless it has been agreed upon initially to pay in less, with a maximum of 75% of the nominal value); and

258. Art. 2:98c(5) BW.
259. Art. 2:98c(8) BW. Similarly these provisions do not apply to banks and similar institutions registered under the Wft, to the extent such transactions are concluded in the normal course of their businesses (Art. 2:98c(9) BW).
260. Art. 2:79(2)/178(1) BW. An issue of shares in excess of the authorised capital will be (partially) void; see Asser/Maeijer, Van Solinge & Nieuwe Weme 2-II* 2009/94.
261. Art. 2:80(1) BW.

(b) the surplus on the share to be paid if so agreed upon by the new shareholder and the company, the so-called 'agreed surplus' (share premium).

With respect to the BV, the law provides that the payment obligation only relates to the nominal value[262] (unless the shares are not fully paid up, see § 4.1.2).

This means that, with respect to the NV, a shareholder subscribing for a new share must pay up the amount of the payment obligation when subscribing for the share and, as a result thereof, the formalities regarding the actual payment, such as the bank statement (only required at the formation of the company) and the auditors statement, must relate to this payment obligation. When paying up the shares in kind, a surplus can be created 'spontaneously'. For instance, a future shareholder subscribes for shares with an aggregate nominal value of EUR 100,000 and agrees to contribute on such shares a participation in another company with a value in excess of EUR 100,000. If the value appears to be EUR 150,000, a spontaneous surplus is created of EUR 50,000. The formalities as described above do not apply to this spontaneous surplus.

With respect to the NV, an agreed surplus on the shares cannot be paid at a later date. If shares are issued above the nominal value and a surplus is agreed upon, this surplus qualifies as agreed surplus and must be paid on the shares upon issue.

With respect to the BV, the agreed surplus does not form a part of the payment obligation. Consequently, the shareholder and the company can agree that the surplus on the shares can be paid at a later stage, provided that this payment of surplus will be made in cash. Since all payments in kind must be made forthwith after the shares are subscribed for, a contribution in kind cannot be agreed at a future date. This restriction also applies to any called up part of the unpaid capital.

The distribution of power within the company for the issuance of new shares, and the pre-emptive rights that existing shareholders may have to these newly issued shares, are discussed below. The power to issue shares is normally accompanied by the power to determine the consideration thereof. If the consideration is below fair market value, the value of the shares of the existing shareholders will be diluted. This may lead to an action in court based on the ground that the determination of the consideration violated principles of good faith.

262. Art. 2:191(1) BW.

The power to issue new shares and to determine the consideration thereof may also be of significance in hostile takeover situations. The key element of this device is the ability of either the management board or holders of a specific type of shares (e.g. priority shareholders, see § 5.2.3) to place preference shares overnight to fend off a raider.

When issuing shares, a distinction should be made between the corporate resolution to issue shares and the actual formalities, based on such resolution, by which the shares are issued and subscribed for. Without a valid resolution to issue shares, the subsequent formalities performed may be invalid.[263] The issued shares are placed by the management board.

In the case of a public offer, the management board must observe the applicable stock exchange regulations.

The formalities for the issuance of shares are similar to the formalities for transfer of shares (see § 5.3). As noted above, a company cannot subscribe for its own shares, and is severely restricted in purchasing shares initially issued to others (see § 4.3.6).

4.4.2 NV

The shareholders' meeting of an NV has the power to decide on the issuance of new shares and to determine the consideration for those shares. The shareholders' meeting may delegate this power to the management board or the supervisory board or another corporate body, for a certain period not exceeding five years, stating the number of shares which may be issued pursuant to this delegation.[264] The delegation gives the corporate body so designated exclusive rights, i.e. during the period of delegation the shareholders are not authorised to resolve to issue shares. During this period, the delegation cannot be revoked, unless otherwise stated in the delegation resolution, but it can be renewed from time to time. For listed companies, it is common practice to renew this delegation on an annual rolling basis. The delegation must be registered with the commercial register within eight days after the resolution has been taken. If there are different types of shares, the power of the shareholders' meeting to issue shares of a specific type and to delegate this power to the board is subject to the prior approval of the holders of that type of share.[265] Within eight days after the issuance of new shares, the company must file

263. Supreme Court 10 Mar 1995, NJ 1995, 595 (*Janssen Pers*). However, see Asser/Maeijer, Van Solinge & Nieuwe Weme 2-II* 2009/237.
264. Art. 2:96(1) BW. Different rules apply to investment companies with variable capital (see § 3.1.3).
265. Art. 2:96(2) BW.

information concerning the type and number of shares with the commercial register.[266]

Certain formalities may need to be observed in addition to the relevant resolution in order to complete the actual issue of shares. A distinction should be made between:

(a) bearer shares: a resolution to issue shares may be followed by a subscription agreement and should be followed by the actual deliverance of share certificates;[267]
(b) registered shares in a non-listed company: a resolution to issue shares must be followed by the execution of a notarial deed to which the company and the subscriber are parties and by which the shares will be actually issued; and
(c) registered shares in a company of which (part of) the issued capital is listed on an official stock exchange:[268] no specific requirements are necessary provided the subscriber appears to accept the shares issued to him.

Shareholders of an NV have a statutory pre-emptive right to subscribe for newly issued shares of the type owned, proportional to their existing shares in the capital of the company.[269] The shareholders can, in various ways, be excluded or restricted from this pre-emptive right. The shareholders' meeting can take a resolution to that effect. The shareholders' meeting can also delegate to a corporate body (the same body to which was originally delegated the power to issue new shares) the right to exclude or restrict the shareholders' pre-emptive rights. This delegation is limited to a period of five years, cannot be revoked, unless otherwise stated in the delegation resolution, and may be renewed from time to time.[270] A shareholders' resolution to restrict or exclude pre-emptive rights or to delegate this power requires a qualified majority of two thirds of the votes cast if less than one half of the issued shares is represented at the meeting.[271] Within eight days after the resolution concerning the restriction or exclusion of pre-emptive rights was taken, the company must file the complete text thereof with the commercial register.[272]

---

266. Art. 2:96(3) BW. A violation of this provision is a criminal offence, see Art. 1(4) WED.
267. One cannot become a holder of a bearer share without a share certificate.
268. Or of which this is expected to happen in the near future, Art. 2:86c(1) BW.
269. Art. 2:96a(1) BW. Different rules apply to investment companies with variable capital (see § 3.1.3).
270. Art. 2:96a(6) BW.
271. Art. 2:96a(7) BW.
272. Art. 2:96a(7) BW. A violation of this provision is a criminal offence, see Art. 1(4) WED.

Pre-emptive rights are not available for new shares issued with a consideration other than cash, unless the articles provide otherwise, or with respect to shares issued to employees of the company or its group companies (see § 3.1.2). Except as otherwise provided in the articles, holders of preference shares have no pre-emptive rights and holders of ordinary shares have no pre-emptive rights with respect to preference shares.[273]

4.4.3 BV

The issued capital of a BV may be increased by a resolution of the general meeting of shareholders. The shareholders can delegate this power to another corporate body. This delegation can be revoked at any time.[274] Furthermore, the articles may confer the power to issue new shares to another corporate body.

In order to complete the increase of the issued capital of the BV, a notarial deed of issue must be executed by which both the company and the subscriber shall be parties.

Unless the articles of association state otherwise, each existing BV shareholder has a pre-emptive right to subscribe for newly issued shares proportional to his or her existing shares in the capital of the company, except for shares issued to employees of the company and its group companies.[275] Unlike the NV, the articles of a BV may provide that the existing shareholders will never have pre-emptive rights. If the articles do not contain such provision, the shareholders can, nevertheless, restrict or exclude the pre-emptive rights of existing shareholders by shareholders' resolution for every issuance of shares, unless the articles provide otherwise.[276] The articles may also designate another corporate body which is or will be authorised to exclude pre-emptive rights.

Except as otherwise provided in the articles, holders of non-profit-sharing shares, non-voting shares and preference shares have no pre-emptive rights with respect to ordinary shares and holders of ordinary shares have no pre-emptive rights with respect to non-profit-sharing shares, non-voting shares and preference shares.[277]

273. Art. 2:96a(2), (3) BW.
274. Art. 2:206(1) BW.
275. Art. 2:206a(1) BW.
276. Art. 2:206a(1) BW.
277. Art. 2:206a(2/3) BW.

4.5 Stock Options

A company can give options either on treasury shares or on newly issued shares. Unless restricted in the articles, treasury shares can be sold by the company on terms that the management board deems appropriate, without restraint. However, if the articles provide for a restriction on the transfer of shares, this restriction must be observed. Options to acquire newly issued shares, however, are subject to the same rules as an original issue of shares (see § 4.4),[278] including the rules for pre-emptive rights.[279]

4.6 Reduction of Issued Capital

4.6.1 General

Two different methods are available for the reduction of issued capital:

(a) redemption of shares (*intrekking*); and
(b) reduction of nominal value (*afstempelen*).

Each method has its merits and limitations. Since 1 October 2012, the procedures regarding capital reduction differ between NVs and BVs.

With respect to NVs capital reduction is subject to strict rules concerning publication and public notification for the benefit of creditors. Public notification must be made by filing with the commercial register and the publication of this filing in a nationally distributed daily newspaper. Creditors may oppose the contemplated action within a two-month period after the date of the publication. Additional waiting periods and posting of security are required in some cases.[280] Disputes are subject to the exclusive jurisdiction of the competent District Court. Irrespective of whether any creditors object, the reduction of issued capital may never bring the issued capital below the statutory minimum capital threshold. If the proposed reduction brings the issued minimum capital below 20% of the authorised capital (which threshold is prescribed by law for NVs (see § 4.1.2), an amendment of the articles is required. An amendment of the articles is also necessary if the nominal value of the shares is reduced.

The resolution to reduce the issued capital of an NV, unless it concerns a reduction of the nominal value as a result of losses (see § 4.6.3), only becomes effective after the two-month period has elapsed. In the event that an amend-

278. Art. 2:96(5)/206(2) BW.
279. Art. 2:96a(8)/206a(6) BW.
280. Art. 2:100 BW.

ment of the articles of association is necessary, the capital reduction becomes effective after the deed of amendment has been executed as well.

With regard to BVs, the procedure has been simplified, as publication and notification of the intended capital reduction is no longer required. Also, the two-month period during which creditors may oppose the intended reduction of capital has been abolished. The procedure currently in place for BVs is that the general meeting resolves to a capital reduction; in order to execute this decision, the approval of the management board is necessary. The management board must refuse its approval if it knows or should reasonably foresee that the company will not be able to keep up with its debt payments afterwards.[281] This is the same test as is applicable for the distribution of dividends (see § 4.8).

4.6.2 Redemption

A redemption *(intrekking)* of shares is only possible: (i) with shares held in treasury; (ii) with shares in relation to which the articles of association prior to their issue provide that this specific type of share can be redeemed with repayment; and (iii) only for BVs with the approval of all holders of the shares of that class or specification. A shareholder whose shares have been redeemed will receive the nominal value of those shares to the extent paid. However, if, prior to the issue of the shares, redemption of a specific type of share is permitted under the articles, the redemption will include all shares of that type (e.g. preference shares), unless such redemption relates specifically to balloted shares (*uitgelote aandelen*), as stipulated in the articles prior to their issuance.[282] With respect to a BV, shares may also be redeemed with consent of the shareholder concerned.[283]

4.6.3 Reduction of Nominal Value

A reduction of nominal value *(afstempeling)* is often effected to make a tax-effective distribution to shareholders of an amount of excess cash held by the company, or when a new capital issuance is being considered and earlier losses have reduced the value of the shares below their nominal value.[284] A nominal value reduction is therefore usually part of a recapitalisation plan. Reduction of nominal value is possible with or without partial payment of

281. Art. 2:208(1) and (6) BW
282. Art. 2:99(2)/208(2) BW.
283. Art. 2:208(2 final sentence) BW.
284. Art. 2:99(3)/208(3) BW.

the nominal value to the shareholders and exemption of their obligation of contribution to shares.[285]

With respect to the reduction of the nominal value with repayment, a notarial deed of amendment[286] of the articles of association must be executed in order to reduce the nominal value of the shares, and – when it concerns an NV – is subject to the requirements concerning filings, waiting periods and any creditors' opposition. The amount to be paid by the company to the shareholder as a result of the reduction of the nominal value shall become due and payable as per the day of the execution of the notarial deed. In the event the reduction of the nominal value serves to make up for losses only, i.e. without any repayments to shareholders, these requirements do not apply.

4.7 Debt Financing of the Group

Due to several major bankruptcy cases in the Netherlands in the past, attention has been given to the financing practice of companies affiliated in a group (see § 3.1.2) whereby the parent company, or a financing subsidiary, creates a debt with collateral from other subsidiaries, including companies that either do not share in the benefits or do not do so in a proportional amount.

The ultra vires doctrine (see § 3.5) provides the framework for determining whether or not the subsidiary may validly make collateral available to its parent and, through the parent, to its sister companies. It can be argued that upstream guarantees are valid even when the financing does not serve the interests of the subsidiary. The best test of the validity of this financial assistance by the subsidiary is whether the pledge on the assets or the guarantee foreseeably jeopardises the company's existence.[287]

4.8 Distributions

4.8.1 Dividends

4.8.1.1 Profit Allocation; Dividend Allocation

The shareholders' meeting has the power to adopt the annual accounts. The right to adopt the annual accounts does not, however, imply the right to allocate profits. The principal rule for NVs is that, unless the articles provide otherwise, profits shall be distributed to the shareholders. Many articles state that the profits are at the disposal of the shareholders' meeting. This rule is

285. Arts. 2:99(3), (4)/208(3), (4) BW.
286. Art. 2:99(1)/208(1) BW.
287. Court of Appeal Arnhem 19 Dec. 1995, NJ 1996, 307 (*Heineken/Telders*).

incorporated in the Dutch Civil Code for BVs, since the modernisation of the BV law as per 1 October 2012. In that case, the shareholders' meeting has the power to create reserves and allocate profits, and consequently to determine the amount of dividends to be distributed.[288] However, the articles may grant the power to create reserves out of profit to another corporate body, such as the management board, the supervisory board, or the meeting of holders of a specific type or class of shares (e.g. priority shares, see § 5.2.3). Unless the articles state otherwise, the claim for payment of dividends is in the case of an NV created by a resolution of the shareholders, which requires the prior adoption of the annual accounts.[289] This applies to NVs, but not to BVs because of the approval of the management board that is prescribed by law (see § 4.8.1.2).

All shareholders share in the profit in proportion to the mandatorily[290] paid in part of the nominal value of their shares in the capital of the company, unless otherwise provided in the articles,[291] provided that no share is completely excluded from dividend rights. With respect to BVs, the law provides more flexibility, where instead of a provision in the articles of association it is also possible that the shareholders unanimously agree to differentiate between shareholders in sharing the profit.[292] Also, a BV can issue non-profit-sharing shares (see § 4.8.4).

Treasury shares of an NV are entitled to dividends, unless the articles state otherwise; a reverse provision (no entitlement to dividends, unless the articles state otherwise) applies to treasury shares of a BV.[293] As generally provided in the articles of association, cumulative preference shares (see § 5.2.2) with payments in arrear rank first with respect to payments of the arrears. Thereafter, payment on all other preference shares must be made in the amount of the stated preferences, followed by payment on ordinary shares. The articles may provide that the profits to which a certain class of shares is entitled be allocated in full or in part to a certain reserve.[294] Dividends may be paid either in cash or in kind. A shareholder's claim for payment expires after five years, unless a longer period is granted under the articles.[295]

288. Art. 2:105(1)/216(1) BW.
289. Art. 2:105(3)/216(3) BW.
290. See § 4.4.1.
291. Arts. 2:92(1), 2:105(6) BW.
292. Art. 2:216(6) BW.
293. Art. 2:105(5)/216(5) BW.
294. Art. 2: 105(10)/216(9) BW.
295. Art. 2:105(7)/216(7) BW.

4.8.1.2 Legality

With regard to payment of dividends, a distinction should be made between: (i) the regular dividend following the adoption of the annual accounts; and (ii) distributions which are made at any other time during a financial year, called 'interim dividends'. Also, a distinction should be made between the NV and the BV. The modernisation of the BV law that entered into force on 1 October 2012 changed the provisions of law in this respect significantly.

4.8.1.2.1 NV

For both categories of distribution the rule for NVs is that dividends can be paid only to the extent that the company's equity (see § 4.1.2) exceeds the total of the actual contributed amount, and the called up part (see § 4.3.5) of the issued capital, plus the statutory reserves and reserves required to be maintained by the articles (the equity preservation test).[296] Consequently, payment of dividends paid out of current profits despite the existence of an accumulated loss that is not eliminated by current profits is not permitted.

There are no statutory solvency or cash flow requirements that an NV must meet before dividends can be paid. Case law, however, indicates that even if the equity preservation test is met, a distribution of dividends which leads to a situation in which the continuity of the company is in danger, may result in liability of managing directors or shareholders of the company.[297]

With respect to the regular dividends, the distribution shall take place after adoption of the annual accounts which demonstrates that the distribution is allowed. A company may, if the articles so permit, distribute an interim dividend, which is declared and paid before the annual accounts are adopted, provided that at that time the equity preservation test can be met.[298] The equity preservation test must be met by a date not earlier than the first day of the third month prior to the month in which the payment of an interim dividend is announced.[299] In addition, the management board must prepare a statement of assets and liabilities as of the date of the test, to be signed by each managing director and filed with the commercial register.[300]

This interim distribution can take place in either of the two following forms, or as a combination of both: (i) distribution out of the free distribut-

296. Art. 2:105(2) BW.
297. See Supreme Court 8 Nov.1991, NJ 1992, 174 (*Nimox*) and Supreme Court 6 Feb. 2004, JOR 2004, 6 (*Reinders Didam*).
298. Art. 2:105(4) BW.
299. Art. 2:105(4) BW.
300. Art. 2:105(4) BW. A violation of this provision is a criminal offence, see Art. 1(4) WED.

able reserves; and (ii) distribution out of profits. In the latter case the profit distribution shall come out of the profits of the current financial year.

To the extent that, upon their adoption, the annual accounts indicate a failure to meet the equity preservation test, the possibility to rescind dividend payments is limited to dividend recipients who knew or should have known that the distribution of the dividend was illegal.[301]

4.8.1.2.2 BV

Until 1 October 2012 the same rules as described above in respect of NVs were applicable to distribution of dividends by BVs. These rules are based on a equity preservation test, a test of the distributable capital of the company. This test has been abolished for BVs and replaced by a system under which two tests must be carried out.

First, under the new rules the general meeting may decide to distribute profits (or reserves) to the extent that the equity capital exceeds the reserves prescribed by law (statutory reserves) or by the articles of association.[302] The decision to distribute can only be executed once the management board has approved it. The management board must refuse its approval if it knows or should reasonably foresee that the company will not be able to keep up with its debt payments afterwards.[303] In this (second) test, the board will have to take notice of all circumstances that might be relevant for the company's capacity to pay its debts during (in general) one year after the distribution.

If the management board grants its approval and it appears later that the company cannot satisfy its debts, the managing directors are then personally liable for the shortfall if – in short – they should have known better. Also, a recipient of the distribution, e.g. a shareholder, is obliged to repay the dividend distributed to him if he knew or reasonably should have foreseen that the company would not be able to meet its debts after the distribution.[304]

With respect to interim dividends no special provisions apply; the two tests referred to above are applicable.

4.8.1.3 Stock Dividends; Bonus Dividends

Dividends can take the form of a distribution of shares of the company. Stock dividends normally mean that shareholders receive newly issued shares out of current profits. The aggregate market value of the newly issued shares is

---

301. Art. 2:105(8) BW.
302. Art. 2:216(1) BW.
303. Art. 2:216(2) BW.
304. Art. 2:216(3) BW.

the amount of the dividend. The issued capital account is increased by the amount of the aggregate nominal value of the issued shares. Bonus dividends are similar to stock dividends, except that the dividend is paid out of a reserve, usually the capital surplus account.[305]

4.8.2 Redemption

A redemption of shares can be achieved by two different means, either: (i) through a repurchase and subsequent cancellation of shares; or (ii) through a direct redemption (see § 4.6.2).

4.8.3 Repayment on Shares by Decrease of the Nominal Value

With respect to repayment on shares, we refer to § 4.6.3.

4.8.4 Non-profit-sharing shares

Since 1 October 2012, shares without any entitlements to profits and/or reserves of the company are allowed in respect of a BV.[306] A holder of such non-profit-sharing shares must, however, always be entitled to exercise voting rights. In other words, shares without any entitlement to profits/reserves and without any voting rights cannot exist under Dutch law.[307]

---

305. Certain statutory reserves may also be converted into issued share capital.
306. Art. 2:216(7) BW.
307. Art. 2:190 BW.

Chapter 5
Shares

5.1 NV and BV Shares; Share Certificates and Registration

5.1.1 Registered Shares and Bearer Shares

NVs may issue bearer shares and shares registered in the name of the holder.[308] BVs on the other hand can only issue registered shares.[309] Share certificates (*aandeelbewijzen*), for both registered shares and bearer shares, can be issued. The legal position of the holder of a certificated registered share and an un-certificated registered share is very similar. The only difference lies in the evidence *vis-à-vis* the issuing company.[310] No difference exists with regard to possible title defects (such as the absence of clean title of the previous owner) or formalities for the transfer of these shares, except for an NV of which all or part of its shares are listed (see § 5.4).

5.1.2. Share Certificates

Share certificates should not be confused with the Dutch word '*certificaten*', which refers to depository receipts (see § 5.5).

Except in cases of fraud, a bearer share certificate evidences title to the shares.[311] NV shareholders with registered shares but without share certificates, and BV shareholders, can prove their title to shares only: (i) if they are founders, or successors to the rights of one or more founders, by reference to the deed of incorporation, together with documents constituting a complete chain of title (e.g. all transfer deeds, see § 5.4.2); or (ii) if they own shares issued after incorporation, by showing the appropriate corporate resolutions and documents constituting a complete chain of title. However, since all registered shares, other than registered shares issued by listed companies, are required to be transferred or issued by a deed of a Dutch civil law notary (who must

308. Art. 2:82(1) BW.
309. Art. 2:175(1) BW.
310. Art. 157(2) Rv.
311. Art. 3:119 BW.

perform a title search) the exposure with regard to title defects is limited (see § 5.4).

The share certificate for an NV share can be in the name of the shareholder (called a registered share certificate) or made out to bearer. A bearer certificate cannot be issued until the full amount of the nominal value of the shares it represents has been paid.[312] The Wge provides the possibility of book-entry share transactions, as a result of which the need of share certificates is decreasing (see § 5.3.3).

For the notification of certain thresholds of voting rights or capital interests in a listed NV, see § 5.3.1.

5.1.3 Shareholders' Register

If the shares are registered, which is always the case for BV shares, the management board must keep a register stating:[313]

(a) the names and addresses of the shareholders;
(b) the class or specification of the shares;
(c) the amount contributed to the nominal value of each share;
(d) any issuance or transfer of shares and the date thereof;
(e) any manifest pledge or life interest (see §§ 5.4.1 and 5.4.3) affecting the shares, the date thereof, together with the names and addresses of the pledgees or the beneficiaries of the life interest, and their meeting and/or voting rights;
(f) the name of a shareholder of the BV that is not bound by certain requirements, like quality requirements, set out in the articles of association; and
(g) the names and addresses of holders of depository receipts with meeting rights for BV shares.

A managing director must sign the shareholders' register every time a new entry is made. Shareholders have the right to inspect the register.[314] The shareholders' register is not, however, open for public inspection, except in relation to shares for which the nominal value has not been fully paid.[315]

---

312. Art. 2:82(3) BW.
313. Art. 2:85(1)/194(1) BW. A violation of these provisions is a criminal offence, see Art. 1(4) WED.
314. Pledgees and beneficiaries of a life interest that have meeting rights (see § 5.5.4) have this right as well, except (for NVs only) with respect to that part of the shareholders' register that is allowed to be kept outside the Netherlands (Arts 2:85(4)/194(5), 2:88(4), 2:89 BW).
315. Art. 2:85(4)/194(5) BW.

Every shareholder and pledgee or beneficiary of a life interest in shares of the company as well as a holder of depository receipts for BV shares with meeting rights has the right to obtain an extract of his registration, free of charge.[316] This extract is not conclusive legal evidence that the registered person is the rightful owner, pledgee, beneficiary, or depository receipt holder or that the shares are properly paid up.

The register must remain at the company's main offices in the Netherlands (except for that part of the register that, under foreign law or stock exchange regulations, must remain in that foreign country).[317] The articles may provide that shareholders are entitled to a certified copy, and that a copy of the register shall be kept in the custody of a Dutch civil law notary or attorney.

5.1.4 Disclosure; Single Shareholder

A company with a single shareholder is subject to certain public disclosure rules. Single-member companies are NVs or BVs with one shareholder who directly holds all of the issued shares. The single shareholder may be another company (including the parent) or a natural person. Treasury shares of the single-member company or shares held by its subsidiaries are ignored when determining the number of shareholders.[318]

Once a shareholder either qualifies as a single bearer shareholder of an NV or loses this qualification, he must notify the company within eight days.[319] Holders of registered shares in an NV or shareholders of a BV company are known to the company, and consequently no special notification by the single shareholder is required. Within one week,[320] the company must notify the commercial register of the name and domicile of the single shareholder. For a single shareholder company special rules apply with respect to transactions between the company and the shareholder if the company is represented by the shareholder. These transactions must be put in writing to avoid the transaction being nullified on behalf of the company. This provision also applies to corporate shareholders.[321]

316. Art. 2:85(3)/194(4) BW.
317. Art. 2:85(4)/194(5) BW.
318. Arts 2:91a(4), 2:137(1)/247(1) BW.
319. Art. 2:91a(1),(2) BW. A violation of these provisions is a criminal offence, see Art. 1(4) WED.
320. Arts 18(1), 20(2) HrW 2007, Art. 22(1)(e) HrB 2008. A violation of these provisions is a criminal offence, see Art. 1(4) WED.
321. Art. 2:137/247(1) BW.

5.1.5 Non-Voting Shares

Unless the articles of association provide otherwise, all shareholders have equal rights in proportion to the nominal value of their shares.[322] Provisions in the articles concerning payment on shares, voting rights, profit-sharing and participation in liquidation proceeds may limit, these inherent rights. These rights can even be eliminated in the articles for a BV, provided that a share must either have voting rights or profit-sharing or participation rights in liquidation proceeds. Non-voting shares only exist in the Netherlands for a BV. Holders of non-voting shares have meeting rights (see § 5.2.5). Alternatively, a trust foundation or other entity is created, which in effect separates the voting power from the beneficial interest in the shares (see § 5.5). Holders of depository receipts of shares issued by that foundation or other trust entity may have meeting rights if so provided in the articles.

5.2 Types of Shares and Other Securities

5.2.1 Ordinary and Common Shares

Ordinary or common shares are shares for which no special provisions are made. When dividends are paid in the form of shares (see § 4.8.1.3), these shares are usually ordinary shares.

5.2.2 Preference Shares

Preference shares have a preference over ordinary shares in the payment of dividends up to – and limited to – a percentage over their nominal value or the total amount of the nominal value and the paid in agreed surplus amount, as stated in the articles of association, or to a fixed interest rate. The articles may state that the preference also relates to liquidation proceeds. Holders of preference shares may have the same voting rights as holders of ordinary shares when the nominal value of the preference shares is the same as the ordinary shares. They may also have limited voting rights or, in the case of a BV, even no voting rights. Preference shares may be used to raise equity when profits do not allow sufficient return to the holders of ordinary shares. Preference shares may also be used as an anti-takeover device. The issuance of these shares to a friendly third party dilutes the voting rights of the holders of ordinary shares. In this scenario, only 25% of the 'protection' preference shares will be paid up, to minimise the cash necessary to finance the subscription. The issuance of

322. Arts 2:118/228, 2:92(1)/201(1) BW.

preference shares may be delegated to the management board for a five-year period in the case of an NV and for an unlimited period in the case of a BV (see §§ 4.4.2 and 4.4.3).

Cumulative preference shares are preference shares with an additional right to carry forward all preference dividends not paid in previous years (because of lack of profits or otherwise), to be paid in full before any payment to the holders of ordinary shares.

Cumulative profit-sharing preference shares (i.e. participating preference shares) are cumulative preference shares which, after payment of their preferred dividend, confer on the holder a claim to dividends on an equal or proportional basis with the holders of ordinary shares.

5.2.3 Priority shares

Priority shares give their holders certain powers as stated in the articles of association.[323] Priority shares may be used to acquire control over certain resolutions of the shareholders' meeting or the management board (called 'oligarchic' control) by shareholders who are usually founders, managing directors or supervisory directors of the company. With respect to a public company, legal title to these shares is for practical reasons often held by a foundation (see § 2.5.2). Priority shares are also a means for minority shareholders to retain control over the company. Their powers may include:

(a) the right to make binding nominations to shareholders regarding the appointment of board members. This right of nomination cannot easily be created when the company is a 'large' company (see § 8.2.3.2). The shareholders cannot appoint persons other than those proposed. However, binding nominations may be rejected by the shareholders by a two thirds' vote if it represents more than one half of the issued share capital;[324]

(b) the right to make proposals to the shareholders' meeting (see § 7.2.1). If priority shares are used to that effect, the articles may also provide that the shareholders may pass the relevant resolution by a simple majority vote and irrespective of the capital represented at the meeting. This provision is often followed by a provision in the articles that, with respect to such proposals not made by the holders of priority shares, a super-majority is required for the shareholders' vote, e.g. a

323. Art. 2:92/201(3) BW.
324. Arts 2:133(2)/243(2), 2:134(2)/244(2) BW.

majority of two thirds representing at least 50% of the issued capital is required in order to adopt the resolution by the shareholders' meeting;
(c) the right to veto the issuance of new shares;
(d) the right to create reserves out of annual profits;
(e) the right to veto proposed amendments to the articles; and
(f) the right to grant or to reject approval when requested by a shareholder in connection with a restriction on the transfer of a registered share (see § 5.4.3).

Alternatively, in the case of a BV, non-profit shares (see § 5.2.6) can be used.

5.2.4 Classes of Shares and (Numeric) Specifications of Shares

It is possible to create different classes of shares for different groups of shareholders within the same type of shares. In practice, this is limited to registered ordinary shares. Normally, each of these classes is identified by a letter, e.g. class A shares, class B shares, etc. Classes are created by a provision in the articles of association, principally to allow pre-emptive rights on shares of the same class, to require the approval of shareholders of a specific class of shares prior to the sale of any shares of that class (see § 5.4.3); or to provide for differences in profit distribution (or profit retention) for each class of shares; or to give the holders of a specific class of shares the possibility to make a binding nomination (see § 5.2.3) for the appointment of a managing or supervisory director, who will be identified by the same letter as the share (e.g. managing director A relates to the class A shares) or to appoint him directly (see § 8.2.3.1) in the case of a BV.

A BV can also distinguish shares by referring to their (numeric) specification, without using classes of shares, to achieve the same result.

5.2.5 Non-Voting Shares

The articles of association of a BV may provide that all shares of a separate class or all shares with a certain (numeric) specification have certain profit-sharing rights and/or participation rights in liquidation proceeds, but do not have voting rights. The articles must refer to these shares as non-voting shares (*stemrechtloze aandelen*).[325] Holders of non-voting shares do not have voting rights in a general meeting for any resolution. The articles may not vary in providing voting rights for certain shareholders' resolutions. The holders of non-voting shares have meeting rights: they must be invited to general

325. Art. 2:228(5) BW.

meetings of shareholders and shareholders' resolutions outside a meeting can only be adopted if they agree to such procedure. (see § 7.2.2). The articles may provide that the holders of non-voting shares have special voting, approval or consent rights as a separate corporate body (e.g. the approval of the meeting of non-voting shareholders is required for an amendment to the articles or for the approval of a board resolution on a specific topic). In principle, non-voting shares do not count as shares for calculating a quorum or a majority of votes (though there are exceptions). Alternatively, profit participation rights (see § 5.2.7) can be used.

If these non-voting shares are introduced by a deed of amendment to the articles, all the shareholders concerned must agree.

5.2.6 Non-Profit Shares

The articles of association of a BV may grant only voting rights to shares, eliminating the profit-rights and/or the participation rights in liquidation proceeds.[326] These non-profit shares may be used in situations where it is important to grant only voting rights to certain shareholders (or third parties, thus making them shareholders). Alternatively, priority shares can be used (see § 5.2.3).

If these shares are introduced by a deed of amendment to the articles, all the shareholders whose rights are decreased must consent to the amendment.

5.2.7 Rights to Other Persons than Shareholders

It is possible to include in the articles of association a provision that permits a profit distribution to persons other than shareholders. A 'profit participation right' (*winstrecht*) created in this way may be issued in negotiable form as a 'profit participation certificate' (*winstbewijs*) and may even be listed on Euronext Amsterdam, subject to the applicable listing requirements. Profit participation rights are of a contractual nature. The creation of profit participation rights must be expressly permitted in the articles.[327] The beneficiary of a profit participation right (i.e. the holder of a profit participation receipt) has a right to share in the company's profits, as outlined in the contractual terms of this right, but can never be granted any rights to cast votes at a shareholders' meeting. In addition to profit sharing, other rights may be granted to these beneficiaries, to the extent that these additional rights are not by law the exclusive prerogatives of the shareholders. These rights cannot be affected or

326. Art. 2:216(7) BW.
327. Art. 2:105(1)/216(1) BW.

abrogated by an amendment to the articles without the consent of every such beneficiary, unless stated otherwise in the articles prior to the creation of such rights. In general, the company has a duty of good faith towards these beneficiaries.[328] Profit participation receipts are sometimes given to the founders of the company and are then called 'founders' receipts' (*oprichtersbewijzen*). Profit participation rights are unusual. Alternatively, in the case of a BV, non-voting shares (see § 5.2.5) can be used.

5.2.8 Convertible Debt Securities

Convertible debentures (including bonds) are debt securities which, under conditions set out in the terms of the loan, provide for an option to convert the debt into shares. Whether this conversion is to be called for at the option of the company or the holder of the debenture, the rules concerning the issuance of new shares must be complied with prior to the issuance of the convertible debentures (see § 4.4.1). Voting rights are not available to the holders of such securities prior to conversion.

5.2.9 Other Securities

Warrants are securities issued by the company that create an option to acquire shares at a specific price during a specific period of time.

Claims are tradeable securities, which allow the holder to acquire shares from the company (upon the issuance of new shares) for a consideration that is usually below market value.

Scrips are securities, to existing shareholders, which are convertible into shares but which do not carry any shareholders' rights until conversion.

5.3 Transfer of Shares

5.3.1 NV Shares

Bearer shares are transferred by surrendering the share certificates, unless the shares have been deposited with Euroclear Nederland (or a similar institution outside the Netherlands), which provides for transfers by book entry, as regulated by law (see § 5.3.3).

Registered shares are transferred by a deed of transfer executed before a Dutch civil law notary.[329] The notarial deed contains certain specific details

328. Supreme Court 27 Jan. 1956, NJ 1956, 48 (*Unipart/RDM*); Supreme Court 11 Jan. 1963, NJ 1964, 433 (*RCMA*).
329. Art. 2:86(1) BW.

about the parties, the company and the shares being transferred.[330] The articles of association may require a share certificate issued for registered shares to be surrendered to the company, in which case transfers may be completed by an endorsement and a replacement of the old certificate by a new certificate in the name of the new owner.[331] Registered shares of a company, all or part of the shares of which are listed on an official stock exchange, or are likely to be admitted to such an official stock exchange in the near future, can be transferred without the involvement of a Dutch civil law notary.[332]

Except when the company is a party to the transfer deed, in respect of an NV that is not listed on an official stock exchange, all shareholder rights can be exercised only by the new shareholder after the company has acknowledged the transfer of the registered shares (*erkenning*), or the notarial deed has been served upon the company by a Dutch court bailiff (*betekening*).[333] In the interim the transferor, who is no longer the legal owner of those shares, may not exercise any rights pertaining to those shares either. The acknowledgement can be placed in the deed of transfer or made by means of a dated statement on a notarial transcript or on a certified copy of the deed.[334] In the absence of a request from any of the parties to the transaction to acknowledge the transfer, the company itself can acknowledge the transfer by entering the new shareholder in the register of shareholders.[335] With respect to registered shares in a listed company, the transfer of shares shall only become effective after the company has acknowledged the transfer of the shares.[336] It is following this acknowledgement that the transferee becomes a shareholder of the NV. If certificates of registered NV shares have been issued, the acknowledgement of transfer is placed on the existing certificate, or a new share certificate is issued upon presentation to the company of the existing certificate. If the amount of the nominal value has not been fully paid, the acknowledgement must occur either in notarised form or the deed of acknowledgement must be filed with the tax authorities.

Actual or potential holders of a direct or indirect interest (in terms of shares or voting rights or both) in the capital of an NV whose shares or depository receipts are admitted to trading on a regulated market must notify the

330. Art. 2:86(2) BW.
331. Art. 2:86c(3) BW.
332. Unless the latter category of shares is listed and deposited with EuroclearNederland, such shares are transferred by a deed of transfer. Unless the company is a party to the transfer, in order to actually transfer the ownership of the shares, this deed must either be acknowledged in writing by the company, or served upon it by a Dutch court bailiff (Art. 2:86c BW).
333. Art. 2:86a(1) BW.
334. Art. 2:86b BW.
335. Art. 86a(2) BW.
336. Art. 2:86c(2) BW.

AFM when any of the following thresholds are reached or passed: 5%, 10%, 15%, 20%, 25%, 30%, 40%, 50%, 60%, 75% and 95%.[337] The AFM must notify the company.[338] Due to a bill adopted in November 2012, a threshold of 3% will be added. This will most likely be enforced in the course of 2013.

5.3.2 BV Shares

BV shares, which are by definition registered shares, are transferred by a deed of transfer executed before a Dutch civil law notary (see § 5.3.1).[339] The procedure for the transfer of registered shares in a BV is similar to that for the transfer of registered NV shares. Unless the BV is a party to the transfer, shareholder rights can only be exercised by the new shareholder (although the transferor no longer has these rights) after the company has acknowledged (*erkend*) the transfer or the notarial deed has been served (*betekend*) upon the company by a Dutch court bailiff (see § 5.3.1).[340] The acknowledgement can: (i) be made in the deed of transfer or made by means of a dated statement on a notarial transcript or on a certified copy of the deed; or (ii) be made by registering the transfer in the shareholders' register.[341] The company itself can also acknowledge the transfer at its own initiative once it has actual knowledge of the transfer,[342] by registration of the transfer in the shareholders' register.

If share certificates are issued for BV shares, the articles of association may provide further requirements for the transfer of the share certificates.

5.3.3 Book-Entry Share Transfers

The Wge provides the possibility of book-entry share transactions. This means that shares are booked on accounts that are specially set up for this reason. Shares can be transferred (and pledged) by means of entries to the balance of those accounts.[343] The transfer of shares under the Wge is solely the crediting and debiting of such security accounts. For this type of transfer no notarial instrument or share certificate is required, nor does an announcement have to be made to the company.

337. Arts 5:35, 5:39 Wft.
338. Art. 5:49 Wft.
339. Art. 2:196(1) BW.
340. Art. 2:196a(1) BW.
341. Arts 2:196a(1), 2:196b BW.
342. Art. 2:196a(2) BW.
343. Securities Giro Act (*Wet giraal effectenverkeer*) Stb. 1977, 333, see further Jennen and Van de Vijver, pages 162-164.

5.3.4 Share Transfer Restrictions

5.3.4.1 NV Shares

Any restrictions on the transfer of NV shares must be set out in the articles of association.[344] Restrictions can only apply to registered shares. Bearer shares are always freely transferable. Permissible restrictions may include a condition that registered shareholders be individuals or entities having certain qualifying characteristics, such as residency in the Netherlands, a specified family affiliation, or the absence of shareholdings in a directly competitive industry. Restrictions shall not, however, render transfer impossible or onerous.[345] Among restrictions considered to be unfair are those which render the amount to be received by the transferor inequitable (e.g. below fair market value, as determined by an independent expert, at the request of the seller).

If transfer restrictions are imposed, it is either an approval procedure, a right of first refusal (offer procedure) or a combination of both.[346]

5.3.4.1.1 Approval Procedure

The articles of association may make the transfer of shares subject to the approval of the management board, the supervisory board, the shareholders' meeting or the holders of a certain type or class of share, such as priority shares. A transfer may also be made subject to the approval of a third party.[347]

After the approval is granted, the seller may offer his shares within three months of such approval to the transferee mentioned in the request for approval. The approval shall be deemed to be granted if the corporate body or third party designated in the articles for that purpose does not grant the approval with a simultaneous designation of an interested party, who will purchase the offered shares for a reasonable price, to be paid upfront in cash.

The seller may, upon determination of the interested parties (designated when the approval is not granted), withdraw his offer. He cannot be forced to transfer his shares to the designated party. For tax reasons, the company may be named as a prospective buyer only if the seller agrees.

---

344. Art. 2:87(1) BW.
345. Art. 2:87(1) BW.
346. Supreme Court 31 Dec. 1993, NJ 1994, 436 (*Verenigde Bootlieden*).
347. Art. 2:87(2) BW.

If the parties fail to agree on the price, the price for the shares must be determined by independent experts.[348] A shareholder may, upon determination of the price by the experts, withdraw his request for an approval to sell.

5.3.4.1.2 Right of First Refusal

The articles may also provide for a right of first refusal. The articles must then provide that the shares shall be offered to all or some other shareholders or to a third party designated by a designated corporate body of the NV.[349]

If the parties fail to agree on the price, the price for the shares must be determined by independent experts. A shareholder proposing to sell may withdraw his offer within one month after the identity of the proposed purchaser and the price offered are made known to him. If it appears that not all shares offered for sale will be purchased upfront for cash, at the request of the seller, and at a price determined by independent experts, the selling shareholder may, within three months thereafter, freely transfer the shares to whomever he chooses.

5.3.4.1.3 Change of Control

Clauses restricting the transfer of shares may be circumvented when shares are held by a corporate shareholder. For example, company A has a transfer restriction provision. Shareholders of company A are company B and Mr. C. The sole shareholder of company B is Mr. B. In order to make the transfer restriction effective, an agreement between Mr. B and Mr. C is required. Otherwise, Mr. B may freely sell his shares in company B, which in practical terms abrogates Mr. C's rights under the transfer restriction. For this purpose, the articles may limit the ownership of the company's shares to individuals.

An alternative to the agreement between Mr. B and Mr. C is to make, in the articles, a change of control provision. This provision will require the shares to be offered to the other shareholders if all or part of the shares in an ultimate corporate shareholder are in any way transferred to a third party, by operation of law, by universal succession of title or otherwise.

---

348. Art. 2:87(2) BW. The experts must also be independent from the company. The external accountant of the company may be appointed as an expert. The internal auditor may be appointed only when the parties consent thereto. Asser/Maeijer, Van Solinge & Nieuwe Weme 2-II* 2009/291.
349. Art. 2:87(3) BW.

5.3.4.2 BV Shares

The restrictions on transfers of shares are far more flexible for a BV than for an NV. Transfer restrictions on BV shares may be restricted and specified in the articles of association. Transfer restrictions set out in the articles must be taken into account, otherwise the transfer is considered to be null and void.[350]

If the articles do not provide for any clause on restrictions on transfer of shares, the transferor must offer the shares on offer to his co-shareholders for a price – if requested by him – to be determined by independent experts.[351] If it appears that not all the shares being offered for sale will be purchased upfront for cash, the selling shareholder may, within three months, freely transfer all shares on offer to whomever he chooses.

The articles may provide for any other form of restrictions on transfer of shares (e.g. the approval by a corporate body or a third party) (see § 5.3.4.1) or for no restrictions at all.[352] The articles may limit the transfer of shares to persons who meet specific criteria (see § 5.3.4.1). Also, transfer restrictions entirely excluding the transfer of shares for a certain period of time (a lock up) may be inserted in the articles.[353] Statutory transfer restrictions that make a transfer (nearly) impossible, are not allowed and will be null and void.[354]

Dutch law provides that a shareholder receives upon his request an amount equal to the value of his shares as determined by one or more independent experts when transferring the shares under share transfer restrictions.[355] The BV articles may provide otherwise and exclude the need for independent experts. The articles may also provide for standards for (expert) valuation of the shares, provided they do not lead to an apparently unreasonable valuation.

The restrictions apply to all transfers, regardless of the underlying reason (sale, contribution, gift, inheritance, foreclosure, etc.) and to all parties (co-shareholders, third parties, group companies, relatives, or the company itself), unless the articles provide otherwise.[356]

350. Art. 2:195 BW.
351. Art. 2:195(1) BW.
352. Art. 2:195(1)(3) BW.
353. Art. 2:195(3) BW.
354. Art. 2:195(5) BW.
355. Art. 2:195(1) BW. For the independent experts, see also 5.3.4.1.1.
356. Art. 2:195(1) BW.

5.3.5 Compulsory Transfers

5.3.5.1 Loss of Qualification or Non-fulfilment Obligations.

A shareholder may be required to sell and transfer his shares in certain situations set out in the articles of association,[357] which may include the holding of shares in competitors, engagement in competitive activities, death (in the case of individuals), bankruptcy or liquidation (in the case of a corporate shareholder) or a change of control (see § 5.3.4.1.3). The articles of a BV may also impose obligations on a shareholder towards the company, a co-shareholder or a third party. If the shareholder does not fulfil his obligations, he may be required to transfer his shares or a part thereof.[358] Again, the selling shareholder must receive an amount which is equal to the value of the shares, offered as determined by one or more independent experts, provided that the BV articles may deviate from the principle of valuation by independent experts.[359] The articles may provide that until the moment of transfer the rights pertaining to the shares to be transferred shall be suspended.[360]

5.3.5.2 Squeeze-out Proceedings

A shareholder owning 95% or more of a company's issued capital and – in the event of a public offer – also 95% or more of the voting rights in a general meeting may initiate legal proceedings to require all of the other shareholders to transfer their shares to him.[361] (See § 10.4.1). Minority shareholders have a similar right to sell their shares to a 95%-majority shareholder who has made a public offer for the shares, within three months after the end of the offer period (see § 10.4.2).[362]

5.3.5.3 Forced Exit Proceedings

A shareholder may, under certain circumstances, require another shareholder to sell and transfer his shares if the other shareholder by his conduct prejudices the 'interests of the company'.[363] A shareholder may also, under certain circumstances, require one or more other shareholders to acquire his shares if the other shareholder(s) is(are) prejudicing his rights or interests to such

357. Art. 2:87a(1)/192(1) BW.
358. Art. 2:192(1)(3) BW.
359. Art. 2:87a(3)/192(3) BW.
360. Art. 2:87a(1)/192(4) BW.
361. Arts 2:92a(1)/201a(1), 2:359c(1) BW.
362. Art. 2:359(d)1 BW.
363. Art. 2:336(1) BW.

an extent that continued shareholding cannot reasonably be expected from him.[364] (See § 10.3)

5.4 Security Interests and Other Encumbrances

5.4.1 Pledge

The existence of the underlying debt determines the existence of the pledge (*pandrecht)*.[365] The pledge automatically ceases to exist once the debt is satisfied.

The pledge on bearer shares (NVs only) can be created by: (i) an agreement between pledgor and pledgee, and compliance with the formalities to remove the share certificates from the pledgor's possession (possessory pledge or *vuistpandrecht*);[366] or (ii) the execution of an instrument before a Dutch civil law notary, or an instrument signed by the pledgor, officially registered with the Dutch tax authorities,[367] in which case it is not necessary to remove the share certificates from the pledgor's possession (non-possessory pledge or *bezitloos pandrecht*).[368] The pledgor is required to state in the instrument that he has the power to pledge the shares and, as the case may be, that certain limited rights are vested in the shares. Any misrepresentation in this respect may give rise to a claim against the pledgor, but it will not protect the pledgee against any defect in the pledge created in his favour.

To create a pledge on registered shares the same formalities must be complied with as for the transfer of such shares (see §§ 5.3.1 and 5.3.2).[369] The management board must register pledges disclosed to it in the shareholders' register (see § 5.1.3). The articles of association of both NVs and BVs may exclude or limit the right to pledge registered shares.[370] The right to pledge bearer shares cannot be excluded or limited by the articles.

Shares which are subject to the Wge (see § 5.3.3) can also be pledged.[371]

364. Art. 2:343(1) BW.
365. Art. 3:7 BW. A pledge may only be created as security for a monetary debt, expressed in any currency.
366. Art. 3:236(1) BW.
367. See *Registratiewet* (Act on Registration), Stb. 1970, 610, as amended.
368. Art. 3:237(1),(2) BW.
369. Arts 3:236(2), 2:86/196, 2:86c BW. Registered shares in a company, and shares or depository receipts of shares which are listed on an official stock exchange, can also be pledged by execution of an instrument before a Dutch civil law notary or by an instrument registered with the local tax registration bureau without acknowledgement by or notification to the company (Art. 2:86c(4) BW).
370. Art. 2:89(1)/198(1) BW.
371. Arts 20, 21, 42 Wge.

The articles may state that the right to vote on the shares may not be conferred to the pledgee. In the event that the articles do not contain such a provision the pledgor and the pledgee may agree that the voting rights pertaining to the pledged shares will remain with the pledgor or will be assigned to the pledgee at the moment the pledge is created. However, if a transfer of the shares concerned to the pledgee will be subject to any transfer restriction included in the articles, the assignment of the voting rights to such pledgee will be subject to the approval of the shareholders' meeting or such other corporate body which, under the articles, is competent to approve any transfer of shares under the transfer restriction provisions. It shall be at the discretion of the shareholders' meeting to grant or deny such approval unless under the company's articles another corporate body is competent to grant approval for any transfer of shares.[372]

5.4.2 Foreclosure

The pledgee can foreclose (*executeren*) the shares without the power of a title of enforcement or court order.[373] Any restrictions on the transfer of shares (see § 5.3.4) will apply.[374] The shares must, in principle, be sold at public auction. Bearer shares that are traded on a stock exchange can be sold by a broker in ordinary trade on such stock exchange.[375] The pledgor or pledgee may, however, seek a court order for a private sale. Until the secured debt has become due and payable, the pledgor and the pledgee may not agree to the foreclosure of the collateral by private sale.[376] The pledgor may also seek a court order for a private sale.

In order to start foreclosure proceedings, the non-possessory pledgee of bearer shares must first obtain possession of the share certificates. If the instrument was not made in notarial form, a court order is required in order to obtain the necessary power to instruct a court bailiff to seize the share certificates.[377]

5.4.3 Life Interest

Life interest (*vruchtgebruik*) is a personal beneficial interest which an owner of assets grants to another person. It is also known as a life estate or *usufruct*. A life interest in shares may include voting rights[378] and the right to receive

372. Art. 2:89/198 BW.
373. Art. 3:248 BW.
374. Art. 2:89(5)(6)/198(6) BW.
375. Art. 3:250(2) BW.
376. Art. 3:251(1)(2) BW.
377. Art. 496(1)(2) Rv.
378. Art. 2:88/197 BW.

distributions,[379] but will normally not include the right to sell or encumber the shares.[380] The articles of an NV or a BV cannot preclude a shareholder from creating a right of life interest in any of his shares,[381] or exclude all or certain persons from exercising the voting rights if they are to become usufructuaries.

5.5 Depository Receipts for Shares

5.5.1 General

Depository receipts (*certificaten*) are instruments issued by a trust foundation or other entity (hereinafter: a trust office) (*administratiekantoor*), representing certain shares of a company held by the trust office. The legal concept applied for transfer to the trust office is *fiducia cum amigo* (*ten titel van beheer*). The trust office is usually a foundation (*stichting*) (see § 2.5.2) formed by the company or the shareholder transferring his shares to the trust office.

For shares in an NV that are transferred to the trust office the issuance of depository receipts may occur with or without the co-operation of the company. If the articles allow the NV to co-operate, and for any specific transfer the NV acts accordingly, the holders of the depository receipts will have certain rights pertaining to these receipts (see § 5.5.4).

For shares in a BV that are transferred to a trust office, it is set out in the BV articles of association, or agreed pursuant to the articles, whether or not the holders of depository receipts have meeting rights.

The receipts refer to the sorts and types of share, but are not identical to the underlying shares. The rights conferred on receipt holders are determined by the provisions according to which the receipts are issued. These provisions are called 'trust conditions' (*administratievoorwaarden*). The financial position of the holder of receipts issued with the co-operation of the company (NV) or having meeting rights (BV) is secured by a statutory pledge on the shares.[382] When creating depository receipts, the legal ownership of the shares is transferred to the trust office. As shareholder the trust office will cast the votes pertaining to these shares. The trust conditions may stipulate that for certain proposals that are subject to a decision of the shareholders' meeting, the trust office must obtain the prior approval of the meeting of depository receipt holders. In most cases, the trust conditions stipulate that distributions by the company to the trust office as shareholder flow to the receipt

379. Supreme Court 23 May 1958, NJ 1958, 458. (*Pierlot/Kremer*); Supreme Court 7 Dec. 1994, NJ 1995, 301 (*Staatssecretaris Financiën/Erven X*).
380. Arts 3:201, 3:212 and 3:216 BW.
381. Art. 2:88(1)/197(1) BW.
382. Art. 3:259 BW.

holder. Depository receipts are often used as an anti-takeover device, or as a means to restrict the involvement of shareholders who are part of a family owning an important block of shares in a company.

5.5.2 Types of Depository Receipts

A distinction can be made between registered depository receipts and bearer depository receipts. For a BV, no bearer depository receipts may be issued.[383] Another distinction can be made between: convertible receipts (*royeerbare certificaten*), which can be converted into the underlying shares upon request and by payment of a nominal fee; partially convertible receipts (*gedeeltelijk royeerbare certificaten*), which can be converted only upon satisfaction of certain trust conditions; and non-convertible receipts (*niet royeerbare certificaten*), which are convertible only upon the liquidation of the trust office.

5.5.3 Independent Trust Office

The Dutch Corporate Governance Code contains special rules for depository receipts and trust offices, and requires the trust office to be independent of the company in which it holds shares.[384] This is of particular importance when the trust office has been formed and its board appointed at the company's initiative, in order to avoid interference by a shareholder or a takeover bid.

5.5.4 Rights of Receipt Holders

Holders of depository receipts do not have the right to vote the underlying shares, unless they have a voting proxy (see § 5.5.5). However, they do have the right to share in the company's profits. For that reason they do not have a direct right *vis-à-vis* the company, but a contractual right *vis-à-vis* the trust office. In addition, if the depository receipts are issued with the company's co-operation (NV) or if the holders have meeting rights (BV), their holders have the right, enforceable against the company, to attend and participate in shareholders' meetings[385] and to obtain any reports, statements and other documents to which shareholders are entitled. For these 'information rights', see § 7.6.

Furthermore, this type of receipt holder may participate in convening a shareholders' meeting through a court order (see § 7.2.1), and they are consid-

383. Art. 2:202 BW.
384. Principle IV.2 CGC.
385. Art. 2:117(2)/227(2) BW.

ered to be among the persons and bodies to which special rules apply requiring reasonable and fair behaviour (see § 10.2.3).[386]

Finally, holders of depository receipts issued with or without the company's co-operation (NV), or with or without meeting rights (BV), have the right to make a request for an enquiry.[387] (See § 10.2.2).

5.5.5 Voting Proxy

Holders of depository receipts that are traded on a regulated stock exchange may ask for a voting proxy.[388] The trust office can only restrict or decline a request or revoke an already-given voting proxy: (i) in the case of a hostile bid; (ii) if the holder of depository receipts has at least 25% of the issued shares; or (iii) the issue of a voting proxy is contrary to the interests of the company.[389] In accordance with the Dutch Corporate Governance Code a trust office must give a voting proxy in all circumstances, without any restrictions.[390]

5.5.6 Meetings of Receipt Holders

The trust conditions may provide for meetings of receipt holders. Most trust offices hold meetings only upon the request of a specified percentage of receipt holders. The receipt holders may have voting rights at such meetings. Only in exceptional cases do the trust conditions require the trust office to cast its vote at the shareholders' meeting in accordance with instructions given by the receipt holders.

5.5.7 Transfer of Depository Receipts

The character of depository receipts may be qualified as claim rights against the trust office. Registered depository receipts may be transferred by deed of assignment.[391] The transfer of bearer depository receipts is effected by surrendering the certificate to that effect to the transferee[392] (unless they are deposited with Euroclear, which provides for transfer by book entry, as regulated by law).

386. Art. 2:8 BW.
387. Art. 2:346(b)(c) BW.
388. Art. 2:118a(1) BW.
389. Art. 2:118a(2) BW.
390. Principle IV 2.8 CGC.
391. Arts 3:93, 3:90(1) BW.
392. Art. 3:94 BW.

5.5.8 Statutory Pledge

For the benefit of the depository receipt holders created with the co-operation of the company (NV), or having meeting rights (BV), a statutory pledge exists[393] on the shares held by the trust office in the company for which the depository receipts are issued, unless specifically stated otherwise. The pledge exists for any and all claims which such depository receipt holders may have against the trust office pursuant to the relationship for which the depository receipts were issued.

393. Art. 3:259 BW.

Chapter 6
Corporate Bodies and their Resolutions

6.1 Corporate Bodies

Although Netherlands law does not define the concept of a corporate body, an accurate description could be that it entails any institution within the company which either by law or by the articles of association received certain powers to make decisions within the company.

All NVs and BVs have at least two corporate bodies: the shareholders' meeting and the management board. In the event that the company qualifies as a 'large' company, it must also, pursuant to law, have a supervisory board or a one-tier board (comprising also non-executive directors). In the event that the company does not qualify as a 'large' company, the articles may or may not provide for a supervisory board (see § 8.1.2).

These corporate bodies are well regulated by law. The powers are divided among these corporate bodies. As will be further described in Chapter 7 and Chapter 8, which deal with these corporate bodies in more detail, no corporate body can legally be deemed to be the ultimate holder of control within the company. The level of control of any corporate body within the company will very much depend on the specific provisions in the articles and the particular circumstances.[394]

Besides these corporate bodies provided by law, the articles may provide for other corporate bodies, as long as their powers are different from those attributed by mandatory law to the former corporate bodies.

Holders of a specific class of shares may form a separate corporate body. For instance, if the company has priority shares, the holders of such shares may form a corporate body to which certain powers are allocated, such as the power to make a binding nomination with respect to the appointment of managing directors, issue of shares and approval of certain resolutions of the management board, etc.

---

394. Much will depend on the actual circumstances of the company in question. It is clear that in a single shareholder company the influence of the shareholders' meeting, then consisting of only one person or legal entity, shall be considerably greater than the influence of the shareholders' meeting in a listed company, where only a limited percentage of the shareholders may be represented.

6.2 Resolutions of Corporate Bodies

Corporate bodies consist of one or more members. As a forum of those members, it may take resolutions. The resolutions are supposed to be the result of the meetings of such corporate bodies.[395] The effects of these resolutions differ in nature, depending on the kind of resolution. Basically, a distinction can be made between the following kinds of resolution.

6.2.1 Resolutions with Internal Effect

The majority of resolutions are adopted only to have an effect within the company, i.e. they aim to deal with an internal situation or to change the structure of the company. An example of a purely internal resolution is the approval of the shareholders' meeting that may be required by the articles of association for a certain decision of the management board. The approval of the shareholders is an internal resolution only and has no external effect.

6.2.2 Semi Internal Resolutions

Certain resolutions may be the first step in a chain of actions. The resolution itself does not work externally but without a valid resolution of the appropriate corporate body the external action cannot have any effect.[396]

For instance, in order to amend the articles of association, the shareholders' meeting must adopt a resolution to that effect. However, the resolution by itself does not result in an amendment to the articles. In addition, a Dutch notarial deed is necessary in order to complete the amendment. If the resolution of the shareholders' meeting was not valid in the first place, the amendment is not valid either. Consequently, the resolution has a certain external effect.

6.2.3 Resolutions with External Effect

Some resolutions have direct external effect as they are directed towards a third party. The resolution itself creates a certain relationship between the company and the third party. Examples of such direct external resolutions are the appointment of a managing director by the shareholders' meeting or a resolution by the appropriate corporate body to issue registered shares in a listed company to a specific shareholder.

395. Supreme Court 15 Jul. 1968, NJ 1969, 101 (*Wijsmuller*).
396. Third parties in good faith may be protected against the effect of an invalid or non-existent resolution. See § 6.3.3.

6.3 Void and Voidable Resolutions of Corporate Bodies

The law contains specific provisions with regard to the consequences of void or voidable resolutions. They apply to NVs and BVs.

6.3.1 Void Resolutions

A resolution taken by a corporate body in violation of the law or the articles of association of the company is void.[397] The resolution is non-existent. It has no effect.

This means for instance that, if in a company (other than a non-exempt 'large' company) a managing director is appointed by resolution of the supervisory board, the appointment is not valid. The resolution was adopted in violation of the articles and the law. The shareholders' meeting, not the supervisory board, is authorised to adopt the resolution.

However, if a resolution is void because it was adopted in violation of the required previous action of, or announcement to, a third party, as provided for in the law or the articles, then the void resolution may be remedied by an act of confirmation by such other party.[398]

6.3.2 Voidable Resolutions

A resolution of a corporate body may be nullified by a court decision[399] in each of the following events:

(a) If the resolution is taken in violation of provisions of law or the articles of association which deal with the manner in which resolutions must be adopted. For instance, the articles of an NV provide that notice for a shareholders' meeting must be given no later than on the seventeenth day prior to the shareholders' meeting. In actuality, the notice is given 15 days prior to the meeting. The meeting takes place and the shareholders' meeting resolves certain issues. These resolutions are subject to nullification.[400]

(b) If the resolution is taken in violation of the principles of reasonableness and fairness.[401] The law provides that the legal entity and all parties

397. Art. 2:14(1) BW.
398. Art. 2:14(2) BW.
399. Art. 2:15 BW.
400. Unless the entire issued capital was represented at that meeting and the resolution was adopted unanimously. Art. 2:115 BW. In the case of a BV this situation can be remedied if all meeting right holders agree to holding the meeting with the shorter notice period. Art. 2:225 BW.
401. Arts 2:15(1)(b), 2:8 BW.

who are connected with the organisation of the legal entity pursuant to law or the articles must behave *vis-à-vis* each other with all due respect towards these principles. The law does not apply to corporate bodies alone, but may also apply to individuals who are connected with the organisation of the legal entity.[402] If a majority shareholder uses his majority vote in a shareholders' meeting and thereby disproportionately harms the interests of the minority shareholder, he might violate this principle, and any resolutions so adopted may be nullified. This provision in the law also has a significant influence on decisions of the management board (see § 9.1.1). When deciding on a certain issue, the management board must consider the effect its decision might have on any other persons connected with the legal entity and may have to reconsider the resolution if it would unreasonably affect the interests of such persons and as a result thereof may be in violation of the principles of reasonableness and fairness.[403]

(c) If a resolution is taken in violation of the by-laws.[404] It should be noted that the concept of by-laws in the Netherlands may differ from the concept of by-laws in other jurisdictions. They are an internal set of rules to be considered more as a code of order. A supervisory board often draws up by-laws regulating, for instance, the number of meetings and to establish a scheme of rotation.

A resolution which is void (see § 6.3.1) is *void ab initio*. A resolution which is subject to nullification remains in existence until it is nullified by a court decision. If it is nullified, then this resolution shall be deemed never to have existed. In other words, the nullification has retroactive effect.

The court may nullify a resolution upon the request of any person who has a reasonable interest in the resolution being nullified or upon the request of the legal entity itself pursuant to a board resolution.[405] However, the power to request the court to nullify the resolution will elapse one year after the day on which either the resolution has been adequately announced or the interested party has obtained actual knowledge of the resolution or has been notified that the resolution has been taken.[406]

402. It is not clear whether a works council falls within the scope of Art. 2:8 BW. No case law exists.
403. Supreme Court 14 Sep. 2007, JOR 2007, 237/239 (*Versatel*).
404. Art. 15(1)(c) BW.
405. Art. 2:15(3) BW.
406. Art. 2:15(5) BW.

Only a resolution which is subject to nullification as described under (ii) above may be remedied by another resolution provided that for the latter resolution all requirements for adopting this resolution have been duly observed.

6.3.3 Protection of a Third Party Acting in Good Faith

A final decision of the court to nullify a resolution or to establish the nullity of a resolution is binding on everybody provided that the company has been a party to the proceedings.[407]

However, resolutions may be directed to specific third parties or may have an effect on the validity of transactions entered into with specific third parties (see § 6.2). The law protects such third party against invalidity of that transaction if this party neither knew, nor ought to have known, that there was a defect in the underlying resolution in terms of its validity. In that case, the void or nullified resolution cannot be held against that party.[408]

This protection does not apply with respect to a resolution by which a director is appointed. The appointment will not be valid, but the company may be held liable for damages.

407. Art. 2:16(1) BW.
408. Art. 2:16(2) BW.

Chapter 7
Shareholders

7.1 Basic Powers

7.1.1 Appointment of Managing Directors and Supervisory Directors

In the Netherlands, the shareholders' meeting does not have supreme authority within the company, and the management board is not subordinate to it.[409] The shareholders have, in fact, a limited role in the management and operations of the company.[410] The shareholders cannot operate as the executive of the company (which is the exclusive power of the management board), or, particularly in the case of 'large' companies (see § 8.3.1.2), overrule decisions of the supervisory board made pursuant to the powers vested in that board by the law or the articles. For the BV, the articles may provide that the management is required to comply with directions given by another corporate body, except when such directions are contrary to the interests of the company.[411] As indicated in § 6.1, it will also depend on the nature of the company, such as the number of shareholders involved, how in effect the powers are divided within the company.

If the company is not a 'large' company, the shareholders' meeting primary power is the power to appoint,[412] suspend and remove[413] managing directors and supervisory directors and to adopt the annual accounts of the company. In the case of an optional supervisory board, i.e. one provided for in the articles[414] but not required by law, the shareholders' meeting may not assign this power to the supervisory board.[415] If, however, the company is a 'large' company and not fully or partially exempt (see § 8.1.2.4), the managing directors are appointed, suspended and removed by the mandatory supervisory board.[416]

---

409. Supreme Court 21 Jan. 1955, NJ 1959, 43 (*Forumbank*).
410. Arts 2:107(1)/217(1), 2:129/239 BW.
411. Art. 2:239(4) BW. Although a similar provision does not exist for the NV, it is argued that this may also apply for NVs (see Asser/Maeijer, Van Solinge & Nieuwe Weme 2-II* 2009/413).
412. Arts 2:132/242, 2:142(1)/252(1) BW.
413. Arts 2:134/244, 2:144(1)/254(1) BW.
414. Art. 2:140(1)/250(1) BW.
415. Arts 2:132/242, 2:142(1)/252(1) BW.
416. Arts 2:162/272, 2:134(1)/244(1) BW.

With respect to the appointment of managing and supervisory directors, the shareholders' meeting may be required to accept nominations made by the management or supervisory board, by a particular type or class of shareholder, usually the holders of priority shares (see § 5.2.3), or by any other person or institution stated in the articles. These nominations can always be overruled by a qualified majority of two thirds of the votes cast, representing more than one half of the issued shares.[417] The articles cannot subject the appointment of directors, managing or supervisory, to the approval of any third parties.[418] The articles of association of a BV that is not a 'large' company may provide that the meeting of holders of shares of a certain class or series of shares may appoint one or more managing directors or supervisory directors.

7.1.2 Annual Accounts; Annual Report; Dividends

The shareholders' meeting has the power to adopt the annual accounts.[419] This right to adopt the annual accounts provides for the possibility to make changes to the annual accounts.

The management board must prepare the annual accounts and make them available to the shareholders within five months following the end of the financial year. In special circumstances, the shareholders' meeting may provide for a time extension of a maximum period of six months.[420] For BVs in which all the shareholders are also a (managing) director, signing of the annual accounts by the (management and supervisory) board members automatically entails adoption of the annual accounts by the shareholders' meeting. For listed NVs a shorter period of four months for the preparation of the annual accounts applies. This period cannot be extended.

The management board must file the annual accounts, once adopted, within eight days, with the commercial register.[421] In the event that the annual accounts are not adopted within two months after the period permitted by law, i.e. within 13 months after the end of the financial year, the management board should file forthwith the draft annual accounts with the commercial register, with a reference to their draft status.[422] The annual accounts must be accompanied by the auditor's opinion[423] and the annual report of the management

417. Arts 2:133(2)/243(2), 2:142(2)/252(2) BW.
418. If the company is not a 'large' company, the articles may provide that one or more supervisory directors with a maximum of one third of the total number of supervisory directors, may be appointed by someone other than the shareholders' meeting. Art. 2:143/253 BW.
419. Art. 2:101(3)/210(3) BW.
420. Art. 2:101(1)/210(1) BW.
421. Art. 2:394(1) BW.
422. Art. 2:394(2) BW.
423. Arts 2:393, 2:394 BW.

board.[424] The annual report of the management board (which does not include the annual accounts)[425] is final and cannot be amended by the shareholders' meeting or the supervisory board. The annual accounts prepared by the management board may include a proposed allocation of profits. Although the right to adopt the annual accounts is vested in the shareholders' meeting the final allocation of profits may be subject, however, to any provisions in the articles of association for the formation of and allocation to certain reserves and to any powers that the articles may vest in that respect in the management board, the supervisory board or the priority shareholders[426] (see § 5.2.4). The allocation of profits includes the determination of amounts available for dividends (for the distribution of dividends, see § 4.8.1). The articles may specifically provide that the management board or the supervisory board may allocate a portion of the profits to a reserve account, which will affect the amount of the profits available for distribution.

If the law or the articles require that the books and accounts be audited, the shareholders have the power to appoint the auditor.[427] The auditor's internal report, known as the management letter,[428] is only submitted to the management board and, where applicable, the supervisory board. This report must include the auditor's findings in respect of the reliability and continuity of the automated data processing.[429] Its findings may become part of the auditor's opinion,[430] which is among the documents that the management board must submit to the shareholders. Any interested person has the authority to enforce the statutory obligation to have the accounts audited.[431]

As a general rule, all companies are subject to the requirement to file their annual accounts and other information with the commercial register (see § 12.1).

Annual accounts may be contested before the Enterprise Court (see § 10.5.1).[432]

---

424. Arts 2:391, 2:394(4) BW.
425. Art. 2:391 BW. The annual report is not the glossy, printed report containing the annual accounts familiar to US lawyers and accountants. It is a report by the management board that explains the annual accounts, and indicates the board's views on the development of the enterprise. It must be in Dutch. The use of another language is permitted only if so resolved by the shareholders' meeting before the beginning of the financial year (Art. 2:362(7) BW).
426. Art. 2:101(6)/2:210(7) BW.
427. Art. 2:393(2) BW. If the shareholders' meeting fails to do so, this power will accrue to the supervisory board.
428. Art. 2:393(4) BW.
429. Art. 2:393(4) BW.
430. Art. 2:393(5) BW.
431. Art. 2:393(8) BW.
432. Art. 2:447 BW.

Annual accounts of listed NVs are also subject to review by the AFM,[433] who may request the Enterprise Court to order that changes be made in the annual accounts.[434]

7.1.3 Approval of Major Corporate Changes

The approval of the shareholders' meeting shall be required for resolutions of the management board regarding an important change in the identity or character of the NV or its business. This includes in any case:

(a) the transfer of all or substantially all of the entire enterprise to a third party;
(b) entering into, or termination of, a long-lasting co-operation with another company or legal entity by the company or its subsidiary, in the event that such co-operation or termination thereof is of fundamental importance to the company; and
(c) taking an interest in, or the divestiture of, a participation by, the company or one of its subsidiaries with a value of at least one third of the amount of the corporate assets pursuant to the annual accounts of the company.[435]

The shareholders also have the right to approve certain major changes in the corporate structure, including amendments to the articles of association, statutory mergers, statutory divisions and dissolution (see Chapter 11).

7.1.4 Good Faith Requirements

The law requires a shareholder to behave reasonably and equitably in all situations towards all parties connected with the company, including other shareholders, the management board, the supervisory board, holders of depository receipts issued with the co-operation of the company (NV) depository receipt holders with meeting rights (BV), the works council and the company itself.[436] This does not imply that shareholders must uphold the company's interests, or that they have any obligation towards other shareholders.[437] These good faith requirements may, however, form the grounds for an action to have a

433. See Wtfv.
434. Art. 2:448(2) BW.
435. Art. 2:107a(1) BW. No similar rule exists for the BV, however, legal commentators have argued that this rule should be applied to the BV by analogy.
436. Art. 2:8 BW.
437. Supreme Court 30 June 1944, NJ 1944, 465 (*Wennex*).

resolution of a corporate body voided by court order (see § 6.3.2).[438] Actions of a shareholder should not unreasonable harm the interests of other parties connected with the company.

7.2 Shareholders' Resolutions

7.2.1 Shareholders' Meeting

Shareholders' meetings of NVs must be held in the Netherlands. BVs are allowed to hold their shareholders' meeting abroad. The meeting must be held at the official seat or at a place designated in the articles of association. Meetings of an NV may be held elsewhere if the entire issued share capital is present or represented. Meetings of a BV may be held elsewhere if all shareholders and other persons with meeting rights have agreed to that and the management board and the supervisory board have had the opportunity to give their advice before the shareholders take their decisions.[439]

A shareholders' meeting must be held at least once a year.[440] All other meetings are referred to as 'special' or 'extraordinary' meetings.

For NVs the annual meeting must be held within six months after the end of the company's financial year, unless the articles specify a shorter period.[441] Notice for meetings must be given by the management board or the supervisory board for the NV at least 15, and for the BV at least eight, days prior to the date of the meeting unless a longer notice period is specified in the articles.[442] For a listed NV, the notice period is 42 days prior to the date of the meeting.[443] Shareholders may request the management board and the supervisory board to convene an extraordinary shareholders meeting. If the board(s) refuse(s) to convene a meeting, one or more shareholders holding in the event of an NV at least 10% and in the event of a BV at least 1% of the issued share capital may convene a meeting by obtaining an order of the president of the competent District Court.[444]

With respect to NVs alone, the management board is under an obligation to convene a shareholders' meeting within three months after it appears

438. Art. 2:15(1)(b) BW.
439. Art. 2:116/226 BW. There is some discussion in legal literature as to whether 'elsewhere' includes abroad for the NV (see Asser/Maeijer, Van Solinge & Nieuwe Weme 2-II*2009/344).
440. Art. 2:108(1)/218(1) BW.
441. Art. 2:108(2)/218(2) BW.
442. Art. 2:115(1)/225 BW.
443. Art. 2:115(2) BW.
444. Art. 2:110/220 BW. This right is also conferred upon holders of depository receipts issued with co-operation (NV) and, for the BV, depository receipt holders with meeting rights, and under certain circumstances, also to pledgees and usufructuaries, provided that the above persons represent at least 10%, or in the case of the BV at least 1%, of the issued share capital.

likely to the management board that the equity of the NV has decreased to an amount equal to or less than 50% of the paid up and called up part of the share capital.[445] At such an extraordinary meeting measures to be taken, if any, shall be discussed.

In the event that there is an obligation pursuant to the law or the articles to hold a shareholders' meeting (e.g. the annual shareholders' meeting or the 'loss' meeting), each shareholder (and for that purpose also the other persons authorised to be present at the meeting, such as holders of depository receipts issued with the co-operation of the company (NV) or depository receipt holders with meeting rights (BV)) has the right to request authorisation from the District Court to convene a shareholders' meeting.[446]

NVs must give notice by an announcement in nationally circulated newspapers. Listed NVs must give notice through the website of the company.[447] The articles may provide for other ways of announcement for registered shareholders and holders of depository receipts issued with the co-operation of the NV. For BVs, the notice must be sent by mail or by e-mail if the shareholder or holder of meeting rights has agreed thereto. Failure to give proper notice may render the meeting voidable,[448] unless notice is waived by a unanimous vote representing all of the issued share capital.[449]

The agenda of the meeting is determined by the party giving notice. Shareholders and holders of depository receipts issued with the co-operation of the company (NV) and meeting right holders (BV) shall have the right to propose issues for inclusion on the agenda of a shareholders' meeting. For BVs this right will exist if they represent jointly at least 1% of the issued capital. For NVs this is also 1% and if it concerns a listed NV, this right also applies to shareholders and holders of depository receipts issued with the co-operation of the company if they represent a market capitalisation of EUR 50 million. Based on the 'Frijns' Act[450] the threshold for NVs will change to 3% of the issued capital and the alternative criterion of EUR 50 million market capitalisation will no longer apply. However, if the articles set out the old thresholds of 1% and/or EUR 50 million market capitalisation, these will

445. Art. 2:108a BW.
446. Art. 2:112/222 BW.
447. Art. 2:113(2)(6) BW.
448. Art. 2:15(1)(a) BW.
449. Art. 2:115(1)/225 BW. For the BV, this vote needs to include all those who are entitled to attend the shareholders' meeting (such as holders of depository receipts), and is subject to the management and supervisory board members having had the opportunity to advise on the issue(s) at hand.
450. *Wet van 15 november 2012 tot wijziging van de Wet op het financieel toezicht, de Wet giraal effectenverkeer en het Burgerlijk Wetboek naar aanleiding van het advies van de Monitoring Commissie Corporate Governance Code van 30 mei 2007*, Stb. 2012, 588.

apply until the articles are amended. The 'Frijns' Act will probably enter into force in the course of 2013.

For the BV, this right to add certain items to the agenda may be overruled if serious interests of the company would not permit any such issue to be dealt with at the shareholders' meeting.

The petition to add an item to the agenda must be submitted to the management board at least 60 days, for an NV, or 30 days, for a BV, prior to the shareholders' meeting.[451] Resolutions on subjects not properly set out in the notice are valid only if carried by a unanimous vote of a meeting at which all shareholders are present or represented.[452] BVs must state the purpose of the meeting in the notice.[453] NVs may refer to an agenda of the meeting that is available for inspection by shareholders at the offices of the company.[454] Any proposal to amend the articles must, however, be mentioned in the notice.[455] In the event that annual accounts[456] or amendments to the articles[457] are to be discussed, the relevant documents must be made available at the offices of the company for inspection by the shareholders prior to the meeting. Copies must be made available, free of charge.

The articles must state who will act as chairman of the meeting. The chairman of the supervisory board or the president of the management board normally serves as chairman of the shareholders' meeting. The chairman may appoint a secretary to keep minutes and prepare the attendance list. The minutes of meetings at which certain important actions are undertaken or discussed must be prepared by a civil law notary.[458] The management board must keep a record of all shareholders' resolutions available for inspection by the shareholders and the holders of depository receipts (see §§ 5.5 and 7.7). They are entitled to receive a copy or excerpt from this record.[459]

For certain topics, such as putting aside a binding nomination or elimination of pre-emptive rights with respect to a new issue of shares, the law requires a quorum. The articles often contain quorum provisions requiring a certain percentage of shareholders to be present, or represented by proxy, when particular subjects (e.g., amendments to the articles or the dissolution of the company) are to be voted on at the shareholders' meeting.

---

451. Art. 2:114a/224a BW.
452. Art. 2:114(2)/224(2) BW. For the BV, the same applies as is noted above for Art. 2:225 BW.
453. Art. 2:224(1) BW.
454. Art. 2:114(1)/(3) BW. Different rules apply to a listed NV.
455. Art. 2:123(1)/233(1) BW.
456. Art. 2:102(1)/212 BW.
457. Art. 2:123(3)/233(3) BW.
458. Arts 2:124(2)/234(2), 2:330(3) BW.
459. Art. 2:120(4)/230(4) BW. For the BV, this right also exists for parties that are entitled to attend the shareholders' meeting (such as holders of depository receipts).

7.2.2 Resolutions without a Meeting

Companies with few shareholders (or just one) may have a provision in the articles of association enabling the shareholders to adopt resolutions without a meeting.[460] These resolutions are valid only if the votes are cast in writing (or by fax or electronically). For an NV, this is only possible if no depository receipts are issued with the co-operation of the company and the resolution is passed by the unanimous vote of all shareholders. For a BV this is only possible if all shareholders and others with meeting rights agree to the fact that the resolutions are taken outside a meeting. The managing directors and the members of the supervisory board have an advisory vote in the meeting of shareholders (see § 7.3). This advisory vote cannot be ignored, even when circumstances would normally indicate concurrence with the resolution.[461] Failure to seek an advisory vote will make the shareholders' resolution subject to nullification. Resolutions without a meeting may be adopted outside the Netherlands and may be executed in counterparts. The management board must keep a record of all such resolutions.

7.3 Voting

The right to vote is concomitant with the ownership of shares. In principle, voting rights can never be separated from the shares.

In order to facilitate the organisation of a shareholders' meeting of NVs, the management board may be authorised by the shareholders' meeting[462] to use a record date to better orchestrate a shareholders' meeting. The purpose of the record date is to determine that the holders of shares registered on a registration list as of a specific day (which is the 28th day prior to the meeting) shall be deemed to be the persons authorised to vote on the shares so registered at the shareholders' meeting, irrespective of whether such persons are still holders of those shares on the day of the shareholders' meeting. The record date aims to facilitate proxy solicitation for Dutch listed companies.

While NVs may have bearer shares, the articles of association of an NV may require that the share certificates be deposited prior to the meeting at the corporate head office or another designated place (often the offices of a commercial bank).[463] The notice of the meeting must state this requirement. An NV shareholder cannot be required to make the deposit more than seven

---

460. Art. 2:128/238 BW.
461. Supreme Court 10 Mar. 1995, NJ 1995, 595 (*Janssen Pers*).
462. Art. 2:119 BW.
463. This does not apply to listed NVs. Shareholders are required to have their shares registered in a register designated for that purpose by the management board (see art 2:119(1) BW).

days prior to the meeting.[464] The articles of a BV may require a shareholder to give notice of his intended presence at the meeting; however, a three day notice is sufficient.[465]

Each shareholder has at least one vote,[466] provided that non-voting shares are permitted for the BV.[467] The voting rights are, in principle, proportionate to the nominal value of the shares.[468] According to detailed provisions of the law, the articles of an NV may grant reduced voting rights per shareholder according to certain non-discriminatory thresholds,[469] provided that the restriction is not more favourable for holders with a large number of shares than for those with a small number of shares. The articles of an NV may also otherwise depart from the proportionality between equity interests and voting interests, provided that a single shareholder, irrespective of the number of shares he holds, shall not have more than a certain number of votes specified by law (six if the authorised capital is divided into 100 or more shares; otherwise the maximum is three).[470] Except for the requirement that each shareholder has at least one vote, the articles of a BV may deviate from the aforementioned restrictions. A change to the articles of a BV with respect to voting rights can only be adopted at a shareholders' meeting at which the total issued share capital is represented.

The managing directors and the supervisory directors have an advisory vote at the shareholders' meeting. A shareholder may be represented by a proxy. The proxy instrument must be in writing. The articles may prohibit certain persons from being a proxy-holder. For the NV, however, attorneys, civil law notaries and registered accountants (*registeraccountants*) may always represent a shareholder as a proxy-holder.[471]

As a general rule, proxies may be revoked at any time before the vote has been taken. Personal attendance of the shareholder at the meeting revokes any proxy given for that meeting.[472] The death or guardianship of the shareholder causes revocation of the proxy by operation of law. The proxy also terminates upon the transfer of the title to the shares. Proxies do not terminate if the NV applies a record date, but this is only with respect to the shares so registered.

464. Art. 2:117(3) BW.
465. Art. 2:227(6) BW.
466. Art. 2:118(1)/228(1) BW.
467. Art. 2:228(5) BW.
468. Art. 2:118(2)/228(2)(4) BW.
469. Art. 2:118(4) BW.
470. Art. 2:118(5)/228(5) BW.
471. Art. 2:117(1)/227(1) BW.
472. Asser/Maeijer, Van Solinge & Nieuwe Weme 2-II* 2009 /356.

Pledgees[473] and beneficiaries of a life interest[474] (see § 5.4) may have voting rights. These voting rights are inherent in and concomitant with their equity interest, and cannot be revoked by the personal attendance of the legal owner of the shares, by the transfer of title to the shares, or by the death or mental incompetence of the shareholder.

The shareholders have access to the shareholders' register (see § 5.1.3). Proxy solicitations and proxy battles are unusual in the Netherlands. There are, therefore, no special rules governing this phenomenon.

The holders of certain types or classes of share, usually priority shares (see § 5.2), may have the right to veto certain shareholders' decisions, especially those providing for amendments to the articles or the dissolution of the company (see § 11.6.2).

7.4 Shareholders' Agreements

Shareholders may enter into agreements concerning certain rights incidental to the ownership of their shares. Shareholders' agreements are, as a general rule, valid and enforceable, but they bind only the parties thereto. Under certain conditions (all shareholders are a party to the agreement, as well as the company itself) arrangements in the shareholders' agreement may be enforceable towards the company: e.g. a shareholders' resolution that has been taken while one of the shareholders violated with the exercise of his voting rights an arrangement in the shareholders' agreement, may be voidable because it violates the corporate principles of reasonableness and fairness (Art. 2:15(1)b in conjunction with Art. 2:8 BW).[475]

The rights and obligations set out in the shareholders' agreement are not incidental to the shares and do not bind future shareholders. The effectiveness of shareholders' agreements may be enhanced by penalty clauses, the use of irrevocable proxies (to the extent legally possible) and covenants to bind a successor or assignee under a penalty provision (*kettingbeding*).

Most joint venture agreements that call for the formation of one or more companies to conduct the joint venture business contain provisions concerning the financing of the joint venture, a right of first refusal in the event that a participant wishes to sell its equity stake and the use that the parties may make of their voting rights. These agreements cannot, however, set aside the powers that the management board and the supervisory board derive from the law and the articles.

---

473. Art. 2:89(3)/198(3) BW.
474. Art. 2:88(3)/197(3) BW.
475. Asser/Maeijer, Van Solinge & Nieuwe Weme 2-II* 2009/387 and District Court of The Hague 1 Aug. 2012, JOR 2012, 286 (*Vanka/Kawat*).

It is generally held by legal commentators that a shareholder cannot sell or otherwise dispose of his voting rights separately from his legal or beneficial ownership rights in the shares, albeit that a voting agreement with other shareholders is allowed. However, a shareholder cannot agree to vote according to instructions from the management board or the supervisory board, and a voting agreement, like any other agreement, cannot violate the law, the articles of association or principles of good morals (*goede zeden*).[476]

Several types of voting agreement have been specifically approved by the Dutch Supreme Court. A voting agreement is valid if it purports to avoid a deadlock at a shareholders' meeting, for instance, by providing that an opinion shall be sought from a third party regarding the resolution to be taken and that shareholders shall vote in conformity with this opinion.[477] The third party must act in good faith. The same practical result can be achieved by a provision in the articles that, in the case of a tied vote among shareholders, a third party will resolve the matter.[478] A voting agreement may provide for a voting pool that requires certain shareholders to vote as a block and in accordance with the majority vote among those shareholders in a pre-meeting.[479] Shareholders may agree with a third party on certain actions of the company (such as the sale of parts of its business) and they may also agree among themselves that they will appoint a new board, if required, in order to ensure proper performance of the agreement with this third party.[480] It is generally accepted that other purposes of voting agreements may also be valid, such as an agreement not to cast votes or to waive a vote under specific circumstances.[481] However, an outright sale of voting rights for a consideration is generally perceived as prohibited and void.[482]

Netherlands law does not permit the formation of a voting trust. However, a similar result can be, and frequently is, achieved by the formation of a foundation (*stichting*) (see § 2.5.2) that holds title to the shares, subject to certain contractual obligations.

476. Asser/Maeijer, Van Solinge & Nieuwe Weme 2-II* 2009/384. The agreement would be void.
477. Supreme Court 30 Jun. 1944, NJ 1944, 465 (*Wennex*).
478. Art. 2:120(1)/230(1) BW.
479. Supreme Court 13 Nov. 1959, NJ 1960, 472 (*Distilleerderij Melchers*).
480. Supreme Court 19 Feb. 1960, NJ 1960, 473 (*Aurora*). A voting agreement to distribute reserves to evade the thresholds for the applicability of the 'large' company rules (see § 8.1.2) may under certain circumstances be void (District Court Alkmaar 15 Dec. 1976, NJ 1978, 319 (*De Zaanlandse c.s.*).
481. Asser/Maeijer, Van Solinge & Nieuwe Weme 2-II* 2009/382.
482. Asser/Maeijer, Van Solinge & Nieuwe Weme 2-II* 2009/384.

7.5 Inspection of Books and Records

Every company must keep books and records, and the management board must store these records for a period of at least seven years.[483] The books and records must be in such a form that, depending on the nature and size of the company, an accurate assessment can be made fairly quickly of its financial status.[484] With the exception of the shareholders' register (see § 5.1.3), shareholders are in principle not entitled to inspect these books and records. Shareholders (or holders of depository receipts) representing either at least 10% of the issued shares or a nominal value of EUR 225,000 (or any lower percentage or amount as provided in the articles of association) may, under certain circumstances, request the Enterprise Court (see § 10.1) to appoint one or more experts to investigate the conduct of the business (see § 10.2.2). For NVs and BVs with an issued capital of EUR 22.5 million or more, the threshold for such a request is 1% of the issued shares or, for a listed NV, shares representing a market value of EUR 20 million. These court-appointed experts are entitled to full access to the books and records.[485]

7.6 Right to Information

The law provides that the management board and the supervisory board shall provide to the general meeting all the information it requests, unless this conflicts with a serious interest of the company.[486]

Every shareholder is entitled to raise specific questions at a general meeting and the company is obligated to answer such questions, unless this would seriously harm the interests of the company.[487] In principle no such right exists outside the general meeting of shareholders.[488]

---

483. Art. 2:10 BW; see § 9.2.2.1 for claims in` bankruptcy upon non-compliance with these provisions.
484. Supreme Court 6 Jun. 1993, NJ 1993, 713 (*Brens/Bülent Sarper*).
485. Art. 2:351 BW.
486. Art. 2:107(2)/217(2) BW.
487. Supreme Court 9 Jul. 2010, JOR 2010, 228 (*ASMI*).
488. The Dutch Supreme Court ruled that the provisions of corporate law for obtaining information are not exhaustive and therefore do not preclude a minority shareholder from obtaining information through a preliminary hearing of witness (Art. 186 Rv) (Supreme Court 20 Oct. 1995, NJ 1996, 120 (*Perrier/Marceau Investissements*). The court may also require the defendant to give the plaintiff access to its books and records but only to the extent necessary to pursue a court case (see also Art. 843a Rv).

7.7 Rights of Holders of Depository Receipts

Holders of depository receipts issued with the support or concurrence of the company (NV) or holders of depository receipts with meeting rights (BV) (see § 5.5) enjoy the following rights on an equal basis with shareholders:

(a) the right to receive the agenda of the meeting;[489]
(b) subject to certain restrictions (see § 7.2.1), the right to add an item to the agenda of a shareholders' meeting;[490]
(c) the right to attend meetings and to participate in discussions.[491] They do not, however, have the right to vote;[492]
(d) the right to obtain the annual accounts and the annual report and auditors' opinion (see § 5.5.4);[493] and
(e) the right to petition for a shareholders' meeting (see § 7.2.1) or for an enquiry into the affairs of the company (*enquête*) (see § 10.2.2).

The same rights may be attributed in the relevant agreement to pledgees and usufructuaries with voting rights and pledgors, pledgees and usufructuaries without voting rights, unless this attribution is not permitted by the articles of association.

489. Arts. 2:113(1)/223(1), 2:114(1)/224(1) BW.
490. Art. 2:114a(2)/224a(2) BW.
491. Art. 2:117(2)/227(2) BW.
492. Holders of depository receipts for shares in a listed company may request the trust office to grant a proxy to cast a vote on the underlying shares and the trust office must, under certain conditions, grant this proxy (see Art. 2:118 BW and § 5.5.5).
493. Art. 2:102(1)/212 BW.

Chapter 8
Distribution of Powers; Management of Business Affairs

8.1 Governance

8.1.1 General

Although Netherlands corporate law is, in many respects, different from corporate law in other continental European countries, historically it has the same basic two-tier management system as exists elsewhere. This consists of a management board (known in France as the *directoire*, and in Germany as the *Vorstand*) which performs executive functions, as well as a supervisory board (in France, the *conseil de surveillance*, and in Germany, the *Aufsichtsrat*) which advises and supervises the management board. In the Netherlands, this system may apply to both NVs and BVs. Each board has its own responsibilities, powers and duties, and each is legally independent of the shareholders.

From 1 January 2013 new legislation is in force in the Netherlands, providing a legal basis for a one-tier system for both NVs and BVs.[494] In this system, the articles of association of a company with a one-tier system allocate specific management powers to executive directors (*uitvoerende bestuurders*) and non-executive directors (*niet uitvoerende bestuurders*). Management powers that have not been allocated will vest in all executive and non-executive directors (the one-tier board). The task of supervising the performance of directors cannot, by such allocation, be withheld from non-executive directors. Powers that may not be allocated to executive directors are the chairmanship of the one-tier board, the nominations for the appointment of directors and the power to determine the remuneration of executive directors.

A system with a supervisory board or non-executive directors is mandatory for companies that have qualified and have been registered with the commercial register to that effect as 'large' companies (see § 8.1.2) for three consecutive years. The status of 'large' company can also be adopted volun-

494. Art. 2:129a(1)/239a(1) BW.

tarily.[495] This may result from negotiations with trade unions or the works council in mergers or other situations. This voluntary 'large' company status can only be adopted if the company, or a company controlled by it, has a works council (see § 13).[496]

In an NV and a BV the shareholders have almost identical powers (and limitations thereto), and the management board (*directie* or *bestuur*) and, where applicable, the supervisory board (*raad van commissarissen*) or non-executive directors (*niet uitvoerende bestuurders*) have almost the same responsibilities. The concept of an 'officer' is unknown in Netherlands corporate law.

The management board is the executive body and may be made up of individuals and/or companies.[497] The management board is responsible for the management of the company and for its representation, i.e. the actions of the company towards third parties (see § 8.2.5).[498] The Dutch management board combines the functions of internal managing directors and senior officers as known in an American company. Consequently, there is no formal position equivalent to that of chief executive officer (although the chairman of the management board is often called the 'CEO'). The management board may, however, consist of a sole member, in which case that person is customarily called the 'managing director' or the 'general managing director' (*algemeen directeur*). If the management board has more than one member, each can have different external powers and internal responsibilities (see § 8.2.1.1),[499] but in principle the entire management board is responsible for proper management.

In the one-tier system, the executive directors will in principle be responsible for the management of the company and the non-executive directors will be responsible for duties similar to those of the supervisory directors in a two-tier system (see § 8.3). However, the non-executive directors and the executive directors serve on the same board and therefore share joint responsibility for proper management. In the one-tier system, the non-executive directors will possibly be more actively involved in the general management of the company than the supervisory directors in the two-tier system. The exact duties and responsibilities of the non-executive director may vary, depending on the articles of association and the allocation of powers set out therein.

In a two-tier system, the supervisory board is distinct from the management board and the same persons cannot serve on both boards. The supervisory

495. Art. 2:157(1)/267(1) BW.
496. Art. 2:157(1)/267(1) BW.
497. For the fiduciary duties of managing directors, see § 9.1.1.
498. Arts 2:129/239, 2:130(1)/240(1) BW.
499. Art. 2:9 BW.

board has a primarily supervisory and advisory function.[500] The articles may give it more specific powers, but in principle the supervisory board cannot exercise executive functions. The supervisory board is not empowered to give specific instructions to the management board or to determine the business policy of the company, and it may not appoint or remove managing directors, unless the company has the 'large' company status (see § 8.1.2). The precise duties and responsibilities of the supervisory board may vary, depending on the articles. The actual duties of the supervisory board often reflect the degree of delegation of power by the shareholders. The shareholders are free, except in the case of a 'large' company which requires the existence of supervisory or non-executive directors, to state in the articles that there will only be a management board and no supervisory board or non-executive directors.

If the NV or BV is a 'large' company, the supervisory board (two-tier) or the group of non-executive directors (one-tier) has a much more prominent position in the corporate hierarchy (see § 8.3.1.2). In no event, however, does the supervisory board have the power to manage the business or negotiate and conclude contracts (except when the management board has a conflict of interest with the company, is absent or is unable to act (*ontstentenis of belet*)) (see § 8.3.1.1).

Furthermore, the shareholders are not the supreme authority within the company. They have certain statutory powers, and the articles may to some extent increase their authority to determine the policy of the company.[501] In 'large' companies, particularly, the shareholders have more limited powers.

8.1.2 'Large' Companies

8.1.2.1 Extended Powers of the Supervisory Board and the Group of Non-Executive Directors

If over a period of three consecutive years an NV or a BV meets the statutory definition of a 'large' company (*structuurvennootschap*) and is not fully 'exempt' (see § 8.1.2.4.1), the law requires it to have a supervisory board or a group of non-executive directors with broad powers.[502] The supervisory board or the group of non-executive directors of a 'large' company is charged with three basic functions: nomination of supervisory directors or non-executive directors, appointment of managing directors or executive directors and approval of certain important decisions of the management board or the one-tier board (see § 8.3.1.2). This mandatory system, intended to reduce the power of

---

500. Art. 2:140(2)/250(2) BW.
501. Art. 2:107(1)/217(1) BW. For the BV, see also Art. 2:239(4) BW.
502. Art. 2:154(1)/264(1) BW.

the shareholders and increase the power of the employee-based works council, is the Dutch alternative to the more direct form of employee participation in management that exists e.g. in Germany (*Mitbestimmung*). Additional rules applicable for 'large' companies are described in §§ 8.2 and 8.3.

8.1.2.2 Definition of 'Large'

In order to determine whether a company qualifies as 'large', the following three cumulative tests apply:[503]

(a) the company's issued capital plus reserves, including its retained earnings, equal at least EUR 16 million;
(b) the company or a 'dependent company' has established a works council, as required by law (see § 13.1); and
(c) the company, together with its dependent companies, normally employs 100 or more persons in the Netherlands.

A dependent company (*afhankelijke maatschappij*), as defined in the Dutch Civil Code, is: (i) a legal person in which the company, or any of its dependent companies, solely or jointly, and for their own account, contributes at least one half of the issued capital; and (ii) a partnership with a business enterprise registered with the commercial register in which the company or a dependent company is a fully liable partner towards third parties.[504] Netherlands law contains special rules for the definition of 'large' in the case of a general partner in a limited partnership.

8.1.2.3 Notification to Commercial Register

A company that qualifies as a 'large' company and is not fully exempt (see 8.1.2.4.1) must notify the commercial register (see § 12.2) thereof within two months after the shareholders' meeting adopted or approved the annual accounts, as the case may be, for the year in which the company meets the statutory criteria.[505] Three years of uninterrupted registration automatically render the rules for 'large' companies applicable.[506] Before the end of the three-year period the articles of association must be amended to comply with the 'large'

503. Art. 2:153(2)/263(2) BW.
504. Art. 2:152/262 BW.
505. Art. 2:153(1)/263(1) BW. Violation of this provision is a criminal offence, see Art. 1(4) WED.
506. Art. 2:154(1)/264(1) BW.

company rules.[507] However, if the articles are not amended before that time, the mandatory provisions will come into force by operation of law.

If the company no longer meets the criteria for qualification as a 'large' company, then it must make a registration to that effect with the commercial register. Except for a few exceptions,[508] only after an uninterrupted period of three years of non-qualification as a 'large' company, the statutory provisions of 'large' companies no longer apply.[509] However, these provisions may thereafter be voluntarily applied provided that the company or its dependent company has a works council.

8.1.2.4 Exemptions

8.1.2.4.1 Fully Exempt 'Large' Companies

The rules for 'large' companies are applicable after the three year registration to that effect with the commercial register. A company which would normally qualify as large is fully exempt (*vrijgesteld*) from the special rules and need not notify the commercial register, if:

(a) the company is 'dependent' on a legal entity to which the special rules concerning a 'large' company apply in full or in part, either mandatorily or voluntarily; or
(b) the company exclusively (or almost exclusively) restricts itself to the management and financing of group companies (see § 3.1.2) and its own and their participation in other legal entities, provided, however, that the majority of the employees of this holding company and all group companies are employed outside the Netherlands; or
(c) the company exclusively or almost exclusively renders management and financial services to a company as set out under (b) above and to other companies of that group; or
(d) at least one half of the issued capital of the company is held as a participation (see § 3.1.2) under a mutual arrangement of co-operation between two or more 'large' companies or companies 'dependent' on 'large' companies.

In practice, the exemptions under (b) and (c) above relate only to international groups of companies with a Dutch-based holding or sub-holding company. In

507. Art. 2:154(3)/264(3) BW.
508. See Asser/Maeijer,Van Solinge & Nieuwe Weme 2-II* 2009/532.
509. Art. 2:154(3)/264(2) BW.

order to be exempted, the holding company must refrain from any activity other than the holding of shares and the financing of its group companies.

A 'large' company to which the exemptions become applicable may transform itself and become a 'regular' company immediately, i.e. without observing the three- year waiting period as described under § 8.1.2.3, by amending its articles of association.[510] However, in some cases the company may want to voluntarily remain a 'large' company in order to avoid any of its Dutch subsidiaries becoming a 'large' company.

8.1.2.4.2 Partially Exempt 'Large' Companies

'Large' company rules apply only partially (*verzwakt regime*) to: (i) companies controlled from outside the Netherlands; and to (ii) international groups with a Dutch-based holding company.[511] Unlike companies with a full exemption, partially exempt companies must register as a company to which the three criteria mentioned in § 8.1.2.2 apply. It will become a 'large' company after three years, but not all the provisions of the rules for 'large' companies will apply. In other words, the company will be partially exempted. This partial exemption affects the special rights of the supervisory board or the non-executive directors with respect to the appointment of members of the management board or the one-tier board and the adoption of the annual accounts in the 'large' company regime. In the partial exempt 'large' company these powers remain with the shareholders.

Control from outside the Netherlands is assumed, or a Dutch-based holding company of an international group is deemed to exist (and therefore the 'large' company rules apply only partially), if at least one half of the issued shares of the company is held by:

(a) a company or another legal entity or its dependent companies, the majority of whose employees (or the employees of their group companies) are employed outside the Netherlands;
(b) a joint venture formed by one or more companies or other legal entities or their dependent companies which meet the criteria under paragraph (a) above; or
(c) a joint venture formed by one or more legal entities which meet the criteria under (a) above and one or more fully or partially exempt 'large' companies.

---

510. Such in contrast to a 'large' company which no longer meets the three criteria as set out in § 8.1.2.3 and will remain a 'large' company for another three years.
511. Art. 2:155(1)/265(1) BW.

However, the partial exemption is not available if the majority of the employees of the group to which the 'large' company belongs, together with the employees of the legal persons or companies referred to in paragraphs (a), (b) and (c) above, are employed within the Netherlands.[512]

8.2 The Management Board and its Agents

8.2.1 Powers of the Management Board

8.2.1.1 Regular NVs and BVs

The members of the management board (often referred to as managing directors) have collective powers and responsibilities. The managing directors share responsibility for all the decisions and acts of the management board and for the acts of each individual managing director. The management board may adopt, for internal purposes, a manual or set of regulations that describes in detail the duties, responsibilities and powers of each managing director, as well as the rules applicable for board meetings. The articles of association may allow the supervisory board to adopt the regulations governing the management board, which may limit the powers of that board. While these manuals and regulations have no external effect, they can be of practical use and may have a significant impact on the liability of a managing director in cases of mismanagement towards the company (see § 9.2).

The law is not specific about the powers of the management board in undertaking 'the management of the company'.[513] The company's business policies must be determined by the management board within the confines of the corporate purposes and in the 'interests of the company' (see § 1.2). The management board oversees the implementation of its policies and the company's day-to-day affairs, in addition to implementing decisions of shareholders' meetings and of the supervisory board (if applicable).

The management board prepares the annual accounts and the annual report (see § 7.1.2). All the members of the management board must sign the annual accounts (see § 9.2.4.2). If a managing director fails to sign, the reasons for his failure to do so must be stated.[514] It is the responsibility of the management board to file the annual accounts within eight days of the adoption or, if the annual accounts are not adopted, within 13 months following the

512. Art. 2:155(2)/265(2) BW.
513. Art. 2:129/239 BW.
514. Art. 2:101(2)/210(2) BW. A violation of these provisions is a criminal offence, see Art. 1(4) WED.

end of the financial year.[515] The articles may empower the management board to resolve to create reserves and thereby allocate profits, and consequently determine the amount of profits available to the shareholders for dividend distribution (see § 7.1.2).

The management board is basically independent in the performance of its duties. It is not subordinate to either the shareholders or supervisory board.[516] The articles may, however, require the management board to obtain the prior approval of the supervisory board (if applicable) or shareholders' meeting with respect to decisions on matters set out in the articles or determined by the supervisory board or the shareholders' meeting.[517] The articles may require that the management board complies with directives issued by the shareholders' meeting, which is especially relevant if the company is part of a group of companies.[518] All these provisions however, are for internal purposes only. Any transactions with third parties concluded by the management board without the required prior approval, or actions in violation of any directive, will nevertheless be binding upon the company. The existence of directives or requirements to obtain any prior approval may not be invoked against the third party concerned.[519] Although the management board may not be legally obliged to accept detailed instructions from another corporate body, especially if they are contrary to the corporate interests of the company and its business, its refusal to do so could result in a serious conflict with the shareholders or the supervisory board, culminating in the suspension or removal of one or more of the managing directors.

The WOR contains several provisions requiring the management board to seek the prior consent or advice of the works council for certain critical decisions. Actions by the company that violate the WOR are subject to judicial recourse (see § 13.2.5).

The management board has no power to fill its own vacancies or to amend the articles of association.

8.2.1.2 'Large' Companies

If an NV or a BV is a 'large' company, special rules govern the powers of the management board. These rules supplement the general rules applicable for the management board and state that in the event of a conflict, the special

515. Art. 2:394 BW.
516. Supreme Court 21 Jan. 1955, NJ 1959, 43 (*Forumbank*).
517. Art. 2:129(3)/239(3) BW.
518. Art. 2:129(4)/239(4) BW. For the BV, the law provides that the management board must comply with such directives, unless this would be contrary to the interests of the company.
519. This third party protection is not available in the event of specific abuse of this protection by such third party. Supreme Court 17 Dec. 1982, NJ 1983, 480 (*Bibolini*).

rules prevail. In a 'large' company, the management board must obtain the approval of the supervisory board or the group of non-executive directors prior to undertaking any of the following:[520]

(a) the issuance or acquisition of shares and debt instruments issued by the company or by a general or limited partnership in which the company is a general partner;
(b) co-operation by the company in the issuance of depository receipts for shares in its capital;
(c) an application for listing or withdrawal of a listing at a stock exchange of shares, debentures, bonds and depository receipts (for NVs only);
(d) the commencement or termination of a major long-lasting co-operation of the company or dependent company (see § 8.1.2.2) with another company or partnership, or participation as a general partner in a general or limited partnership if this co-operation or the termination thereof is of major significance to the company;
(e) any acquisition by the company or a dependent company of a participation (see § 3.1.2) in another company that exceeds the amount of one quarter of the participating company's issued capital and reserves as shown on its balance sheet and the notes thereto, and any substantial increase or decrease in any such participation;
(f) any investment of an amount equal to at least one quarter of the company's own issued capital and reserves as shown on the balance sheet and the notes thereto;
(g) any proposal to amend the articles of association;
(h) any proposal to dissolve the company;
(i) the filing of a petition for bankruptcy or for a suspension of payments;
(j) the termination of the employment of a significant number of employees of the company or of a dependent company, at the same time or within a short time span;
(k) a substantial change in the employment conditions of a significant number of employees of the company or of a dependent company; and
(l) any proposal to reduce the issued capital.

The articles may further supplement these requirements.

If the management board enters into a transaction in violation of these provisions, the company is nevertheless bound. The violation may, however, form the grounds for removal of a managing director or for other legal actions (see § 9.2).

520. Art. 2:164(1)/274(1) BW.

A supervisory board cannot force the management board to take action on any of the matters set out above. This initiative is at the sole discretion of the management board.

8.2.2 Structure of the Management Board

The management board may consist of individuals or legal entities, either Dutch or foreign, resident or non-resident. The management board must have at least one member. Its size is as determined by the articles of association and is the result of the appointment and removal of managing directors from time to time. The size of the board is not determined by the management board itself.

Most managing directors are employed full-time by the company. The concept of an 'officer' does not exist in the Netherlands. The articles of the company may provide for the allocation of duties (e.g. financial affairs) to one or more members of the management board.[521] Duties that have not been allocated remain the responsibility of all members of the management board.[522] These allocated responsibilities remain within the power of the management board as a whole and are part of its general responsibility for corporate affairs. Consequently, the title of president or general director (*algemeen directeur*) does not always imply a more prominent legal position than that of the other managing directors.

The articles may require certain qualifications or expertise for managing directors.[523] The managing director's name, residential address (or, if the director is a company, its head office address) and other particulars must be entered in the commercial register (see Chapter 12).

8.2.3 Appointment, Compensation, Suspension and Removal

8.2.3.1 Appointment in Regular NVs and BVs

The initial management board is appointed by the founders when the company is first incorporated.[524] Their names appear in the deed of incorporation. Thereafter, managing directors are appointed by the shareholders' meeting. The articles of association of a BV may state that managing directors are appointed by the meeting of holders of shares of a specific class or type, provided that every shareholder who has voting rights can participate in the decision-making process regarding the appointment of at least one managing

521. Art. 2:9(1) BW.
522. Art. 2:9(2) BW.
523. Art. 2:132(2)/242(2) BW.
524. Art. 2:132/242 BW.

director.[525] In a one-tier system a director will be appointed as 'executive director' or as 'non-executive director'. It is not uncommon for the articles to provide that certain members of the (management) board be identified as members A, members B, etc. This distinction between the board members may be made to show a distinction between the (managing) directors and their powers to bind the company (see § 8.2.5.3). It is also used to show a direct link between any such (managing) director and a class of shareholders with a corresponding identity (class A, class B, etc.), having special nomination rights. For BVs alone an alternative structure can be considered with the right to appointment attributed to the meeting of holders of shares of a specific class or type. If binding nomination rights for the appointment of (management) board members are granted in the articles to a particular type or class of shareholders (usually holders of shares with a class indication or priority shares, see § 5.2) or to the supervisory board (or any other person or institution stated in the articles), then the shareholders' meeting must, in principle, appoint one of the candidates from the binding nomination thus made. However, this nomination can be overruled by a qualified majority of two thirds of the votes cast if they represent more than one half of the issued shares.[526] Appointment by the holders of one class or type of shares of all (for the BV) or part (for the NV) of the board is prohibited. Shareholders may, however, conclude a shareholders' agreement (see § 7.4) requiring the parties thereto to vote in favour of a proposal made by holders of one class or type of shares.

If the company has a works council (see § 13.1), the management board is required to give the works council prior notice of any proposed candidate for appointment to the board, in order to give the works council an opportunity to render non-binding advice before the appointment is made.[527] The works council of an NV has the right to determine its position (*standpuntbepaling*) with respect to the appointment (suspension and removal) of a managing director and this position will be presented to the shareholders' meeting together with the proposal to appoint (suspend or remove) a managing director.[528]

Managing directors are usually appointed for an indefinite period of time. Annual appointments or re-appointments are uncommon and, to the extent managing directors have employment agreements with the company, are incompatible with Dutch labour law. The latter does not apply to listed companies, where directors are often appointed for periods of four years. Dutch law

525. Art. 2:242 BW.
526. Art. 2:133(2)/243(2) BW.
527. Art. 30(1) WOR. This consultation right assumes that the managing director qualifies as a director under the WOR.
528. Art. 2:134a(1) BW.

specifically provides that the relationship between the managing director and the listed company does not qualify as an employment agreement.[529]

8.2.3.2 Appointment in 'Large' Companies

In the case of a non-exempt 'large' NV or BV, the members of the management board are appointed by the supervisory board and, in the case of a one-tier board, the executives are appointed by the non-executives.[530] This power cannot be made subject to a nomination by any class or type of shareholders, including priority shareholders (see § 5.2). The shareholders must be notified prior to the appointment, although they cannot veto the appointment results. The works council (see § 13.1) must also be notified and given the opportunity to render advice prior to the appointment.[531]

In a partially exempt 'large' company (see § 8.1.2.4) the appointment of a managing director is subject to the same rules as apply to ordinary companies (see § 8.2.3.1).

8.2.3.3 Limitation on 'Significant' Board Positions in BVs, NVs and Foundations

A person who holds more than two 'significant' positions as supervisory director or non-executive director or who holds a 'significant' position as chairman of the supervisory board or as chairman of the board in a one-tier system, cannot be appointed as 'significant' managing director, or as 'significant' executive director of a one-tier board. For this purpose the membership of a supervisory body set out in the articles of association is deemed to be a supervisory board position, and the appointment as supervisory director at different companies within a group counts as one supervisory board position.[532]

A 'significant' board position is a board position in an NV, BV or foundation in relation to which at two consecutive balance sheet dates at least two of the following criteria are met:

- the value of assets, as given in its balance sheet (together with explanatory notes) on the basis of their acquisition price and production costs, is more than EUR 17.5 million;
- its net turnover in the applicable financial year is more than EUR 35 million; and

529. Art. 2:132(3) BW.
530. Art. 2:162/272 BW; and for the one-tier board: Art. 2:164a(2)/274a(2) BW.
531. Art. 30(1) WOR.
532. Art. 2:132/242a BW.

- the average number of employees in the applicable financial year is at least 250.

8.2.3.4 Compensation; Employment Contracts

Members of the management board are in most cases employed by the company. The terms of employment are determined by the shareholders, unless otherwise provided in the articles of association (e.g. that the terms shall be fixed by the supervisory board).[533] In a 'large' company, whether or not partially exempt, the terms of employment are also determined by the shareholders, unless otherwise provided in the articles.[534] Although the company, in its capacity as employer, is managed by the management board, the board cannot, by virtue of an employment agreement alone, give instructions to an individual managing director. Moreover, if the managing director is also employed by another company, e.g. a parent company, he might appear to be in an ambiguous position. His responsibilities as a managing director cannot be subordinated to his employment relationship with either company.

A managing director's salary is often indexed to or subject to annual revision based on the cost of living. NVs which do not only have registered shares, have no restrictions on the transfer of shares provided for in its articles and do not allow bearer depository receipts to be issued with the co-operation of the company, must disclose in the explanatory notes to the annual accounts (on an individual basis for each managing/supervisory director) defined payments regarding salary, redundancy and profit sharing as well as any rights to subscribe for shares in the NV, including the exercise price.[535]

In the event that a managing director is a legal entity, the contractual relationship between the company and such legal entity has the legal qualification of a contract for professional services.[536] As per 1 January 2013 all contracts of newly appointed managing directors of listed NVs who are natural persons, will also be legally qualified as a contract for professional services and not as employment contracts.

NVs are required to formulate a remuneration policy for the management board or the executives. This policy is established by the shareholders' meeting. If the company has a works council, it should be given the opportunity to make its views known.

---

533. Art. 2:135(5)/245 BW. If another corporate body determines the terms of employment, the grant of shares or any options on shares requires the approval of the shareholders (see Art. 2:135(5) BW).
534. Asser/Maeijer/Van Solinge & Nieuwe Weme 2-II* 2009/310.
535. Art. 2:383b-383e BW.
536. Art. 7:400 BW.

8.2.3.5 Suspension

A managing director may be suspended at any time by a resolution of the shareholders' meeting if the shareholders have the power to appoint managing directors. The suspension has the effect that the managing director remains in office, but without any of the emanating powers. A supervisory board always has the power to suspend a managing director, unless otherwise stated in the articles of association. In a one-tier system the board may at any time suspend an executive director.[537] In a 'large' company that is not fully exempt, this power to suspend is usually vested in the supervisory board. A suspension may always be lifted by the shareholders, unless the suspended director was originally appointed by the supervisory board (which is the case in a 'large' company which is not fully or partially exempt). For a BV the right to appoint a managing director may be vested in the meeting of holders of shares of a certain type or class of shares. In that case they are the ones that may suspend the managing director and they may also lift the suspension. Suspension does not in itself terminate the director's employment contract with the company.

An irregular or unreasonable resolution to suspend a managing director may be contested in court (see § 10.2.3). Suspensions must be recorded at the commercial register (see § 12.2).

8.2.3.6 Removal; Termination of Employment Contract

The removal of a managing director requires a resolution of the body authorised to appoint the managing director. The articles of association of a BV that is not a 'large' company may provide that a managing director can also be removed by another corporate body. In the case of a 'large' company, the supervisory board must first consult with the shareholders' meeting.[538] In cases of mismanagement, the Enterprise Court may also remove a managing director (see § 10.2.4).

If the company has a works council (see § 13.1), the management board must give the works council prior notice of an anticipated removal, in order to allow the works council time to render advice prior to the actual removal.[539] In an NV a representative of the works council can explain its point of view at the shareholders' meeting.

The articles may stipulate that any shareholders' resolution regarding the removal of a managing director requires a special quorum or qualified

537. Arts 2:147(1)/257(1), 2:134(1) BW.
538. Art. 2:162/272 BW. In a one-tier board, these responsibilities are exercised by the non executive members, see Art. 2:164a(2) BW.
539. Art. 30(1) WOR.

majority vote, or that no quorum or qualified majority will be required when the removal is proposed by a certain class or type of shareholder (e.g. priority shareholder) or by the supervisory board. There is, however, a statutory limitation[540] on both the quorum and the qualified majority of vote, being a maximum of two thirds of the votes cast which represent a maximum of one half of the issued share capital.

A shareholders' resolution to remove a managing director can be voided by the court if the managing director concerned has not been properly heard at the shareholders' meeting prior to the resolution.[541] Managing directors and supervisory directors have an 'advisory vote' at the shareholders' meeting,[542] including in respect of a resolution to remove a managing director.[543] The removal of a managing director must be recorded at the commercial register (see § 12.2).

A resolution to remove a managing director from the management board results, in principle, automatically in the termination of the employment contract of that managing director.[544] The legislation applicable for termination of employment is similar to that which applies to termination of employment of other types of employees, except that no permit is required from the UWV (Benefits Agency for Employee Insurances).[545] Disputes and claims fall, in most cases, under the jurisdiction of the District Court,[546] rather than the cantonal Division of the District Court (which has jurisdiction over ordinary labour disputes). The District Court cannot order the company to reinstate a managing director.[547] If the court finds that the termination of employment was obviously unreasonable, the managing director may be entitled to a substantial severance payment from the company. In most cases, a settlement is reached with the board member whereby his employment is terminated with a so-called 'golden handshake'.

---

540. Art. 2:134(2)/244(2) BW.
541. Supreme Court 29 Jan. 1943, NJ 1943, 198 (*Bouw- en Handelmaatschappij Sinis I/Schipper*); see also Court of Appeal Amsterdam 18 May 1990, NJ 1990, 591 (*WTC Amsterdam/Van der Wiel*).
542. Art. 2:117(4)/227(4) BW.
543. Supreme Court 10 Mar. 1995, NJ 1995, 595 (*Janssen Pers*).
544. Supreme Court 15 Apr. 2005, JOR 2005, 144 (*Bartelink/Ciris Television*); Supreme Court 15 Apr. 2005, JOR 2005, 145 (*Eggenhuizen/Unidek Volumebouw*).
545. Art. 6(5) *Buitengewoon Besluit Arbeidsverhoudingen* (Decree on Labour Relations), Stb. 1945, F214, as amended; *Ministeriële Beschikking* (Ministerial Decree) of 10 December 1954, Stcr. 1954, 242.
546. Art. 2:131/241 BW.
547. Art. 2:134(3)/244(3) BW. See further Grapperhaus and Verburg, 2009, Chapter 5.

8.2.4 Resolutions by the Management Board and Managing Directors

8.2.4.1 Resolutions passed in Meetings

Meetings are scheduled informally. There are no statutory notice requirements. Meetings are customarily held at the company's head office, but may be held elsewhere, even outside the Netherlands. The board's manual or regulations (see § 8.2.1.1) may provide detailed rules concerning the scheduling of board meetings. A managing director may be represented at a board meeting only by a fellow managing director. The system of alternate/substitute managing directors does not exist under Netherlands law and is not permitted. Although members of the management board, including the chairman, normally have equal powers and voting rights, the articles of association or board regulations may provide that a specific managing director or a managing director with a defined function (e.g. the chairman) has more votes than the others, or a casting vote. However, no managing director, including the chairman, may have voting powers that allow him to override the votes of all other managing directors.[548] Managing directors may not vote by blank proxy. A managing director may give a specific power of attorney to a fellow member of the management board to vote on his behalf in his absence, but this may only take place for a specific meeting and not on a continuing basis. The articles may give the supervisory board or another corporate body a casting vote in the event of a deadlock.

8.2.4.2 Resolutions without a Meeting

The management board may adopt resolutions without a meeting if the managing directors unanimously agree to the resolution.

8.2.5 Binding the Company

8.2.5.1 General

Except when specifically stated otherwise in the law (and as explained below), the management board has the exclusive power to represent the company. Unless otherwise provided in the articles of association, each managing director has the authority to represent the company in respect of third parties (including appearing in court on behalf of the company).[549] This authority does not

548. Art. 2:129(2)/239(2) BW.
549. Art. 2:130(2)/240(2) BW.

require any specific action by the management board as a whole. However, especially with respect to important actions on behalf of the company, an underlying board resolution is assumed.

The law prohibits any limitations on the basic power of an individual managing director to enter into transactions with third parties, except that either or both of the following may be imposed by the articles (assuming more than one managing director is in office):[550]

(a) the company will be bound only if a minimum number of managing directors have acted jointly; and/or
(b) the company will be bound only if one or more managing directors with defined functions have acted, either individually or jointly, with fellow managing directors, or with designated agents of the company.

It is not possible to limit the transactional power of managing directors to specific subject matters, or according to the size or nature of the transaction in the articles. The limitation set out in (a) and (b) above may, however, be supplemented by a provision in the articles enabling a managing director to obtain a permanent power of attorney from the other directors. The power of attorney may then set out certain limitations concerning the size or nature of the transactions allowed.[551] This power must be registered with the commercial register (see § 12.2). Third parties can then, by examining the company's filing at the commercial register, easily ascertain whether the managing director has the power he purports to have.

8.2.5.2 Statutory Exemptions on the Authority to Represent the Company

The law specifically states that for certain transactions the management board is not authorised to represent the company.

(a) Contribution in kind on shares:[552] The management board is only allowed to accept contributions in kind on shares to be issued if the articles of association expressly authorise the management board to do so. Otherwise the management board may accept contributions in kind only if the shareholders' meeting grants approval. Without this approval the company is not bound to the transaction.
(b) Issuance of shares and setting aside pre-emption rights.[553] A resolution to issue shares in the company and a decision to set aside pre-emption

550. Art. 2:130(2)/240(2) BW.
551. Arts 3:60-79 BW.
552. Art. 2:94(2)/204(2) BW.
553. Arts 2:96/206; 2:96a/206a BW.

rights of shareholders has to be taken by the shareholders' meeting, unless another corporate body has been designated in the articles or by the shareholders' meeting.

(c) Repurchase of shares:[554] The management board of an NV (not a BV) is only authorised to repurchase shares in the company if (among other formalities, see § 4.3.6) the shareholders' meeting has granted specific authorisation to that effect, as well as with respect to the number of shares, method of repurchase and price. Without this authorisation the management board is by law precluded from repurchasing the shares. The company is not bound to the transaction in the event the repurchase concerned registered shares. Managing directors may then be held personally liable for the damage of the sellers. If the repurchased shares are bearer shares, the repurchased shares must be transferred to the managing directors by virtue of law. Each of them shall be liable to the company for compensation of the purchase price.

Certain matters fall within the exclusive domain of the shareholders (e.g. adoption of the annual accounts) or the supervisory board and may not be delegated. Managing directors have no authority whatsoever in these areas, except for advisory votes regarding shareholders' resolutions.

Transactions with third parties which violate either the law or any of the acceptable limitations on the transactional powers of the management board are not enforceable against the company if the limitations are properly disclosed at the commercial register.[555] A managing director who lacks the required authority for his actions but implicitly or explicitly warrants that he has this authority may be liable to third parties for any resultant damages.[556] If the unauthorised actions injure the company, the company may also be entitled to damages.

When a managing director exceeds his authority a distinction should be made between: (i) an action which should have been taken by others (e.g. by the management board as a whole, or jointly with one or more other managing directors, the supervisory board, or shareholders); or (ii) an action to which the company is not authorised. In the latter case the action is null and void,[557] in the former, depending on the nature of the action, the unauthorised act can

554. Arts 2:98(4); 2:98a(1-2) BW.
555. Art. 2:6(2) BW.
556. Supreme Court 26 Jun. 1981, NJ 1982, 1 (*Van den Broek/Van Willigen Vuren*).
557. For example: the issue of shares in excess of the authorised share capital, the subscription by the company to its own shares (Art. 2:95/205 BW), the acquisition of shares in its own capital which are not fully paid (Art. 2:98(1)/207(1) BW) and the acquisition of shares in its own capital in violation of Art. 2:98(2)/207(2) BW.

be ratified through acquiescence or acceptance by the company of the benefits of the transaction with knowledge of the material facts.

The articles often contain other provisions limiting the power to transact with third parties. As discussed above, these provisions have no third party effect and only serve internal purposes. Transactions that violate these provisions are under normal circumstances binding on the company. The managing director involved may be liable to the company for non-compliance with the articles. Among these internal provisions are provisions requiring the management board to obtain prior approval for certain actions (e.g. acquisition of property) from the shareholders or the supervisory board, including the approval required for the types of actions set out above in 'large' companies (see § 8.2.1.2),[558] as well as provisions conferring certain management responsibilities on a specific managing director (e.g. the finance director).

Apart from his individual power to bind the company, each managing director has a right of access to shareholders' meetings as well as the right to give his advice on all matters under discussion.[559] This is of particular significance when an individual managing director disagrees with the majority position of the management board.

8.2.5.3 Managers and Agents

Netherlands law does not recognise the concept of officers. All executive authority emanates from the management board,[560] which may appoint persons who are not members of the board to certain management positions. These positions may involve the management of all or part of the company's routine affairs. The authority to delegate this power may be set out in the articles of association. In the absence of a provision in the articles, the management board is free to appoint one or more managers. The management board then determines the scope of their powers, which determination may be subject to the prior approval of the supervisory board or the shareholders' meeting. At all times, the persons appointed as managers shall act under the responsibility of the management board.

The power of a person to act on behalf of the company with respect to third parties is, for the most part, controlled by ordinary agency principles.[561] The most significant difference, however, between ordinary agents and agents of companies is the applicability of the *ultra vires* doctrine: the corporate agent cannot act beyond the scope of the company's purposes (see § 3.5). Other-

558. Art. 2:164(2)/274(2) BW.
559. Art. 2:117(4)/227(7) BW.
560. Art. 2:129/239 BW.
561. Arts 3:60-79 BW.

wise, the agent's power can be general, without any limitations. Limitations on the authority of corporate agents should be clearly defined in a power of attorney. The powers of agents and the limits on their authority to act for the company must be filed at the commercial register (see § 12.2).

In addition to employees whose express authority is normally conferred in writing, corporate employees may have implied authority to engage the company in any act incidental to the employee's title or office. Thus, while a 'sales director' may not be a managing director, he may nevertheless enter into sales transactions which are concluded in the ordinary course of business on the company's behalf. The use of titles for specific offices can therefore create corporate liability even though the holder of the office is not expressly empowered to bind the company, i.e. to make the company responsible. When the employee holds an executive office or title[562] and his course of conduct leads third parties to believe that he has the required power to act on behalf of the company in that specific area, third parties may rely on this apparent authority.[563] This is particularly true if, with or without authority, the person has previously represented the company in similar transactions which the company did not seek to challenge.[564] An effective means of advising third parties about the proper authority of corporate executives is by recording the extent of each power in the commercial register (see § 12.2), and by strict enforcement. A corporate agent who is registered with the commercial register, but is not on the board, is referred to in Dutch as a *procuratiehouder*.

An agent who lacks the required authority for his actions but who implicitly or explicitly warrants that he has actual authority may be liable to third parties for any resultant damages.[565] If the unauthorised actions cause injury to the company, the company may also be entitled to damages.

8.2.5.4 Proof of Authority

Dutch companies do not have a secretary or other person capable of testifying to the authority of a person who transacts business with third parties on behalf of the company. Consequently, certificates of incumbency are unknown. However, as far as third parties are concerned, the company's filings at the commercial register (the company's unique registration number must be on the letterhead of the company, see § 12.1) form conclusive evidence of the

562. The title '*directeur*' alone, or in combination with other designations, is often used for key employees, who are not managing directors, even though the Dutch word '*directeur*' literally implies board membership.
563. Asser/Van der Grinten/Kortmann 2-I 2004/27.
564. Supreme Court 19 Mar. 1942, NJ 1942, 445 (*De Gruyter NV/NV De Voorschotbank*).
565. Arts 3:70, 3:78, 3:79 BW.

extent of the powers of each individual managing director, manager and agent to sign on behalf of and thereby bind the company.[566]

The commercial register will provide excerpts from registrations on request.[567] These excerpts are legal evidence and normally make it unnecessary to obtain the types of resolutions of the management board that are customary in other jurisdictions.

8.2.5.5 Conflicts of Interest

A managing director abstains from participating in the deliberations and decision making process of the management board if he has a direct or indirect personal interest that conflicts with the interests of the company. If, as a result, no management board resolution can be passed, the decision will be taken by the supervisory board, or in absence thereof, by the general meeting of shareholders, unless otherwise provided in the articles of association.[568] Violation of this rule does, in principle, not restrict the power to represent the company.

8.3 The Supervisory Board

8.3.1 Powers of the Supervisory Board

8.3.1.1 Regular NVs and BVs

The members of the supervisory board (referred to individually as supervisory directors) have collective powers and responsibilities. The supervisory directors share responsibility for all the decisions and acts of the supervisory board and for the acts of each individual supervisory director.[569] From a legal point of view the supervisory board is not subordinate to the shareholders' meeting and need not accept instructions from it. Its sole concern is the 'interests of the company' (see § 1.2) and its business enterprise. The management board is not subordinate to the supervisory board and remains responsible for any action taken in response to a decision of the supervisory board.[570]

The primary responsibility of the supervisory board is to supervise the policy of the management board and the general course of corporate af-

566. Under certain circumstances, this evidence is not conclusive due to actions of the company which are misleading third parties about the scope of the authority of a managing director or a proxy holder: Supreme Court 15 Jan. 1993, NJ 1993, 301 (*Henkel*); Supreme Court 23 Oct. 1998, NJ 1999, 582 (*Nacap/Kurstjens*).
567. Art. 22 HrW 2007; Art. 51 HrB 2008.
568. Art. 2:129(6)/239(6) BW.
569. Art. 2:140(2)/250(2) BW.
570. Art. 2:151/250 and Asser/Maeijer, Van Solinge & Nieuwe Weme 2-II* 2009/486 BW.

fairs.[571] This supervision includes the power and duty to intervene, whenever necessary, and to take such corrective actions as may be required in the 'interests of the company', always within the confines of the articles of association and the law. The management board must consult the supervisory board on all important matters including, but not limited to, any matters delineated in the articles. The supervisory board may also, on its own initiative, provide the management board with advice and request any information it deems appropriate. The articles usually provide for the right to inspect the books and records and for unrestricted access to the corporate premises. The management board has the statutory duty to provide the supervisory board in a timely fashion with the information necessary to carry out its responsibilities and perform its duties.[572] The management board shall at least once a year provide the supervisory board with information in general, in writing, about the strategy of the company, the financial risks and the management and control system of the company. The supervisory board may in principle rely on the information if it appears to be in good order. However, this does not mean that the supervisory board should not ask for additional information if it seems appropriate.[573] The articles may require the management board to obtain prior approval from the supervisory board for actions concerning matters set out in the articles or in resolutions of the supervisory board. For the NV, the management board may be required to comply with the supervisory board's directives on the general course of policy of the company in such areas as further defined in the articles (see § 8.2.1).[574] For the BV, the management board may in the articles be required to comply with specific instructions of the supervisory board.

The articles of association may provide that, with respect to the appointment of managing directors, the supervisory board, or some other person or institution as provided for in the articles, may make binding nominations that can only be rejected by the shareholders' meeting in a stipulated qualified majority. Any such nomination can always be overruled by a qualified majority of two thirds of the votes cast representing more than one half of the issued capital. The articles may give additional powers to the supervisory board, provided that these powers are not of an executive nature and do not affect the statutory powers of the shareholders.

Each supervisory director must sign the annual accounts. The reasons for any missing signatures must be stated.[575] Since annual accounts are normally

---

571. Art. 2:140(2)/250(2) BW.
572. Art. 2:141/251 BW.
573. District Court of Breda 1 May 1990, NJ 1990, 740 (*Tilburgsche Hypotheekbank*). See also § 9.3.4.
574. Art. 2:129(4)/239(4) BW.
575. Art. 2:101(2)/210(2) BW.

open for public inspection (see § 12.2), this statutory requirement emphasises the power that a supervisory director may be able to exercise by threatening to refuse to sign.

Each supervisory director has access to all shareholders' meetings and may at all times give his advice on matters on the agenda, whether or not he agrees with the position of the majority of the board.[576]

The works council (see § 13.1) meets twice annually with a managing director in what is known as a 'consultation meeting' for the purpose of discussing general business affairs. At least one supervisory director usually attends this consultation meeting.[577]

The supervisory board may acquire executive powers when all the members of the management board have a conflict of interest with the company on a matter (see § 8.2.5.5).[578] If the company does not have a supervisory board, the executive powers on that matter vest in the shareholders' meeting, unless the articles provide otherwise (see § 8.3.5). The articles may also grant executive powers to the supervisory board in the event that the members of the management board cannot or may not act.[579] The supervisory board is also responsible for retaining the auditor of the company if an audit of the accounts is required by law or the articles, but only if the shareholders' meeting fails to take the necessary action.[580]

8.3.1.2 'Large' Companies

If an NV or a BV is a 'large' company, special rules apply with regard to the powers of the supervisory board or, in the case of a one-tier board, the non-executive members of the board (see § 8.1.2). These special rules supplement the general rules for supervisory directors and non-executive directors. In the event of a conflict, the special rules prevail. The special rules must be incorporated into the articles of association within three years after the company gives notice to the commercial register that it qualifies as a 'large' company (see § 12.2).

The special powers of the supervisory board, or of the non executive directors, vary, according to whether the 'large' company is non-exempt or partially exempt (see § 8.1.2.4). The supervisory board (or the non executive directors) of a non-exempt 'large' company has the following special powers:

576. Art. 2:117(4)/227(7) BW.
577. Art. 24 WOR.
578. Art. 2:129(6)/239(6) BW.
579. Art. 2:134(4)/244(4) BW.
580. Art. 2:393(2) BW.

(a) the power to appoint, suspend and remove the managing directors (see § 8.2.3); and
(b) the power to approve or reject certain specified actions of the management board (see § 8.2.1.2).

The special powers of the supervisory board (or the group of non-executive directors) of a partially exempt 'large' company are limited to those set out under (b) above. The powers of a supervisory board (or the group of non-executive directors) of a company that has adopted the 'large' company status voluntarily (see § 8.1.1) are at least equal to the powers of a supervisory board in a partially exempt 'large' company. The appointment of managing directors may remain within the domain of the shareholders.[581]

8.3.2 Structure of the Supervisory Board

Unlike the management board, which in the Netherlands may have (executive) corporate members, the supervisory board must consist of individuals.[582] Supervisory directors may be Dutch or foreign, resident or non-resident. The number of supervisory directors is determined by the articles of association or by a shareholders' resolution. The supervisory board may consist of a single supervisory director, unless it is a 'large' company, in which case it must have at least three supervisory directors.[583]

Although all supervisory directors, including the chairman of the supervisory board, have equal powers and duties, the articles may provide in certain cases for a 'designated supervisory director' (*gedelegeerd commissaris*). This designated supervisory director represents the supervisory board in the period between meetings and supports the management board in its daily executive responsibilities.

The chairman of the supervisory board often acts as the chairman of the shareholders' meeting. The articles, however, may provide for a different chairman. In a 'large' company, certain persons are ineligible for the office of supervisory director, or in the case of a one-tier board, the office of non-executive director.[584] These include employees of the company or of other companies in which the company holds at least one half of the issued capital, as well as officials or employees of any trade union that is a party to a collective bargaining agreement covering any employees of the company. The

581. Art. 2:157(1)/267(1).
582. Art. 2:140(1)/250(1).
583. Art. 2:158(2)/268(2).
584. Art. 2:160/270.

supervisory directors' names, residential addresses, and other particulars must be entered in the commercial register (see § 12.2).

8.3.3 Appointment, Compensation, Suspension and Removal

8.3.3.1 Appointment in Regular NVs and BVs

The initial supervisory board, if there is to be one, can be appointed by the founders when the company is incorporated.[585] Their names appear in the deed of incorporation. Thereafter, supervisory directors are appointed by the shareholders' meeting. The articles of association of a BV may state that supervisory directors are appointed by the meeting of holders of shares of a specific class or type, provided that every shareholder who has voting rights can participate in the decision-making process regarding the appointment of at least one supervisory director.[586] If the articles so provide, a maximum of one third of the members of the supervisory board may be appointed by someone other than the shareholders' meeting.[587] The articles of a BV may state that a maximum of one third of the members of the supervisory board may be appointed by a third party, provided that every shareholder who has voting rights can participate in the decision-making process of at least one supervisory director.[588]

The basic rules concerning nominations and qualifications for the appointment of members of the management board (see § 8.2.3.1) apply equally to members of the supervisory board. The articles may, however, provide that holders of certain classes or types of share, or other persons, have the power to nominate all or some of the members of the supervisory board. However, any such nomination can be rejected by the shareholders' meeting by a two thirds' qualified majority vote representing more than one half of the issued share capital.[589] A classified supervisory board is not allowed.

The proposal or nomination of a candidate for appointment to the supervisory board must state the candidate's age, his occupation, his ownership (if any) of shares in the company, other relevant positions currently or previously held, and the names of other companies in which he serves as a supervisory director. The reasons for the proposal or nomination must be given.[590]

---

585. Art. 2:142(1)/252(1).
586. Art. 2:252(1) BW.
587. Art. 2:143/253 BW.
588. Art. 2:253 BW.
589. Arts 2:142(2)/252(2) and 2:133/243 BW.
590. Art. 2:142(3)/252(3) BW.

Supervisory directors are usually appointed for a specific period of time, often between three and six years. When a term of office expires, the member may be re-appointed, unless the articles provide otherwise. The proposal to appoint or reappoint a supervisory director must be explained. If it concerns a reappointment, the previous performance of his duties as a supervisory director must be taken into account.[591] The by-laws or the regulations of the board usually provide for a staggered appointment of the supervisory board members, whereby a proportion of the supervisory directors will be appointed over two or more years.

The works council of an NV has the right to determine its position (*standpuntbepaling*) with respect to the appointment (suspension and removal) of a supervisory director and this position will be presented to the shareholders' meeting together with the proposal to appoint (suspend or remove) a supervisory director.[592]

8.3.3.2 Appointment in 'Large' Companies

The supervisory directors of 'large' companies are appointed for a four-year term by the shareholders' meeting on nomination by the existing supervisory directors (see § 8.1.2.1).[593] This rule does not apply at the incorporation stage, when the founders appoint the first supervisory directors, or in the initial three-year period during which the company qualifies as a 'large' company but is not yet subject to the special statutory rules (see § 8.1.2.4).[594] During this period, the shareholders' meeting retains the right to appoint supervisory directors. A supervisory director will resign at the latest at the end of his four-year term. He may be reappointed immediately.

As from the date the 'large' company rules become applicable (see § 8.1.2.2), supervisory board members are appointed by the shareholders on nomination by the supervisory board, to the extent their nomination was not already made in the deed of incorporation or before the 'large' company rules applied to the company.[595] The supervisory board must inform the shareholders and the works council of its nomination. Both the shareholders and the works council may recommend persons to the supervisory board for nomination.

With respect to the appointment of one third of the members of the supervisory board, the works council has an 'enhanced' right of recommen-

591. Art. 2:142(3)/252(3) BW.
592. Art. 2:144a(1) BW.
593. Arts 2:158(4)/268(4) and 2:161(1)/271(1) BW. In this paragraph references to 'supervisory directors' include non-executive directors and references to 'supervisory board' include the group of non-executive directors, in the event of a one-tier board (see also § 8.4).
594. Art. 2:154/264 BW.
595. Art. 2:158(4)/268(4) BW.

dation.[596] In such case, the supervisory board must nominate the person recommended by the works council, unless it expects that: (i) the recommended person is not capable of fulfilling the duties of a supervisory board member; or (ii) the supervisory board will not be properly constituted if an appointment is made in accordance with the recommendation.

If the supervisory board objects, it must so notify the works council and it must consult with the works council in an attempt to reach agreement on the nomination. If no agreement can be reached, an application to the Enterprise Court in Amsterdam must be lodged no earlier than four weeks from the start of the consultation with the works council. The supervisory board shall place the recommended person on the nomination list if the Enterprise Court declares the objection unfounded. If the Enterprise Court declares the objection well founded, the works council may make a new recommendation.

The shareholders may reject a nomination by the supervisory board by an absolute majority of the votes cast representing not less than one third of the issued capital, in which case the supervisory board must nominate a new person.[597] If the shareholders do not appoint the nominated person and do not resolve to reject the nomination, the supervisory board itself can appoint the nominated person.

With the consent of the supervisory board and the works council, the shareholders can to a large extent deviate from the appointment system for a 'large' company as set out in the Dutch Civil Code, by the incorporation of an alternative system in the articles of association.[598]

8.3.3.3 Limitation of 'Significant' Supervisory Positions

The maximum number of 'significant' supervisory positions that one person can hold in Dutch NVs, BVs and foundations is limited to five, unless such person (also) holds a 'significant' position as managing director, in which case the maximum number of 'significant' supervisory positions is limited to two. (See for a definition of 'significant' board positions § 8.2.3.3). In calculating the number of 'significant' positions, the post of 'significant' chairman is deemed to equal two 'significant' supervisory board positions. The limitations on significant supervisory positions apply to supervisory directors, non-executive directors and members of other supervisory bodies set out in the articles.[599]

596. Art. 2:158(6)/268(6) BW.
597. Art. 2:158(9)/268(9) BW.
598. Art. 2:158(12)/268(12) BW.
599. Art. 2:142a/252a BW. This applies to 'significant' board positions in companies or foundations that meet at least two of the criteria set out in Art. 2:397(1)/(2) BW.

The appointment as 'significant' supervisory director at different companies within a group counts as one 'significant' supervisory board position.

8.3.3.4 Compensation

A supervisory director is not considered to be an employee. The relationship between the supervisory director and the company is deemed to be an agreement for professional services.[600] This applies equally to a designated supervisory director (see § 8.3.2), despite the fact that this office may in fact be a full-time position.

The shareholders' meeting can determine to pay remuneration to the supervisory directors.[601] The supervisory directors are entitled to be reimbursed for their costs, including out-of-pocket expenses. The aggregate compensation for supervisory directors must be disclosed in the notes to the annual accounts.[602]

8.3.3.5 Suspension and Removal

A supervisory director of a 'regular' NV or BV may be suspended or removed at any time by the appointing authority without any compensation. In the majority of the cases that will be the shareholders' meeting.[603] The articles of association of a BV may provide that a supervisory director may also be removed by the general meeting of shareholders. In cases of mismanagement, a supervisory director may be removed by the Enterprise Court (see § 10.2.4).

Any suspension or removal must be recorded in the commercial register (see § 12.2). An individual supervisory director of a 'large' company can only be suspended by the supervisory board. The removal of a supervisory director of a 'large' company prior to the end of his term of office falls under the exclusive jurisdiction of the Enterprise Court, and is based on a petition filed by the supervisory board, the shareholders, or the works council.[604] The grounds for removal are dereliction of duties or other serious lapses, or any drastic change of circumstances as a result of which the company cannot reasonably be required to keep the supervisory director in office.

The general meeting of shareholders of a 'large' company may pass a motion of 'no confidence' in the supervisory board as a whole (or the whole

600. Asser/Maeijer, Van Solinge & Nieuwe Weme 2-II* 2009/503. Art. 7:400 BW.
601. Art. 2:145/255 BW.
602. Art. 2:383(1) and Arts 2:383b and 383c BW.
603. Art. 2:144/254. See § 8.3.3.1.
604. Art. 2:161(2)/271(2). In this paragraph references to 'supervisory directors' include non-executive directors and references to 'supervisory board' include the group of non-executive directors, in the event of a one-tier board (see also § 8.4).

group of non-executive directors in a one-tier board) (see § 8.3.3).[605] Such resolution can only be adopted after the management board has first notified the works council of the proposal for the resolution and the reasons thereto, which notification shall be made not less than 30 days prior to the general meeting in which the proposal will be considered. The works council can explain its position in the general meeting of shareholders. The resolution shall be taken with an absolute majority of the votes cast representing not less than one third of the issued share capital. This resolution shall result in the immediate removal of all the members of the supervisory board (or all non-executive directors). Without delay the management board shall then request the Enterprise Court to temporarily appoint one or more supervisory board members (or non-executive directors). These supervisory board members (or non-executive directors) shall procure that a new board shall be constituted in accordance with the regular statutory provisions.

8.3.4 Resolutions by the Supervisory Board

The rules concerning meetings of and resolutions by the management board (see § 8.2.4) apply similarly to the supervisory board, except that individual supervisory directors cannot act on behalf of the supervisory board without specific authorisation.

A supervisory director abstains from participating in the deliberations and decision-making process of the supervisory board if he has a direct or indirect personal interest that conflicts with the interests of the company. If, as a result, no supervisory board resolution can be passed, the decision will be taken by the general meeting of shareholders, unless otherwise provided for in the articles of association.[606]

8.4 The One-Tier Board

When introducing the one-tier board, the legislator did not provide a new set of rules governing the one-tier board, but introduced the concept of executive and non-executive directors (see § 8.1.1) and basically only provided that the rules governing the appointment and dismissal of supervisory board members in a 'large' NV or BV also apply to the appointment and dismissal of non-executive directors. The role and rights of the supervisory board in the appointment, suspension and dismissal of members of the supervisory board in 'large' companies (see §§ 8.3.3.2 and 8.3.3.5) will be assumed by the group

605. Art. 2:161a/271a BW.
606. Art. 2:140(5)/250(5) BW.

of non-executive directors in the one-tier board in relation to the appointment and dismissal of the non-executive directors.

Otherwise, the rules governing the management board will basically apply to the one-tier board, except for the distinction between the roles of the executives (day-to-day management) on the one hand and the non-executives (supervision of the management) on the other hand.

8.5 Gender Diversity on Boards

Recent legislation has provided for temporary rules on more even distribution of management and supervisory board seats between men and women at certain large companies.[607] The rules are temporary and will, in principle, be cancelled as of 1 January 2016. The starting point is that a board should comprise at least 30% men and 30% women. The rules apply to all appointments following enactment, including reappointment.

The statutory percentages for a more even distribution of board seats are target figures. The act does not require an increase in the number of board members or the dismissal of board members before the end of their tenure, but merely compliance with the criteria for a more even distribution of board seats. It is up to the general meeting of shareholders to decide whether or not the composition of the board needs to be changed.

If an NV or BV to which these provisions apply fails to distribute its board seats according to the target figures, it must explain in its annual accounts:

- why the seats have not been distributed according to the target figures;
- how the company has tried to achieve a more even distribution; and
- how it intends to achieve distribution according to the target figures in the future.

607. Art. 2:166/2:275 BW. This applies to NVs and BVs that meet at least two of the criteria set out in Art. 2:397(1)/(2) BW. These are the same criteria used in relation to the limitation of 'significant' board positions. See § 8.2.3.3.

Chapter 9
Duties and Liabilities of Board Members

9.1 Introduction

9.1.1 Fiduciary Duties

With regard to the fiduciary duties of directors, common law jurisdictions traditionally distinguish between the duty of care and the duty of good faith (also known as the duty of loyalty). In the Netherlands, the duty of care is expressed in terms of a duty to 'properly perform' management or supervisory duties.[608] The duty of good faith is part of the reasonableness and fairness requirement[609] that Netherlands corporate law imposes on relationships between the management board, supervisory board, shareholders, holders of depository receipts (with meeting rights, or issued with co-operation of the company), certain pledgees,[610] certain usufructuaries[611] and the works council (see § 6.3.2),[612] and that general contract law imposes on the parties to a contract.[613]

9.1.2 Internal and External Liability

A breach of the fiduciary duties may give rise to a cause of action to hold directors liable. A distinction must be made between the contractual or 'internal' and non-contractual or 'external' liabilities of directors. Internal liability exists towards the company and arises from the contractual relationship between the directors on the one hand and the company on the other hand. External liability arises in relation towards third parties, such as creditors, individual shareholders, employees and the tax authorities.

608. Arts 2:9, 2:138/248 and 2:149/259 BW.
609. Art. 2:8 BW.
610. Art. 2:89(4)/198(4) BW.
611. Art. 2:88(4)/197(4) BW.
612. Resolutions or actions of the management board which would result in an unreasonable violation of the rights of any of the parties involved may be voidable. Art. 2:15(1)(b) in conjunction with Art. 2:8 BW.
613. Art. 6:248(1) BW.

9.1.3 Uniformity of Liability Standards

In its recent case law, the Dutch Supreme Court has attempted to establish a certain uniformity of liability standards. Internal liability occurs if a director is 'seriously to blame' (*ernstig verwijt*) for the improper performance of his duties. External liability can occur in the event of 'serious blame' (*ernstig verwijt*) *vis-à-vis* a shareholder, or 'sufficiently serious blame' (*voldoende ernstig verwijt*) *vis-à-vis* a creditor. These concepts are converging towards the standard of 'serious blame' *(ernstig verwijt)*.[614]

9.2 Liability of Managing Directors

9.2.1 Liability towards the Company

9.2.1.1 Grounds for Liability

Under Art. 2:9 BW each managing director is obliged to 'properly fulfil' the duties assigned to him. If a managing director fails to properly fulfil his duties, he is then liable for the damage that the company sustains as a result. In practice, former directors could face liability under Art. 2:9 BW on the initiative of a (partially) new board of managing directors, or of a trustee if the company is bankrupt.

The management of a company is a duty of the managing directors collectively. There is a collective, collegial responsibility for the performance of management duties. The financial policy and matters of major importance concern all managing directors, regardless of any division of duties. Each managing director is, in principle, wholly liable for any failure. An individual managing director can only exculpate himself by proving that he cannot be blamed, either directly for the failure or for not taking measures to avert its consequences (e.g. because the matter did not fall within the scope of his duties). The burden of proof lies with the managing director.

When does a managing director fail to perform his duties? According to case law, a managing director is required to perform his duties conscientiously in accordance with what can be expected of a reasonable and competent managing director under the same circumstances.[615] Taking risks is inherent to conducting business and a managing director has a certain freedom in the performance of his management duties. His policy must be assessed at the time he acted and not with hindsight. He is allowed to make mistakes, but the

614. Supreme Court 20 Jun. 2008, NJ 2009, 21 (*Willemsen/NOM*). See further Asser/Maeijer, Van Solinge & Nieuwe Weme 2-II* 2009/441.
615. Supreme Court 8 Apr. 2005, NJ 2006, 443 (*Laurus*).

mistakes cannot be so serious as to constitute improper performance of duties or an unlawful act.

There is a relatively high threshold of liability under Art. 2:9 BW. The criterion is that a managing director is liable for the improper performance of his duties if he is seriously to blame (*ernstig verwijt*).[616] Whether a managing director has performed his duties improperly and whether he is seriously to blame for that must be assessed on the basis of all the circumstances of the case. There is no general standard similar to the 'business judgment rule' in the United States. The following must be taken into consideration: the types of activity conducted by the company and the related risks, the division of duties of managing directors on the board, any regulations applicable for the managing directors, the information at their disposal or which should have been at their disposal at the time of the decision or conduct for which the managing director concerned is being reproached, as well as the knowledge and due care that can be expected of a managing director who is competent to fulfil his duties and does so conscientiously.[617]

Case law assumes improper performance of duties within the meaning of Art. 2:9 BW, *inter alia*, in the following situations: withdrawing funds of the legal entity, mixing private affairs with those of the legal entity,[618] taking unnecessarily large risks, not taking out general insurances, taking important decisions without investigation or without proper information[619] and acting contrary to statutory provisions that are intended to protect the company.[620]

Since the modernisation of the law for BVs as per 1 October 2012, managing directors of a BV are personally liable towards the company in the event that the management board approved a resolution of the general meeting of shareholders to distribute dividend (or reserves) as a result of which the company cannot satisfy its debt payments.[621] Managing directors can only be held liable in the event they knew or reasonably should have known that the distribution would cause a situation of inability to pay (see also § 4.8.1.2.2). A managing director who is liable can exculpate himself if he cannot be blamed and if he did not fail to take measures to avoid that situation of inability to pay. This ground for liability is in line with Art. 2:9 BW (described above) and expresses the particular responsibility of the management board with respect to distributions to shareholders. This liability of managing directors may also

---

616. Supreme Court 10 Jan. 1997, NJ 1997, 360 (*Staleman/Van de Ven*).
617. Non-exhaustive list from Supreme Court 10 Jan. 1997, NJ 1997, 360 (*Staleman/Van de Ven*).
618. See Court of Appeal The Hague 26 Sep. 2006, JOR 2007, 61 (*Recourt/Kruiper*) where engaging the majority of the employees in a business newly started by the managing director qualified as improper performance of duties.
619. District Court of Utrecht 12 Dec. 2007, JOR 2008, 10 (*Ceteco*). Settled in appeal.
620. Supreme Court 29 Nov. 2003, NJ 2003, 455 (*Schwandt/Berghuizer Papierfabriek*).
621. Art. 2:216(3) BW.

apply in the event of repurchase of shares by the BV[622] and reduction of the issued capital of the BV with repayment to its shareholders.[623]

9.2.1.2 *Liability of an Employee*

In the context of internal liability, the general liability of an employee for damage to his employer and third parties should be considered. Art. 7:661 BW provides that an employee who causes damage to his employer or to a third party whom the employer is bound to compensate for the damage is only liable towards the employer if the damage is due to (wilful or) deliberate recklessness (*bewuste roekeloosheid*). If the managing director has an employment agreement with the company, as is often the case, this rule will also apply, in principle, to the managing director. In the literature, it is assumed that in assessing the actions of a managing director, the criterion of 'serious blame' is equivalent to 'deliberate recklessness'.

A company that holds a managing director liable on the basis of Art. 2:9 BW or Art. 7:661 BW can also base its action in tort (see § 9.2.3).

9.2.2 Liability for a Deficit in an Estate

9.2.2.1 *Grounds for Liability*

Pursuant to Art. 2:138/248 BW (also known as the Third Act on the Prevention of the Abuse of Companies), each managing director is jointly and severally liable for a deficit in the estate of an insolvent company if the board of managing directors 'appears to have performed its duties improperly' in the three years preceding the bankruptcy and if it is apparent that the insolvency has, to a large extent, been caused by such improper performance of duties. There is improper management if it is established that no reasonable managing director would have acted in such a manner in the same circumstances.[624] An individual managing director can exculpate himself by proving that he cannot be blamed for the lack of proper management and by showing that he has not failed to take measures to avert the consequences of it.[625] A court can mitigate the amount for which the managing director is liable on various grounds.

---

622. Art. 2:207(3) BW.
623. Art. 2:208(6) BW.
624. Supreme Court 7 Jun. 1996, JOR 1996, 68 (*Van Zoolingen*); Supreme Court 8 Jun. 2001, JOR 2001, 171 (*Panmo*).
625. Art. 2:138/248(3) BW. Such proof will not be easy. But a managing director who refrains from voting for a decision that obviously implies an improper performance of duties, and as a result of his resignation refrains from lending his cooperation to such improper performance of duties, will have adequately exonerated himself (MvA II 16 631, No. 6, p 19).

The liability of managing directors pursuant to the Prevention of Abuse Act is not liability towards the bankrupt company but liability towards the estate (the joint creditors). This means that a managing director cannot set off his liability against an old claim he has on the company.[626] The receiver (*curator*) acts on behalf of the estate and is the only person who can lodge a claim for liability against a managing director for the deficit.

The division of the burden of proof, as between the receiver and the managing director, is regulated by Art. 2:138/248(2) BW, which contains two statutory presumptions. There is an *irrebuttable* presumption that a board of managing directors has improperly performed its duties (throughout) if it has not complied with its obligation under Art. 2:10 BW to keep proper records or with its obligation under Art. 2:394 BW to publish the annual report and accounts on time (that is, within 13 months of the end of the financial year). In this case there is a *rebuttable* presumption that the improper performance of these duties was a major cause of the insolvency.

A managing director can produce proof to the contrary. He has to prove that facts and circumstances other than improper performance of duties were an important cause of the bankruptcy.[627] If a managing director is successful, it is then up to the receiver to show that, despite this, the improper performance of his duties was also an important cause of the bankruptcy, in which case his claim will be granted.[628]

The receiver may initiate a procedure as described in this paragraph simultaneously with a procedure on the basis of Art. 2:9 BW (see § 9.2.1.1).[629]

9.2.2.2 *Immaterial Omission*

It follows from Art. 2:138/248(2) BW that an immaterial omission in fulfilling an obligation to keep records and an obligation to publish annual accounts in time does not qualify. Whether a failure of the board of managing directors in respect of these obligations can be considered to be an immaterial omission depends on the specific circumstances of the case. A managing director who was in office for 25 days was not liable even though there was evidence of maladministration.[630] In another case the filing of the annual accounts a few days later than was prescribed by law was not, in the circumstances, considered to give rise to a liability.[631]

---

626. Supreme Court 18 Sep. 2009, NJ 2009, 438 (*B./Van den End q.q.*).
627. Supreme Court 20 May 1988, NJ 1989, 676 (*Koster/Van Nie*).
628. Supreme Court 20 Oct. 2006, NJ 2007, 2 (*Schilt/Jansen q.q.*).
629. Art. 2:138/248(8) in conjunction with Art. 2:9 BW.
630. Supreme Court 28 Jun. 1996, NJ 1997, 58 (*Bodam Jachtservice*).
631. Supreme Court 11 Jun. 1993, NJ 1993, 713 (*Brens q.q./Sarper*) and Supreme Court 2 Feb. 1996, NJ 1996, 406 (*Pfennings/Niederer*).

9.2.2.3 Actual Managing Director or Policy-Maker

The liability of managing directors in bankruptcy is extended in Art. 2:138/248(7) BW to anyone who determines or co-determines the policy of a company as if he were a managing director. Examples include a shareholder who is intensively involved in policymaking or a supervisory director who performs management tasks. The law aims at people exercising decisive influence, but who hide behind front men. It is important here to keep in mind that a managing director who advises or who accepts conditions or instructions and acts afterwards allows himself to be guided by the insights of third parties, but does not as a result absolve himself of his managerial responsibilities. As long as a managing director can weigh up the competing interests himself, it is he who is acting as a managing director and not any third party concerned, and the latter cannot be held liable. A managing director who is registered at that capacity at the commercial register cannot avoid liability by arguing that he is only a formal managing director.

9.2.3 Liability towards Third Parties on the Basis of Tort

9.2.3.1 General

A managing director may be liable towards third parties on the basis of tort (*onrechtmatige daad*).[632] Third parties may be creditors, but also various other persons involved with the company, such as individual shareholders. Tortuous actions are violations of a right and acts or omissions breaching a duty imposed by law or by a rule of unwritten law pertaining to proper societal conduct.

In fulfilling his duties, a managing director represents his company. His acts or omissions are primarily acts or omissions of the company; if he acts unlawfully in the performance of his duties, this unlawful act will be attributed to the company and deemed to be an unlawful act of that company. The managing director is still not personally liable. The personal liability of a managing director is a secondary liability, where it concerns subjective or individual blame. This is different in the event that a managing director is held liable on the basis of tort because he violated a personal duty of care towards a third party. Then, there is no 'secondary liability' as his specific role within the company is not relevant. In that case, the normal requirements of a tort-based claim apply.[633]

---

632. Art. 6:162 BW.
633. Supreme Court 23 Nov. 2012, LJN: BX5881.

9.2.3.2 *Liability towards Shareholders*

The managing director only has a contractual relationship with the company, and not with its shareholders. This means that any legal action by a shareholder or by a group of shareholders against a managing director cannot be based directly on Art. 2:9 BW but only on tort.

In 2008, the Supreme Court rendered judgment on a managing director held liable by an individual shareholder.[634] It ruled that in a claim based on tort by a shareholder, the high threshold of Art. 2:9 BW, referred to above, applies and that therefore a shareholder can only bring an action against an individual managing director in the event of 'serious blame'. The Supreme Court considered '… that the circumstance that acts have been committed contrary to the provisions of the articles of association intended to protect an individual shareholder, implies, in principle, liability on the part of the managing director *vis-à-vis* the individual shareholder'. The managing director has the opportunity to produce proof to the contrary.

It remains an open question as to whether this rule can be generalised to include other rules to protect the interests of shareholders, such as the rules for public offers or the Dutch Corporate Governance Code, so that violation of these rules, in principle, would create a liability on the managing director *vis-à-vis* the shareholders. A second unanswered question is whether, once liability has been established, a shareholder can claim compensation for the damage assessed (usually a reduction in the value of his shares, which is a 'derivative loss'). Case law seems to indicate that the latter is not the case, if and in so far as the company itself has sustained damage as a result of the same acts and can institute legal proceedings itself.

9.2.3.3 *Liability towards Creditors*

The Supreme Court has made it clear that in the event that a company's creditors sue a managing director personally on the basis of tort, more is required than 'ordinary blame'. The Supreme Court has ruled that, in general, it can only be assumed that a managing director has acted unlawfully towards a creditor of a company when, in view of his obligation to perform his duties properly as referred to in Art. 2:9 BW, 'sufficiently serious blame' (*voldoende ernstig verwijt*) can be attributed to him.

According to established case law, a managing director is liable on the basis of tort if he has concluded an agreement on behalf of the company and knew, or reasonably should have known, when he concluded the agreement

634. Supreme Court 20 Jun. 2008, NJ 2009, 21 (*Willemsen/NOM*).

that the company would be unable to fulfil its obligations resulting therefrom or would be unable to fulfil them within a reasonable period of time and would not offer recourse for the damage suffered by the contractual party as a result of the breach of contract.[635] Personal blame is then obvious since the managing director can foresee that the creditor will sustain damage. The burden of proof in such a case lies, in principle, with the harmed creditor. Personal blame can be rebutted if the managing director can produce reasons to justify his actions. If at the time of entering into the transaction there was indeed a risk that the obligations ensuing from it could not be satisfied, and neither could recourse be assured, but there was also a real chance of survival, then the managing director is not deemed liable.

A distinction has to be made between the above-described situation and a case where a managing director permits, or causes, a company to fail to perform an agreement that was previously concluded by it and thus causes damage to a creditor. Whether there is then personal liability on the part of the managing director depends on whether sufficiently serious blame can be attributed to him, and this in turn depends on the circumstances of the case.[636] There must be an unwillingness to pay on the part of the managing director. The sole fact that a managing director of a company does not ensure that the company complies with its payment obligations towards its creditors is inadequate to assume personal liability on his part.

In the event of selective payment by managing directors of an insolvent company to itself or to group companies, there is also the risk of personal liability for the managing directors.[637]

9.2.3.4 Liability towards other Third Parties

Sometimes managing directors are held personally liable by third parties (such as the State) on the basis of tort because of pollution of the environment. However, in the field of environmental law, personal liability tends to be the exception. The claimant will have to prove that the director knew or could have known of the polluting activities and that he did nothing to prevent or counter them.

In judgments of the lower courts directors' liability against third parties has been assumed on other grounds, e.g. if pension premiums deducted by a company are not turned over to the pension provider, but are applied to

---

635. Supreme Court 6 Oct. 1989, NJ 1990, 286 (*Beklamel*).
636. Supreme Court 3 Apr. 1992, NJ 1992, 411 (*Van Waning/Van der Vliet*); Supreme Court 18 Feb. 2000, NJ 2000, 295 (*New Holland/Belgium*) and Supreme C ourt 8 Dec. 2006, NJ 2006, 659 (*Ontvanger/Roelofsen*).
637. Supreme Court 12 Jun. 1998, NJ 1998, 727 (*Coral/Stalt*).

ordinary business operations. In one such case a court held that a managing director was liable for the damage sustained by the employees of the now bankrupt company because he was aware that the premiums had not been paid and he had kept the employees 'in the dark'.

9.2.4 Other Forms of Liability

9.2.4.1 Liability for Tax Debts, Social Insurance Contributions and Contributions to Company Pension Funds

Managing directors are liable to the tax authorities for specific taxes, social insurance premiums and compulsory contributions to company pension funds.[638] The act that introduced this liability is often referred to as the Second Act on the Prevention of Abuse of Companies. The obligation on a company (and therefore its managing directors) to make immediate written notification to the competent authorities in the event it is unable to fulfil its payment obligations is at the centre of this legislation.

If a company does not fulfil, or does not properly fulfil its notification obligation, each managing director is jointly and severally liable for payment of the amounts due. A managing director can exculpate himself only by showing that: (i) he is not to blame for the company having failed to (properly) fulfil its notification obligation; and (ii) he is not to blame for the non-payment of the relevant amounts. A managing director accepts responsibility for his company's financial policy upon his appointment. He cannot shirk this by, e.g., distancing himself and concentrating on other duties. A managing director is expected to be aware of the financial position of a company and to take adequate measures in this respect.

If the notification obligation has been fulfilled, a managing director is only liable if the relevant authorities can show that the non-payment is due to apparent improper management by the managing directors jointly in the period of three years preceding the time of the notification. For the purposes of Art. 36(3) Inv. 1990, apparent improper management is involved if no reasonable managing director would have acted in the manner concerned in the same circumstances.[639] An individual managing director can exonerate himself by showing that he is not to blame for the improper management.

In these regulations a managing director means the (former) managing director during whose term of management the premium or tax debt occurs; this

638. Art. 36 Inv. 1990, Art. 60 Wfsv and Art. 23 Sectoral Pension Fund (Obligatory Participation) Act (*Wet verplichte deelneming in een bedrijfstakpensioenfonds*).
639. Supreme Court 7 Jun. 1996, NJ 1996, 695 (*Van Zoolingen*). See also Supreme Court 8 Jun. 2001, NJ 2001, 454 (*Panmo*).

also includes those determining or co-determining policy and, if the managing director is a legal person, its managing directors.

Liability as described in this paragraph can be invoked outside bankruptcy.

9.2.4.2 Liability for Misleading Annual Accounts, Annual Report and Interim Figures

A special case of tort can be found in Art. 2:139/249 BW, relating to liability for balance sheets. If the annual accounts, the annual report or interim figures published by a company misrepresent the financial situation of the company, the managing directors are jointly and severally liable *vis-à-vis* third parties for the damage suffered by these third parties as a result. A managing director who can prove that he is not to blame for the misrepresentation is not liable. Third parties – including creditors and shareholders and employees – must show the causal link between the misleading representation in the annual accounts and the damage sustained in order to bring a successful claim under Art. 2:139/249 BW. There is almost no case law in relation to liability for misleading balance sheets.

9.2.4.3 Liability for Defective Incorporation of the Company

If the court declares that, in the absence of an executed deed of incorporation by a Dutch notary, the company never came into existence, persons who acted in the name of the non-existent company will be personally bound to fulfil all of its agreements with third parties.[640] This is a rather theoretical ground for liability.

9.2.4.4 Liability for Pre-Incorporation Transactions

The founders, their representatives and others who entered into agreements with third parties on behalf of the company to be formed are, unless specifically agreed otherwise, personally bound by pre-incorporation transactions until the date of ratification by the company (see § 3.3.2.4) following its incorporation.[641]

If, following ratification, the company fails to perform such obligations, the persons who acted on behalf of the company may be held liable if they knew or ought to have known that the company would not be able to comply with these obligations. Knowledge of the companies' inability to comply will be presumed if the company is declared bankrupt within one year of

640. Art. 2:4(4) BW.
641. Art. 2:93(2)/203(2) BW.

formation.[642] In addition, the managing directors may be held liable if at the moment they ratified such transactions they knew, or reasonably should have known, that the company would not be able to meet these obligations.

9.2.4.5 Liability after Incorporation of the Company

The managing directors of a company are required to register their company in the commercial register and subsequently to file an original copy of the deed of incorporation at the office of the commercial register.[643] In addition to the company, managing directors are jointly and severally liable *vis-à-vis* third parties for each act performed during their term of management and as a result of which the company is legally bound in the period before:

(a) the initial registration in the commercial register, accompanied by the copies to be filed, has been effected;
(b) the paid up part of the capital is at least the minimum capital prescribed at incorporation (only applicable to NVs); and
(c) at least one fourth of the nominal amount has been paid upon the capital being issued by the incorporation (only applicable to NVs).

9.2.4.6 Capitalisation

The rules concerning capitalisation of the company are of critical importance, especially for the NV (see § 4.3). Non-compliance can result in personal liability of the managing directors for any shortfall and for damages incurred by third parties. Furthermore, managing directors will be personally liable for reimbursement to the company of the value of treasury shares being held by the company in excess of the thresholds of respectively 10% (for a listed NV) and 100% minus one share for BVs and non-listed NVs.[644]

9.3 Liability of Supervisory Directors

9.3.1 General

In relation to the liability of supervisory directors, one should bear in mind that the duties of supervisory directors are different from those of managing direc-

642. Art. 2:93(3)/203(3) BW.
643. Art. 2:69/180 BW.
644. Art. 2:98a(3)/207a(2) BW. As non-listed NVs may buy in shares up to 100% minus one share (and listed NVs up to 50%) of the issued share capital (see § 4.3.6), the threshold in Art. 2:98a (3) BW seems an obvious mistake by the legislator.

tors. According to the law, supervisory directors are charged with supervision of the policies of managing directors and of the general course of affairs of a company. They also advise the managing directors. Just like managing directors, supervisory directors must serve the interests of the company (including the interests of the corporate group, especially if the company is the holding company of that group).[645]

In the past few years more and more requirements have been established for the supervision of the management of companies. The latter applies in particular to listed companies that must comply with the Dutch Corporate Governance Code which provides detailed provisions with regard to the responsibilities of the supervisory directors.

In the performance of their duties, supervisory directors are largely dependent on information furnished by managing directors; the board of managing directors is obliged to provide the required information in time to the board of supervisory directors.[646] Supervisory directors may, in principle, rely on the information provided by the board of managing directors. However, there may be circumstances in which they have reasons to doubt the correctness or completeness of this information, in which case they are required to ask critical questions and/or to request further documents.[647]

Given that supervisory directors are not directly responsible for policy but only for its supervision, in general they would less easily be assumed to be or actually held personally liable in the same way as managing directors would be. In case law only a few limited cases are known where supervisory directors have been held personally liable for damage sustained by a company and third parties. In enquiry proceedings (*enquêteprocedure*) it is often the case that a supervisory director will be held jointly responsible for mismanagement that has been established due to failed supervision. A decision like this from the Enterprise Court, however, does not imply the personal liability of supervisory directors for the damage sustained (see § 10.2).

9.3.2 Liability towards the Company

Liability towards a company pursuant to Art. 2:9 BW also applies to the performance of duties by a supervisory director.[648] Again, in general, liability will arise only if the board of supervisory directors is 'seriously to blame' for the

645. Art. 2:140(2)/250(2) BW.
646. Art. 2:141/251 BW.
647. Supreme Court 10 Jan. 1990, NJ 1990, 66 (*Ogem*); Enterprise Court 16 Oct. 2003, JOR 2003, 85 (*Laurus*).
648. Art. 2:149/259 BW.

manner in which it has performed its (supervisory and advisory) duties. This is no different for supervisory directors than for managing directors (see § 9.2).

The influence of a board of supervisory directors on the policy of a company is, in principle, collaborative and corrective. The supervisory directors are required to discharge their duties completely independently (this also applies in relation to the shareholders who nominate or appoint them). The board of supervisory directors is subject to the obligation to provide all the information the general meeting of shareholders requires, unless this conflicts with a serious interest of the company.[649]

One example of where supervisory directors have been held liable due to the improper performance of their duties was the bankruptcy of *Ceteco*, in which they endorsed the policy of the managing directors, which was aimed at unsustainable growth, without any further investigation and without taking any account of the related risks to the company.[650]

9.3.3 Liability for a Deficit in an Estate

9.3.3.1 Grounds for Liability

Supervisory directors may also be liable in bankruptcy.[651] Supervisory directors are not required to adhere to the obligations laid down in Arts 2:138(2)/248(2) BW to keep records and publish annual accounts, even if the board of managing directors fails to fulfil these obligations, but it is their duty to supervise the fulfilment of this obligation by the managing directors. For this purpose, they must allow themselves to be briefed by the managing directors and to advise them regarding the fulfilment of these obligations and, where necessary, intervene, e.g. by suspending a managing director or by facilitating his dismissal.[652]

In the bankruptcy of *Ceteco* the District Court ruled that in addition to the managing directors the supervisory directors were liable for the deficit in the estate, because 'it can be expected of a reasonable supervisory director that he (…) would investigate whether the policy can be continued to give priority to growth over bringing order to its internal organisation, before giving permission for any further expansion'.[653]

The burden of proof of improper performance of duties by the supervisory director lies with the receiver. When it is established that the managing

649. Art. 2:107(2)/217(2) BW; see also § 7.6.
650. District Court of Utrecht 12 Dec. 2007, JOR 2008, 10 (*Ceteco*). Settled in appeal.
651. Art. 2:149/259 BW in conjunction with Art. 2:138/248 BW.
652. Supreme Court 28 Jun. 1996, NJ 1997, 58 (*Bodam Jachtservice*).
653. District Court of Utrecht 12 Dec. 2007, JOR 2008, 10 (*Ceteco*). Settled in appeal.

directors have not fulfilled their obligation to keep records and to publish annual accounts, the supervisory director must furnish adequate factual information to dispute the argument of the receiver that the supervisory director has improperly performed his duties.[654]

9.3.3.2 Actual Managing Director or Policy Maker

A supervisory director can also be held liable for determining or co-determining the policy of a company (see § 8.3.1).[655] He also can be held liable if he performs management tasks pursuant to the articles of association or to a resolution of the general meeting of shareholders for a certain period of time in certain circumstances.[656]

9.3.4 Liability towards Third Parties on the Basis of Tort

A supervisory director may also be held liable towards third parties on the basis of tort.[657] An example of this, under the old act and in the context of bankruptcy, was the bankruptcy of Tilburgsche Hypotheekbank NV. The District Court of Breda ruled that the board of supervisory directors should have intervened when it saw that the management was making large loans to third parties that were not secured. It should have independently verified that the loans were secured and not completely relied on the information supplied by the management. Since they did not intervene, the supervisory directors were held liable for the damage.[658]

9.3.5 Other Forms of Liability

9.3.5.1 Liability for Tax Debts, Social Insurance Contributions and Contributions to Company Pension Funds

The Second Act on the Prevention of Abuse of Companies does not affect supervisory directors as such. However, the Act remains relevant in respect of their advisory and supervisory position (see § 9.3.3).

654. Supreme Court 28 Jun. 1996, NJ 1997, 58 (*Bodam Jachtservice*).
655. Art. 2:138/248(7) BW.
656. Art. 2:151/261 BW.
657. Art. 6:162 BW.
658. District Court of Breda 1 May 1990, NJ 1990, 740 (*Tilburgsche Hypotheekbank*).

9.3.5.2 *Liability for Misleading Annual Accounts, Annual Report and Interim Figures*

In addition to the managing directors, supervisory directors are also jointly and severally liable for damage sustained by third parties as a result of annual accounts (*jaarrekening*) that misrepresent the financial position of a company. As opposed to managing directors, supervisory directors are not liable for misleading representations appearing in annual reports (*jaarverslag*) or for misleading interim figures published by a company. A supervisory director who can prove that he is not to blame for misrepresentation can avoid liability.[659]

9.4 Liability of Members of a One-Tier Board

Pursuant to Art. 2:129a/239a BW, that came into force on 1 January 2013, it is possible to create a one-tier board with executive and non-executive directors. As executive and non-executive directors of a one-tier board are essentially members of one and the same corporate body (namely the management board), they operate under the same principle as applies to members of a management board and a supervisory board in the Netherlands, in that members of such boards are collectively responsible for the proper performance of the relevant board's duties and responsibilities.

It has been argued[660] that in view of this collective responsibility the liability of a non-executive member of a one-tier board will increase *vis-à-vis* the position of a member of a supervisory board in a two-tier system. Presumably, for this reason the law introducing the one-tier board has elucidated that a director is *responsible* for all the tasks that are not by law or in the articles of association allocated to one or more of the other directors and that he is generally *liable* unless in view of the allocation of tasks to other directors no 'serious blame' can be attributed to him.

In view of the above, the liability of an executive director can be judged in the same way as that of a managing director (see § 9.2).

The extent of the liability of a non-executive director will in due course become clear from case law. One may expect, however, that in general the increased involvement of the non-executive director (as compared to the involvement of a supervisory director) in the general governance of a company with a one-tier board may lead to enhanced liability of the non-executive director as compared to the supervisory director in a two-tier board system.

---

659. Art. 2:150/260 BW.
660. See contributions of: L. Timmerman and J.B. Wezeman in ' Bestuur en Toezicht', Kluwer, Deventer 2009.

9.5 Liability of Others

9.5.1 The Incorporator

The incorporators may be held liable, as if they were managing directors, if they have bound the company at its incorporation and did not act with proper caution (see § 3.4.4).[661]

9.5.2 Director-Company

In the Netherlands a company can be appointed managing director of another company. In these cases, which are not uncommon in group structures, the individual managing directors of the director-company may be held personally liable, jointly with the director-company.[662] This also applies to a foreign director-company of a Dutch company.[663]

9.5.3 Foreign Company

In determining the nationality of a company, Dutch law follows the 'incorporation theory'. Foreign companies therefore operate in the Netherlands under their own national corporate laws (*lex societas*). However, certain Dutch statutory rules concerning directors' liability for mismanagement do apply to directors of foreign companies.

The liability for a deficit in an estate, according to Art. 2:138/248 BW (see § 9.2.2), is also applicable for directors of foreign companies that are declared bankrupt in the Netherlands and are subject to Dutch corporate income tax (whether or not any tax is actually owed). Local managers of these foreign companies may be held liable as if they were managing directors.[664]

9.6 Enquiry Proceedings and Liability

The conclusion by the Enterprise Court that there has been mismanagement at a company is binding on all parties that have participated in the last stage of the enquiry proceedings leading up to such verdict.

Such a conclusion, however, does not establish *personal* liability of the director involved. This must be established in separate, ordinary, civil procedures whereby the claimants (a trustee in bankruptcy, banks, the company

---

661. Art. 2:93/203(4) BW.
662. Art. 2:11 BW.
663. Supreme Court 18 Mar. 2011, JOR 2011, 144 (*D Group*).
664. Art. 10:119 and Art. 6 Wfbv.

involved, etc.) will need to assert and prove that directors are personally responsible, and therefore liable, for the damages incurred as a result of the mismanagement of the company. As a consequence of the outcome of the enquiry proceedings the burden of proof may, however, shift to the directors involved. Consequently, enquiry proceedings are regularly the overture to procedures whereby damages are claimed.[665]

9.7 Protection against Liability

9.7.1 General

There are options available to limit the risk of liability for managing directors and supervisory directors. The following measures can be taken:

(a) discharge, where the managing director or supervisory director is released from liability for his previous management of the company;
(b) exoneration, where the managing director or supervisory director exonerates himself contractually *vis-à-vis* the company from the harmful consequences of his actions;
(c) indemnity, where the managing director or supervisory director is indemnified by the company or by a shareholder *vis-à-vis* claims from third parties, e.g. on the basis of tort or Art. 2:138/248 BW (also known as the Third Act on the Prevention of Abuse of Companies); and
(d) insurance, where the managing director or supervisory director insures himself against the consequences of internal and external liability.

9.7.2 Discharge

Discharge is a power vested in the general meeting of shareholders of an NV/BV. Discharge granted to a managing director for the policy pursued by him in a certain period, in principle, prevents him from being held liable by the company for his policy during that particular period. Discharge therefore does not preclude any external liability. Discharge is also possible in the case of a one-man company in which (almost) all the shares are held by the sole managing director. As a rule a resolution to discharge only results in release from liability for the policy pursued if this policy appears from the annual accounts or has become known to the general meeting by other means.[666] Moreover, in

665. See Van Hooijdonk & Eijsvoogel, p. 74.
666. Supreme Court 10 Jan. 1997, NJ 1997, 360 (*Staleman/Van de Ven*); Supreme Court 25 Jun. 2010, JOR 2010, 227 (*Dingemans/De Rouw*).

some cases a managing director cannot invoke discharge granted if this would conflict with the principles of reasonableness and fairness. Also, a resolution granting discharge can be nullified by a court upon a claim by an interested party that it conflicts with the principles of reasonableness and fairness[667] or as part of enquiry proceedings.[668] If the company instituted legal proceedings against a managing director in relation to a specific dispute, and afterwards discharge is granted in the general meeting, the managing director cannot in general invoke that he could believe in good faith that the company would discontinue the proceedings. Discharge implies the waiver of the company's right to file a claim. A company is free to grant or not to grant discharge. Therefore, managing directors and supervisory directors have no right to discharge.

9.7.3 Exoneration

Discharge only offers limited protection. The same applies to an exoneration clause between the company and the managing director for claims of the company (on the basis of Art. 2:9 BW). In general, this type of clause will be deemed null and void, because it is contrary to the mandatory nature of Art. 2:9 BW, which stipulates that a managing director must perform his duties properly. The thinking behind this is that a managing director to whom a company can attribute 'serious blame' cannot hide behind a statutory or contractual provision exonerating him. It is permissible, however, for a company to agree with the managing director or supervisory director upon his taking office that the company will reimburse all the costs incurred by him in order to enable him to defend himself against a claim of liability by the company.

9.7.4 Indemnity

Indemnifying managing directors against claims by third parties is, in general, a possibility, and, certainly in the case of listed companies, also very common. Indemnification can cover the obligation to pay damages to third parties as well as the costs of legal proceedings, and the terms can be laid down in an agreement or in the articles of association of the company. Contractual indemnification has the advantage that, in principle, no approval is required from the shareholders. Indemnification offers limited protection in the sense that no valid claim for indemnification will be possible if intent or gross negligence can be attributed to the managing director. Moreover, indemnification does not provide any protection if the company is declared bankrupt.

---

667. Art. 2:15 BW.
668. Art. 2:356 BW.

9.7.5 Insurance

Each managing director or supervisory director can take out insurance. The D&O (Directors' & Officers') liability insurance offers cover to managing directors and supervisory directors for personal liability. Frequently, a company too enjoys cover for compensation it has paid to managing directors and supervisory directors as a result of claims from third parties. In the case of a group, D&O insurance is in practice taken out by the holding company of the group as the policyholder. The policy then states that the insurance applies in respect of all or part of the managing directors within the group. An individual managing director will have to ensure that the sum insured is adequate – even after payments to other insured parties – in order to cover any liability to which he may be exposed. He could push to have an apportionment formula included in the terms and conditions of the insurance or elect to have individual liability insurance.

The damages covered by the insurance consists, on the one hand, of amounts for which the managing director or supervisory director has been found liable for in relation to third parties (and where great attention must be paid to the exclusions applied by the insurer) and, on the other hand, the costs incurred for the defence at law by the managing director or supervisory director. The costs of the defence are deducted from the sum insured. In practice, it is possible for the entire sum insured to be used to pay the costs of the defence.

D&O insurance is, in principle, taken out for a term of one year, after which an extension may be permitted. The insurer can, however, refuse the extension. D&O insurance is based on the claims-made principle, which means that for cover under the policy it is necessary for a claim to be filed or received by an insurer within the term of the insurance. In principle, it is not important when in the past the provoking event occurred. In the event of bankruptcy of a company most D&O insurances end. The majority of insurances also provide for the option of extended cover, and there is an option, if the end of the insurance period is imminent and a situation presents itself that could fall within the terms of the cover, to report this situation as a 'circumstance'. If a claim is filed relating to this circumstance after the insurance has expired, then this will still fall within the terms of the cover.

A claim by a managing director on an insurer may be subject to an attachment or garnishment by the creditors of the managing director. The problem with this is that the managing director will be hindered in his defence, as the entire claim will be affected by the attachment, and the money required for the defence will no longer be available. Nevertheless, on the basis of the most recent case law, it is fair to assume that an attachment levied on insurance payments will also, in principle, be available for the amount of the costs of the defence.

Chapter 10
Corporate Litigation

10.1 Jurisdiction

Corporate litigation can take place by means of standard proceedings in the District Court. The District Court, e.g., has jurisdiction for claims to annul corporate resolutions on the grounds of violation of the law or of the articles of association,[669] or violation of the principles of reasonableness and fairness (see § 6.3).[670] It also has jurisdiction for directors' liability claims (see Chapter 9).

However, corporate litigation in the Netherlands is to a large extent under the exclusive jurisdiction of the specialised Enterprise Court, a division of the Amsterdam Court of Appeal.[671] The Enterprise Court is made up of five judges with expertise in corporate affairs. Three legally trained judges are accompanied by two lay judges, who in practice are experts in business, socio-economics, accounting and tax matters.[672]

The most important proceedings in which the Enterprise Court has exclusive jurisdiction are the so-called enquiry proceedings. In these proceedings the Enterprise Court can investigate the alleged mismanagement of a company and take measures to address that mismanagement (see § 10.2). Two other procedures that can be brought before the Enterprise Court are the forced exit proceedings (only on appeal) (see § 10.3) and the squeeze-out proceedings (see § 10.4). Finally, the Enterprise Court has jurisdiction over disputes concerning the form and content of the annual accounts (see § 10.5.1), over appeals by a works council against certain proposed actions of the management board (see § 10.5.2) and over the composition of the supervisory board of 'large' companies (see § 10.5.3).

---

669. Art. 2:14 BW.
670. Art. 2:15 BW.
671. Van Hooijdonk & Eijsvoogel 2012.
672. Art. 66(2) RO.

10.2 Enquiry Proceedings

10.2.1 General

The law provides for a unique Dutch procedure regarding an enquiry into the affairs of the company (referred to below as the 'enquiry proceedings').[673] These enquiry proceedings are divided into three distinct stages. All stages fall under the exclusive jurisdiction of the Enterprise Court of the Amsterdam Court of Appeal. Decisions of the Enterprise Court are subject to appeal to the Supreme Court with regard to matters of law and reasoning only.

10.2.2 First Stage: Request for Enquiry

The enquiry proceedings start with a written request (*verzoekschrift*) by the petitioner to the Enterprise Court to initiate an investigation into the policies of the company and the general course of its affairs.[674] From that moment onwards the Enterprise Court takes charge of the proceedings and may pursue the matter *sua sponte*. This investigation may relate to all or part of the 'policy' of the company, an undefined term which includes implemented or anticipated decisions or events, and a single action or series of actions within a specific or unspecified period of time. It is not limited to the policy of the management board. It may concern every corporate body or person who holds office in any such corporate body and who is involved with the policy of the company. The investigation may concern the legal entity of the company or the enterprise which it operates.

The law defines the persons who are authorised to request an enquiry. In the case of an NV or BV with an issued capital of no more than EUR 22.5 million, the petition can be filed by shareholders or holders of depository receipts and certain pledgees and usufructuaries holding alone or together at least 10% of the issued shares or shares with a nominal value of EUR 225,000 (or any lower percentage or amount provided in the articles of association).[675] In the case of an NV or BV with an issued capital that exceeds EUR 22.5 million, the petition can be filed by shareholders or holders of depository receipts and certain pledgees and usufructuaries holding alone or together at least 1% of the issued shares and, if the shares of the company are admitted to trading on a regulated market or multilateral trading facility as meant in Art. 1:1 Wft,[676] also by shareholders (or holders of depositary receipts and certain pledgees

673. Arts 2:344-359 BW.
674. Art. 2:345 BW.
675. Art. 2:346(1)(b) BW.
676. Or a comparable trading platform in a non-EU Member State.

and usufructuaries) holding alone or together shares representing a value of at least EUR 20 million according to the closing quotation on the last trading day before the request to the Enterprise Court is made.[677]

Even beneficial owners of depository receipts that meet these criteria have the right to ask for an enquiry.[678] A request for an enquiry can also be filed by the Attorney General if matters of public interest are involved[679] and by a trade union with members employed by the company.[680] The right to request an enquiry can also be granted by virtue of the articles of association or an agreement with the company,[681] e.g. to a works council,[682] employees,[683] or supervisory directors.[684] Finally, with effect from 1 January 2013, the company itself is entitled to ask for an enquiry. Such a request will have to be made by a duly authorised representative of the company. Normally speaking this will be the board of directors or one or more individual directors, but for the purpose of enquiry proceedings the supervisory board of the company is also entitled to submit a request on behalf of the company.[685]

The Enterprise Court shall only honour the petition if there are sufficient grounds to doubt as to whether the company is pursuing a proper policy or a proper course of affairs.[686] This means that there must be circumstances which justify the assumption that there is a reasonable chance that after investigating the matter the conclusion of the enquiry will be that the company was not following a proper policy or a proper course of affairs. It is at the sole discretion of the Enterprise Court to determine whether such 'sufficient grounds' exist.[687]

Before submitting the request to the Enterprise Court, the petitioner must notify in writing the management board and the supervisory board, if there is one, as to the complaints made against the policy of the company. In the absence of this notice the request will be inadmissible. The company must be given a reasonable period of time to investigate the complaints and to take measures to remedy these.[688] The notice requirement does not apply if it is

677. Art. 2:346(1)(c).
678. Supreme Court 6 Jun. 2003, NJ 2003, 486 (*Scheipar*) and Enterprise Court 17 Feb. 2009, ARO 2009, 45 (*Butôt*).
679. Art. 2:345(2) BW.
680. Art. 2:347 BW.
681. Art. 2:346(c) BW.
682. Enterprise Court 5 Oct. 2005, JOR 2005, 269 (*Smith Transformatoren*).
683. Enterprise Court 16 Oct. 2007, ARO 2007, 166 (*E-traction*).
684. Enterprise Court 31 Dec. 2009, JOR 2010, 60 (*Inter Access*).
685. Art. 2:346(1)(d) BW.
686. Art. 2:350 BW.
687. In the event that this test is not met and as a result the Enterprise Court declines the petition, the company has the right to claim damages from the persons requesting the investigation (Art. 2:350(2) BW).
688. Art. 2:349(1) BW. A trade union must first solicit the views of the competent works council as well (Art. 2:349(2) BW).

the company itself that is asking for an enquiry. In such case, the supervisory board or, if the petition is filed by the supervisory board, the board of directors and the works council must be informed as soon as possible about the intention of the company to file the request.

10.2.3 Second Stage: Enquiry

If the Enterprise Court sustains the request for an enquiry, it will appoint one or more independent investigators.[689]

The investigators will be free to conduct the investigation in any way they wish, and may determine what information they want access to or whom they want to cross-examine as a witness.

The Enterprise Court will also appoint an examining justice (*raadsheer-commissaris*), who will oversee the work of the investigator(s). Upon the request of the petitioners or an interested party, the examining justice can give directions to the investigator(s) about the way the investigation should be carried out.[690]

The investigator(s) will prepare a report which must contain the findings of the enquiry. This report will be filed with the court. The persons who have petitioned for the enquiry will be sent a copy of the report. The official report will be open to public inspection, if so ordered by the Enterprise Court.

With the official report being filed, the second stage of the enquiry proceedings is concluded.

10.2.4 Third Stage: Decision

The third stage concerns the measures to be taken once there has been a finding of mismanagement in the enquiry report. The petitioners and all other parties named above may then request the Enterprise Court to take certain measures. This additional request must be filed separately, within two months after the report is issued, in the same form as the initial request for the investigation.[691] If the Enterprise Court shares the view that mismanagement has taken place

---

689. The costs of the investigation must be borne by the company. However, if it is concluded that the enquiry was not made on reasonable grounds, i.e. there are no reasons to doubt the company's policy, then the company may seek compensation for the costs incurred in connection with the enquiry from the requesting persons. If the report of the investigators indicates that certain officers of the company, i.e. managing directors, supervisory directors or someone else employed by it, are responsible for the improper policy, the company may request that these officers cover the costs paid by the company with respect to the investigation.
690. Art. 2:350(4) BW.
691. Art. 2:355(1)(2) BW.

within the company, the Enterprise Court may take one or more of the following measures:[692]

(a) the suspension or nullification of a resolution of the management board, the shareholders' meeting or any other corporate body;
(b) the suspension or removal of one or more managing directors or supervisory directors;
(c) the temporary appointment of one or more managing directors or supervisory directors;
(d) the temporary deviation from such provisions of the articles of association as shall be specified by the Enterprise Court;
(e) the temporary transfer of shares to a nominee; and
(f) the dissolution of the company.[693]

The Enterprise Court can only determine mismanagement following the conclusion of an enquiry.[694]

The Enterprise Court is not under an obligation to take any of the abovementioned measures. It can also limit itself to the determination that there has been mismanagement.[695] The Enterprise Court can impose measures other than the measures requested, but it cannot take any measures other than those stated above.

As explained above, the concept of mismanagement is not limited to an improper policy of the management board of the company, but may also relate to other corporate bodies and to the shareholders or to certain shareholders. The cases vary in nature. A finding of mismanagement may e.g. be arrived at in the event that a managing director has violated the principles of sound entrepreneurship.[696] In a significant number of the cases where there was a finding of mismanagement, there was a deadlock situation, with the effect that the company was unmanageable and therefore could not properly function as a legal entity.[697]

Other cases in which the Enterprise Court has found mismanagement related to violations of the mandatory rules of law or the articles of association of the company concerning the distribution of powers between the various corporate bodies within the company.[698] Furthermore, a conclusion of mis-

692. Art. 2:356 BW.
693. This latter sanction cannot be imposed if this would be contrary to the interests of the shareholders or the employees or contrary to the public interest (Art. 2:357(7) BW).
694. Supreme Court 27 Sep. 2000, NJ 2000, 653 (*Gucci*).
695. Supreme Court 10 Jan. 1990, NJ 1990, 466 (*Ogem*).
696. Supreme Court 10 Jan. 1990, NJ 1990, 466 (*Ogem*).
697. Enterprise Court 8 Oct. 1998, JOR 1998, 166 (*Hoffman Beheer*).
698. Enterprise Court 22 Mar. 2005, JOR 2005, 176 (*Van Doorn*).

management may be arrived at in the event that the interests of the company have become subordinate to a personal interest or that there was no proper distinction between the interests involved.[699]

The enquiry proceedings will not result in a court decision that imposes liability on certain persons for the improper policy. Claims for damages resulting from the improper policy must be instituted by way of a separate civil case before the competent court (see § 9.6).

10.2.5 Provisional Measures

At every stage of the proceedings the Enterprise Court may impose provisional measures.[700] The Enterprise Court cannot impose provisional measures on its own initiative. A request of the petitioner is necessary. Once a request is made, all other interested parties can themselves also apply for provisional measures.[701] However, the Enterprise Court is not restricted by the measures asked for; it can impose such provisional measures as it deems necessary.[702] The imposed measures must be provisional in nature, but the consequences of the measures can be irreversible.[703] The duration of the measures can in any event not exceed the duration of the proceedings.

Examples of provisional measures are: a prohibition on the management board from taking actions that could change the status quo of the company,[704] a prohibition on shareholders from exercising their voting rights[705] or the dismissal of directors together with the appointment of temporary directors.[706]

10.3 Forced Exit Proceedings

Dutch corporate law provides a shareholder with the right, in certain circumstances, to force out another shareholder or, alternatively, to force other shareholders or the company to acquire his shares. Translated literally, these proceedings are called dispute resolution proceedings (*geschillenregeling*), but this rather general term is replaced herein by 'forced exit proceedings'.

---

699. Enterprise Court 8 Oct. 1987, NJ 1989, 270 (*Van der Klis II*).
700. Art. 2:349a(2) BW.
701. Enterprise Court 25 Jun. 2002, JOR 2002, 126 (*AND*), Enterprise Court 24 Nov. 2008, JOR 2009, 9 (*Fortis*) and Supreme Court 23 Mar. 2012, JOR 2012, 41 (*e-Traction*).
702. Supreme Court 4 Oct. 2002, Supreme Court 4 Oct. 2002, NJ 2002, 556 (*Zwagerman*).
703. Supreme Court 19 Oct. 2001, Supreme Court 19 Oct. 2001, JOR 2002, 5 (*SkyGate*).
704. Enterprise Court 4 Jul. 2001, JOR 2001, 149 (*HBG*) and Enterprise Court 3 May 2007, JOR 2007, 143 (*ABN AMRO*).
705. Enterprise Court 30 Jul. 2001, JOR 2001, 206 (*Cohere*) and Enterprise Court 31 Oct. 2002, JOR 2003, 59 (*ZDS Trading*).
706. Enterprise Court 17 Mar. 2005, ARO 2005, 39 (*Masa Transportation*) and Enterprise Court 10 Dec. 2003, ARO 2003, 186 (*ERU*).

Forced exit proceedings are available only for BVs and for closely held NVs (of which the articles of association provide for registered shares only, contain a blocking clause and do not permit the issuance of bearer depository receipts).[707]

One or more shareholders representing at least one third of the issued share capital of a company may require another shareholder to transfer his shares to himself or themselves, if the other shareholder by his conduct prejudices or has prejudiced the interests of the company to such an extent that his continued shareholding cannot reasonably be tolerated.[708]

A comparable remedy exists vis-à-vis a pledgee or holder of a right of usufruct who has been granted the voting rights on the shares. If such a pledgee or usufructuary by his actions prejudices the interests of the company to such an extent that his continued exercising of the voting rights cannot reasonably be tolerated, one or more of the shareholders representing at least one third of the issued share capital can claim that the voting rights will revert to the pledgor and legal owner of the shares.[709]

Conversely, a shareholder may require that his fellow shareholders buy him out, if one or more of the other shareholders have prejudiced his (rather than the company's) rights or interests to such an extent that his own continued shareholding cannot reasonably be expected of him.[710] A claim to be bought out may also be made against the company if the company itself has prejudiced the shareholder's rights or interests to the same extent. A claim cannot be made against the company, however, if the buy-back of the shares by the company would violate statutory rules of capital protection.[711]

Forced exit proceedings are not available if a procedure for the resolution of shareholder conflicts is already provided for in the articles of association of the company or in a shareholders' agreement, unless it has become apparent that the procedure provided for 'cannot be applied'.[712] The procedure in the articles of association or in the agreement should provide the claimant with a remedy comparable to the forced exit proceedings.

A claim in forced exit proceedings is brought against the defendant shareholder (and/or the company) in the District Court in the district where the company has its seat. A copy of the writ is served on the company, which then notifies in writing the shareholders who have not been summoned, so that the company and the other shareholders can join the proceedings, if they wish to

707. Art. 2:335(2) BW.
708. Art. 2:336(1) BW.
709. Art. 2:342 BW.
710. Art. 2:343(1) BW.
711. Art. 2:343(1) BW; Art. 2:98/207 BW.
712. Art. 2:337 BW.

do so.[713] An appeal must be brought before the Enterprise Court.[714] The articles of association or a shareholders' agreement may deviate from this jurisdiction, for instance by providing that forced exit claims will immediately be brought in the Enterprise Court (appealable only to the Supreme Court, on limited grounds) or in arbitration.[715]

The court adjudicating a forced exit claim automatically has jurisdiction with respect to other claims (such as claims for damages) between the same parties (and/or the company) relating to the same actions on which the forced exit claim is based.[716] It may also grant injunctive relief (such as an order suspending the voting rights of the defendant) for the duration of the proceedings and even beyond that until the forced exit, ordered by the court, has actually been effected.[717]

The proceedings in the court of first instance progress through two stages.

First, the District Court will have to determine whether the conditions for the forced exit have been proven by the claimant. Second, if it awards the forced exit claim, the Court will appoint one or more experts to determine the price of the shares. However, if the litigating parties agree on the price, or if the articles of association or a shareholders' agreement provide(s) such a clear measure for determining the price that the appointment of experts is not necessary, the court can skip the second stage altogether and order the transfer of the shares against payment of the relevant price immediately at the end of the first stage.[718]

If the parties are in agreement that one or more shareholders should exit the company and their disagreement merely relates to price, they can (instead of going through the entire forced exit proceedings) petition the court to determine the price of the shares and appoint experts for that purpose. In connection therewith they can request the court to take into account certain agreed valuation principles.[719]

Alternatively, they can request the court to appoint experts whose findings will have the force of binding advice without, therefore, the court itself giving a judgment on the price of the shares.[720]

---

713. Art. 997a Rv.
714. Art. 2:336(3) BW.
715. Art. 2:337(2) BW.
716. Art. 2:336(5) BW.
717. Art. 2:338(3) BW.
718. Art. 2:339(3); 2:340(2) BW.
719. Art. 2:343c BW.
720. Art. 2:343c (4) BW.

10.4 Squeeze-Out Proceedings

10.4.1 General Squeeze-Out Proceedings

A shareholder who owns, either alone or with one of its group companies, 95% or more of a company's issued share capital may initiate legal proceedings to require all of the other shareholders to transfer their shares to him.[721] Squeeze-out proceedings are subject to the jurisdiction of the Enterprise Court, with a right of appeal to the Supreme Court on questions of law and reasoning only.[722] The price of the shares to be transferred is determined by the Enterprise Court, which may order expert valuation. The Enterprise Court must refuse the mandatory transfer of a minority interest of 5% or less (i) if the seller would suffer considerable financial damage that would not be compensated by the squeeze-out price; (ii) one or more minority shareholders hold one or more priority shares;[723] or (iii) if the majority shareholder has renounced his right to initiate squeeze-out proceedings (which may be particularly relevant in joint ventures).

10.4.2 Squeeze-Out and Sell-Out Proceedings after a Public Bid

In 2007 a specific squeeze-out procedure was introduced.[724] The procedure is only applicable after a public offer on the shares of a listed company. The majority shareholder (holding at least 95% of the shares) has to initiate the proceedings within three months after the time period for acceptance of the offer has lapsed.[725] If at least 90% of the shares to which a voluntary public offer relates have been acquired as a result of the public offer, the public offer price is presumed to be a reasonable squeeze-out price. In the case of a mandatory public offer, the price offered in the public offer is presumed to be a reasonable squeeze-out price.[726]

At the same time a sell-out right for the minority shareholder was introduced.[727] The requirements are similar to the requirements for squeeze-out proceedings of Art. 2:359c BW.

721. Art. 2:92a(1)/201a(1) BW.
722. Art. 2:92a(2)/201a(2) BW.
723. Supreme Court 16 Jan. 2004, NJ 2004, 184 (*Goglio*).
724. Art. 2:359c BW.
725. Art. 2:359c(3) BW.
726. Art. 2:359c(6) BW.
727. Art. 2:359d BW.

10.5 Other Proceedings before the Enterprise Court

10.5.1 Proceedings to challenge Annual Accounts

Any interested party can apply to the Enterprise Court to have a company amend its annual accounts, annual report or other ancillary information if these do not comply with the legal provisions regarding annual accounts.[728] A petition to this effect can also be filed by the Attorney-General of the Court of Appeal in Amsterdam, if the Attorney-General considers such a petition to be in the public interest. The AFM also has the right to file a petition, but only in relation to the annual accounts, annual reports and ancillary information of issuing entities within the meaning of Art. 1(b) Wtfv. As regards claims concerning compliance with audit rules, the involvement of auditors[729] and the filing of the annual accounts[730] or other financial information, these fall within the jurisdiction of the District Courts. Any interested party (e.g. shareholders, works council, etc.) may bring an action before the District Court.

10.5.2 Proceedings regarding Works Council Act

Certain decisions by the management board that have potentially a major impact on the company or its employees must be submitted to the works council for its prior advice (see § 13.2.4.3).[731] If the procedural rules are not properly complied with, or if it finds that the contemplated action by the management board could not reasonably have been taken if the board had 'weighed all interests involved', the Enterprise Court may prohibit or order the reversal of the action by the management board.[732] Certain other management decisions require not only the prior advice but actually the consent of the works council (see § 13.2.4.4). The cantonal division of the District Court may enforce this right of the works council by ordering that those decisions cannot be made or implemented without the approval of the works council.[733]

728. Arts 2:447 and 448 BW.
729. Art. 2:393(8) BW.
730. Art. 2:394(7) BW.
731. Art. 25(1) WOR.
732. Art. 26(4) WOR.
733. Art. 27 WOR.

10.5.3 Proceedings regarding Composition Supervisory Board of 'Large' Companies

The Enterprise Court also has exclusive jurisdiction in disputes regarding the composition of the supervisory board in 'large' companies (*structuurvennootschappen*) (see § 8.3.1.2). The Enterprise Court decides on objections against the appointment of supervisory directors specifically recommended by the works council.[734]

The removal of a supervisory director of a 'large' company also requires an action by the Enterprise Court.[735] However, claims based on violations of statutory or other procedural rules for the appointment are brought before the District Courts.

734. Arts 2:158(7)/268(7)and 2:159(3)/269(3) BW.
735. Art. 2:161(2)/271(2) BW.

Chapter 11
Corporate Changes

11.1 General

The corporate structure of a company can be changed during its existence, e.g. by amendment of the articles of association. A statutory merger with another company may also cause a corporate change, especially for the company that disappears as a result of the merger. Other examples of corporate changes are: statutory demergers, adoption of another legal form and dissolution.

11.2 Amendment of the Articles of Association of NVs/BVs

The articles may be amended upon a resolution by the shareholders and the subsequent execution of a notarial deed containing the amended provisions.[736] The amendment becomes effective upon the execution of the notarial deed and not from the moment the resolution is taken.[737] The articles may contain provisions that restrict or exclude the right to amend all or certain provisions. An amendment of these provisions is nevertheless possible, by a unanimous vote of a meeting at which all shareholders are present or represented.[738] Unless the articles state otherwise, no qualified majority or quorum is required for an amendment of any other provision, including the provisions concerning the corporate name, capital, purposes, quorum requirements and distributions.

As per 1 October 2012, however, the law regarding BVs prescribes certain requirements or consequences regarding an amendment of the articles of association. For example, an amendment which provides for a change in voting rights of shareholders can only be taken unanimously by all the shareholders.[739] When an obligation of shareholders is introduced by means of amendment of the articles, it cannot be imposed on a shareholder against its will; a shareholder voting against this amendment cannot be bound by this obligation.[740]

---

736. Art. 2:124(1)/234(1) BW.
737. Art. 2:124(1)/234(1) BW.
738. Art. 2:121(3)/231(3) BW.
739. Art. 2:228(4) BW.
740. Art. 2:192(1) BW.

A resolution regarding amendment of the articles of association of a BV that is particularly detrimental to any right of holders of shares of a specific class or specification, requires the prior approval of the group of holders of these shares. Such approval is not required if this has been stated explicitly at the time the right that is detrimental, was granted.[741] This provision e.g. concerns the situation in which certain rights of holders of non-voting shares will be changed as a result of an amendment of the articles: the approval of this group of holders of non-voting shares is then required.

If the articles require a quorum, and at the first properly notified shareholders' meeting no quorum is present, a second meeting can, unless the articles provide otherwise, ignore the quorum requirement and take a valid vote, provided that the notice for the second meeting specifically refers to this objective.[742] The second meeting can only be convened after the first meeting has been held.

No amendment can abrogate, without their consent, the rights of third parties under the articles.[743] For example, directors' bonus provisions contained in the articles cannot be changed without the approval of each managing director who is effectively or potentially entitled to a bonus payment under the articles (unless the articles provide otherwise).

Shareholders adversely affected by a shareholders' resolution cannot insist on receiving payment of the fair market value of their shares. They may, however, seek a court order invalidating the shareholders' resolution on the basis that the resolution violates good faith principles (see Chapter 6 and § 10.2).[744]

If a proposed amendment appears on the agenda of a shareholders' meeting, this must be set out in the notices of the meeting. The text of any proposed amendments must be made available to the shareholders in a timely fashion at the main office of the company, and copies must be available upon request.[745]

An amendment may be proposed by any party entitled to convene a shareholders' meeting (see § 7.2.1). If the amendment involves a reduction of capital, special rules for the protection of creditors must be satisfied if it concerns an NV (see § 4.3).

The complete amended text of the articles must be filed with the commercial register. Only upon this filing will the amendment have effect with respect to third parties.

741. Art. 2:231(4) BW.
742. Art. 2:120(3)/230(3) BW.
743. Art. 2:122/232 BW.
744. Arts. 2:92(2)/201(2), 2:8, 2:15(1)(b) BW.
745. Art. 2:123/233 BW.

11.3 Statutory Merger

11.3.1 Introduction

11.3.1.1 Types of Statutory Merger

The statutory merger[746] (*juridische fusie*) is a means of obtaining control over other business operations. The same economic result can often be reached by framing the transaction in the form of a share acquisition or an asset acquisition. Statutory mergers may take place between NVs, BVs, associations, co-operatives, mutuals and foundations, provided that, in the latter three cases, as a general rule, the merging entities must have the same legal form (see §§ 2.5.1 and 2.5.2).[747] Only the forms of statutory merger involving NVs and BVs as constituent legal entities are discussed here.

Since 2008, a statutory merger is possible between an NV/BV and similar legal entities from other member states of the EU.[748] Consequently, a Dutch statutory merger can be used as a device for changing the law governing the legal person, but only within the borders of the EU.

A statutory merger can take several different forms. For example, a company (the 'surviving company') absorbs another company, so that this second company ceases to exist by operation of law, and the shares of the absorbed company are exchanged for shares in the surviving company by operation of law.[749] An 'upstream merger' is an example of a type of merger involving a parent company that absorbs a subsidiary, so that the subsidiary ceases to exist. Alternatively, in a 'downstream merger', the subsidiary is the surviving entity and the parent company ceases to exist.

A triangular merger is slightly more complicated. The surviving company absorbs one or more companies, which cease to exist by operation of law, and the shares of the absorbed companies are, by operation of law, exchanged for shares in a third company (the 'acquiror') that belongs to the same group as the surviving company. All the shares of the surviving company must be held by the acquiror, either alone or together with another company that is part of its group (see § 3.1.2).[750] Through the use of a triangular merger, a parent company can avoid the existence of minority interests in one of its subsidiaries.

---

746. The provisions concerning the statutory merger were introduced into Netherlands law to implement the Third EC Company Law Directive (see § 1.3.3).
747. Arts. 2:308(1), 2:310(1),(3) BW. Art. 2:310(4) BW provides an exception to this general rule.
748. Art. 2:333b *et seq.* BW.
749. Art. 2:309 BW.
750. Art. 2:334 BW.

In a consolidation merger, a new corporate entity is formed upon the merger of two or more constituent companies that are absorbed by the new company, so that the absorbed companies cease to exist.[751] References to statutory mergers include consolidation mergers, and the same rules apply to both legal forms, unless otherwise indicated.

A 'sister merger' is deemed to exist with respect to a statutory merger between two or more wholly owned subsidiaries.[752]

For 'short-form' mergers, with simplified procedures, see § 11.3.5.

11.3.1.2 No 'Merger Force-Outs'

Netherlands law does not recognise the right to 'force out', 'freeze-out' or 'squeeze-out' unwanted shareholders by means of a merger (see § 5.3.5.2 for force-outs of small minorities), and a merger can be used only to a limited extent to compel certain shareholders to accept cash or notes for their shares.[753] A statutory merger is not, therefore, the appropriate mechanism for either eliminating public shareholders in a 'going private' effort or for forcing shareholders to accept a tender offer on penalty of being 'mopped up' later for a less attractive consideration subsequent to the merger of the target into the aggressor company (known in the U.S. as a 'front-end loaded' tender offer).

11.3.1.3 Trade Unions and Works Council

The Merger Code applies to the acquisition of direct or indirect control (more than 50%) over all or part of the activities of another enterprise as well as the formation of a co-operation of enterprises (the definition includes joint ventures between two or more companies). The Merger Code must be observed in any merger involving one or more enterprises that: (i) are established in the Netherlands and regularly employ 50 employees or more; or (ii) belong to a group of enterprises with one or more of the enterprises being established in the Netherlands that in aggregate employ 50 employees or more.[754]

If the Merger Code applies, trade unions must be consulted.[755] The WOR requires the prior consultation of the works council in several situations, including: the transfer of control of all or part of the enterprise; the establishment, takeover or relinquishment of control of another enterprise; or the

751. Art. 2:309 BW.
752. Art. 2:333(2) BW.
753. Art. 2:325(1) BW. See also Enterprise Court 20 Dec. 2007, JOR 2008, 36 (*Shell*) and Supreme Court 14 Sep. 2007, JOR 2007, 237 (*Versatel I*).
754. Art. 2 Merger Code 2000 (*SER-besluit Fusiegedragsregels* 2000), <www.ser.nl>.
755. Art. 4 Merger Code. The consultation must take place in such a manner that the opinion of the trade unions can still be of significance with respect to the proposed merger and its structuring.

establishment, substantial modification or discontinuation of long-term co-operation with other enterprises, including a substantial financial participation by or on behalf of such an enterprise (see § 13.2.4.3).[756] A statutory merger almost invariably falls within the scope of these provisions. No merger can be effected before completion of the consultation process,[757] which may take some considerable time.

Collective bargaining instruments may also have independent provisions requiring prior consultation with the trade unions or the works council in the event of mergers and consolidations. Any written opinion given by the works council or the trade unions must be disclosed to shareholders (see § 11.3.4.2).

11.3.2 Legal Effect

Upon the statutory merger taking effect, by operation of law:

(a) the absorbed company(ies) cease(s) to exist;[758]
(b) all of the assets and liabilities of the disappearing company(ies) are absorbed by the surviving company by way of universal succession of title, thereby becoming part of its own assets and liabilities;[759] and
(c) except in certain limited cases defined by law (see §§ 11.3.3 and 11.3.5), the shareholders of the disappearing company(ies) become shareholders of the surviving company.[760]

11.3.3 Consideration

11.3.3.1 Shares

A statutory merger is essentially an exchange of shares, and cash is used only to account for exchange ratio discrepancies, such as when the value of each newly issued share in the share capital of the surviving company is less than the value of each share in the absorbed company. The total amount of cash or promissory notes involved in the transaction cannot exceed 10% of the aggregate nominal value of the newly issued share capital.[761] In making payments in cash to third party minority shareholders, the good faith requirement

756. Art. 25(1) WOR. Art. 4.7 Merger Code states that the parties will allow the relevant works councils to take notice of the opinion of the trade unions in order to enable the works councils to take that opinion into account in their advice under Art. 25 WOR.
757. Art. 25(2) WOR.
758. Art. 2:311(1) BW.
759. Art. 2:309 BW.
760. Art. 2:311(2) BW.
761. Art. 2:325(1) BW.

(see § 6.3.3), in this context meaning the requirement of equal treatment of shareholders, should be applied to the extent possible.[762] This precludes the use of high nominal value shares exclusively to create a 'merger force-out' of minority shareholders. Property cannot be used as consideration for these discrepancies.

No shares in the capital of a surviving company will be received in the case of a 'sister merger', an 'upstream merger' involving wholly owned subsidiaries or a triangular merger (see § 11.3.1.1).[763]

In view of the modernisation of Dutch BV law per 1 October 2012, non-voting shares and non-profit-sharing shares can be issued by BVs. An NV cannot issue such shares; NV shares always carry voting and profit rights. In the event of a merger between a BV (as the disappearing company) and an NV, a holder of non-voting shares and non-profit-sharing shares may request compensation because he cannot receive such shares (in return) in the acquiring NV. In that case this shareholder receives cash instead of NV shares.[764] The amount of the compensation will be determined by one or more independent experts, taking into account (possible) relevant provisions in the articles of association or shareholder agreement regarding the pricing of shares. When such provisions are unambiguous, no experts have to be appointed.[765] A request for compensation must be filed by the shareholder in writing to the company, within one month after the company notified the shareholder of its right to ask for compensation. The civil law notary cannot execute the merger deed before payment of the compensation, unless the companies involved in the merger agreed that the acquiring company will pay the compensation.[766]

11.3.3.2 Treasury Shares

The notarial merger deed by which the merger is completed (see § 11.3.4.4) may provide for a cancellation by the surviving company of treasury shares or other shares in the surviving company held by the absorbed company, but not in excess of the total nominal value of the newly issued share capital.[767] The detailed statutory provisions for a reduction of issued capital (see § 4.6) are not applicable with respect to this cancellation of shares.

762. Asser/Maeijer, Van Solinge & Nieuwe Weme 2-II* 2009/576.
763. Art. 2:311(2) BW.
764. Art. 2:330a(1) BW.
765. Art. 2:330a(2) BW.
766. Art. 2:330a(3) BW.
767. Art. 2:325(2) BW.

11.3.4 Procedure

11.3.4.1 Merger Plan

The merger plan is a joint proposal by the management boards of the absorbed and surviving companies.[768] It forms the basis for the notarial deed that completes the merger procedure. The merger plan must be signed by all the managing directors and approved and signed by all the supervisory directors, where applicable. If a director fails to sign, a reasoned explanation is required.[769] Drawing up a merger plan is a prerequisite to a statutory merger. The joint nature of the required plan makes a statutory merger inconceivable as part of a hostile acquisition.

The merger plan must describe in detail the proposed actions, including, as a minimum:[770]

(a) the legal form, name and statutory seat of each of the companies to be merged;
(b) the articles of the acquiror in its then existing form and in its post merger form or, if the acquiror is newly established, the draft deed of incorporation;
(c) the rights or compensatory payments which are chargeable to the acquiror and which are granted to persons who, other than as shareholders, have special rights *vis-à-vis* the companies ceasing to exist, such as profit rights or share subscription rights, and their effective date;
(d) the benefits in connection with the merger, conferred on managing directors, supervisory directors or other persons involved in the merger;
(e) the proposed composition of the management board and the supervisory board, if there is to be one;
(f) in respect of each of the companies ceasing to exist, the effective date from which financial information shall be incorporated in the annual accounts or other financial accounts of the acquiror;
(g) the proposed measures in connection with the transfer of the share ownership of the absorbed companies;
(h) the proposed continuation or discontinuation of the business activities of the absorbed companies;
(i) who must approve the merger resolution;
(j) the proposed exchange ratio for the shares, and any cash consideration;

768. Art. 2:312(1) BW.
769. Arts 2:312(4), 2:326(2) BW.
770. Arts 2:312(2), 2:326(1) BW.

(k) the date from which and the extent to which the shareholders of the absorbed company will share in the profits of the surviving company;
(l) the impact of the merger on the amounts in the balance sheet for goodwill, capital surplus and distributable reserves of the surviving company;
(m) the number of shares that will be cancelled (see § 11.3.3.2);
(n) the consequences of the merger for holders of non-voting or non-profit-sharing shares;
(o) the amount of compensation offered for a non-voting or non-profit-sharing share; and
(p) the total amount of compensation that can be requested as compensation by holders of non-voting shares and non-profit-sharing shares.

11.3.4.2 Supporting Documents

The merger plan must be supported by an explanatory memorandum prepared by the management board of each company involved. This memorandum must describe the reasons for the merger and must comment on the legal, economic and employment ramifications of the merger.[771] It must also explain: the method or methods applied in determining the exchange ratio for the shares, whether such method or methods are justified under the circumstances; the valuation resulting from each method applied; if more than one method has been applied, whether the relative weights attributed to the valuation methods applied may be considered generally acceptable; and whether there have been any particular difficulties in the valuation and the determination of the exchange ratio.[772] The explanatory memorandum does not have to be prepared if each shareholder of the merging companies consents to this.[773]

If more than six months of a company's financial year have elapsed by the time the plan of merger and accompanying documentation are filed with the commercial register (see § 12.1.1), its management board must either prepare annual accounts or an interim statement of assets and liabilities, consistent with the applied valuation methods, as of a date which is not earlier than the first day of the third month preceding the month of the filing.[774]

Each company must retain an auditor to examine the plan of merger and certify whether in his opinion the exchange ratio for the shares is reasonable, and the auditor must also give an opinion on the statements made in the

771. Art. 2:313(1) BW.
772. Art. 2:327 BW.
773. Art. 2:313(4) BW.
774. Art. 2:313(2) BW. This provision does not apply to listed companies that comply with the obligations of Art. 5:25d Wft to publish half-yearly results; see Art. 2:313(5) BW.

explanatory memorandum with respect to the valuation method or methods.[775] These requirements regarding the examination and opinion of the auditor can be waived, but only if each shareholder of the merging companies consents to this.[776] The auditor must also certify that the equity of the absorbed company is as a minimum equal to the aggregate nominal value of the shares that will be issued, plus any cash consideration and plus the total amount of compensation that will be paid to holders of non-voting shares or non-profit-sharing shares of a BV that merges into another entity than a BV (see § 11.3.3.1). The auditor must have access to the books and records of all the companies involved.[777]

Each company must file with the commercial register the plan of merger, the annual accounts for the three preceding years together with the relevant auditors' opinions, the annual reports for the three preceding years, and any interim statements or annual accounts not yet adopted. Filing can be done electronically. These documents, together with the explanatory memorandum, as well as any advice from or recommendations by the works council and the trade unions, where applicable, must also be deposited at each company's head office for inspection by shareholders and others who have a similar interest *vis-à-vis* the company. A notice that the filings have been made, the 'notice of deposit', must be published in a daily newspaper with national circulation.[778]

11.3.4.3 Decision-making

As a general rule, a merger resolution must be taken by the shareholders' meeting.[779] No resolution can be taken on the merger within the one-month period following the notification in a national newspaper referred to under § 11.3.4.2 (for timing, see § 11.3.4.4).[780] A merger resolution is similar to a resolution to amend the articles (see § 11.2), except that if less than one half of the issued capital is represented at the shareholders' meeting, a qualified majority of two thirds of the votes is required.[781] The surviving company may authorise the merger by resolution of its management board, provided that this procedure is not opposed by shareholders representing 5% or more of the issued capital, and provided the articles so permit and the intention to do so

775. Art. 2:328(1) and (2) BW.
776. Art. 2:328(6) BW.
777. Art. 2:328(3) BW.
778. Art. 2:314 BW.
779. Art. 2:317(1) BW. The shareholders' meeting does not have the right to amend the merger plan (Art. 2:317(2) BW). Although not specifically mentioned in Art. 2:107a BW, a resolution of the management board of an NV regarding the merger may fall under the scope of this Article.
780. Art. 2:317(2) BW.
781. Arts. 2:317(3) and 2:330(1) BW.

has been stated in the notice of deposit (see § 11.3.4.2).[782] The same possibility exists for the management board of the absorbed company in the event of an upstream merger with its parent company that holds all the shares of the absorbed company, unless the articles provide otherwise.[783]

11.3.4.4 Timing

Creditors may, under certain conditions, oppose the proposed merger in order to satisfy their claims against a merging company and require the merging company to provide security in that respect. The works council, where applicable, and, if the Merger Code apply, the trade unions, have the right to be consulted well in advance of the resolution or the authorisation (see § 11.3.1.3).[784]

If, as a result of the merger, a contract of a merging company should, in all reasonableness and fairness, not remain in force unamended, a party to such contract may request the court to have the contract amended or rescinded by court order, and damages may be awarded.[785] This course of action does not arise until the merger is completed, but it may be prudent to attempt to avoid it in advance.

Pledgees and beneficiaries of a life interest (right of usufruct) (see § 5.4) in shares of the disappearing company will, as a general rule, receive a similar right in shares of the surviving company.[786]

The merger is completed by the execution of a deed before a Dutch civil law notary, effective the following day.[787] The deed must be executed within six months of the date of the notice of deposit (see § 11.3.4.2). The civil law notary is responsible for compliance with the mandatory statutory requirements and the requirements of the articles and must render an opinion that all the requirements have been satisfied.[788] Within an eight-day period following the execution of the merger deed, the surviving company must file a certified copy of the merger deed with each of the commercial registers (see § 12.1.1) with which filings have been made by any of the companies involved.[789]

---

782. Art. 2:331 BW.
783. Art. 2:331(4) BW.
784. Their recommendations must be deposited for shareholder inspection (see § 11.3.4.2).
785. Art. 2:322 BW.
786. Art. 2:319(1) BW.
787. Art. 2:318(1) BW.
788. Art. 2:318(2) BW.
789. Art. 2:318(3) BW.

11.3.5 Short-Form Merger

A 'short-form' merger, with simplified procedures, is available, *inter alia*, for upstream mergers of a company with a wholly owned subsidiary[790] and for 'sister mergers', i.e. mergers between two or more wholly owned subsidiaries.[791]

The simplified procedures for a 'short-form' merger entail exemptions for: (i) the items in the merger plan (see § 11.3.4.1 (j) to (n)); (ii) the approval of the plan of merger by the supervisory directors; (iii) the explanatory memorandum for the absorbed company;[792] (iv) the valuation statements in the explanatory memorandum; and (v) the auditors' reports (see § 11.3.4.2).[793]

11.4 Statutory Divisions

11.4.1 Introduction

11.4.1.1 General

Statutory divisions (*juridische splitsingen*) may take place between NVs, BVs, associations, co-operatives, mutuals and foundations (see §§ 2.5.1 and 2.5.2), provided that in the latter three cases, as a general rule, the parties to the division have the same legal form.[794] Only the forms of divisions involving NVs and BVs as constituent legal entities are discussed here. Under current Netherlands law, a cross border division, involving Dutch and foreign legal entities, is not possible, even if it considers entities within the EU.

Although a statutory division can take several forms (see § 11.4.1.2), it basically entails the absorption of the whole or a part of the business of a company by one or more other companies (the 'recipient companies') through the exchange of shares. For consideration other than in shares, see § 11.4.3. By means of a statutory division, economic groups can be restructured or broken-up and joint ventures formed or terminated, by means of one single legal act whereby assets and liabilities are transferred under universal succession of title.

To a certain extent, a statutory division is the mirror of a statutory merger. In particular, this is the case with respect to the prescribed procedure (see

790. Art. 2:333(1) BW.
791. Art. 2:333(2) BW.
792. This exemption does not apply if other parties than the surviving company have a special right *vis-à-vis* the company ceasing to exist, such as profit rights or share rights.
793. Art. 2:333, 2:313(3) BW.
794. Arts 2:308 and 2:334b(1), (3) BW. Art. 2:334b(4) BW provides for an exception to this general rule.

§ 11.4.4). Moreover, the consultation requirements with the trade unions and works councils (see § 11.3.1.3) are similarly applicable in the context of divisions. However, whereas in a statutory merger one or more businesses are transferred in their entirety to one company, in a statutory division there may often be a transfer of part of the assets and liabilities of a company to more than one recipient company. This requires specific forms of protection for third parties (see § 11.4.6).

11.4.1.2 Types of Statutory Division

The law distinguishes between two different methods of a division: the division (*zuivere splitsing*) and the demerger (*afsplitsing*).[795]

In a division, two or more recipient companies absorb all the assets and liabilities of an existing company (the 'dividing company'), such that the dividing company by operation of law ceases to exist.[796] As a general rule, the shares of the dividing company are exchanged for shares in the recipient companies (for exceptions, see § 11.4.3). A species of this form is the 'qualified division' whereby different shareholders of the dividing company receive shares in different recipient companies.[797]

In a demerger, one or more recipient companies absorb the whole, or a distinct part, of the assets and liabilities of an existing company (the 'demerging company'), whereby the demerging company does not cease to exist (such company after the demerger the 'surviving company'). In a demerger the shareholders of the demerging company receive shares in all of the recipient companies, or one more recipient companies will be incorporated by the demerging company in the demerger.[798]

In a triangular division, the shares of the dividing or demerging company are by operation of law exchanged for shares in a third company that belongs to the same group (see § 3.1.2) as the recipient company.[799] All of the shares of the recipient company must be held by the group company, either alone or together with another company in the group of the recipient company.[800]

For 'short form' demergers, with simplified procedures, see § 11.4.5.

In both a division and a demerger, the recipient companies can be existing companies or can be incorporated at the time of the division. While the law defines the dividing or demerging company and each recipient company (with

795. Art. 2:334a(1) BW.
796. Art. 2:334a(2) BW.
797. Art. 2:334cc BW.
798. Art. 2:334a(3) BW.
799. Art. 2:334ii(1) BW.
800. Art. 2:334ii(2) BW.

the exception of companies that are incorporated at the time of the division) as a 'party to the division', such parties to the division may also be referred to below as 'companies involved'.[801]

11.4.2 Legal Effects

Upon the division taking effect, by operation of law:

(a) the dividing company ceases to exist (only in the event of a division);[802]
(b) the transferred assets and liabilities of the dividing or demerging company are absorbed by the recipient company(ies) by way of universal succession of title (*algemene titel*), so becoming part of its, or their, respective assets and liabilities;[803]
(c) except in certain limited cases defined by law (see § 11.3.3) the shareholders of the dividing company become shareholders of (all) the recipient company(ies).[804]

11.4.3 Consideration

A statutory division is essentially an exchange of shares, and cash is used only to account for exchange rate discrepancies, such as when the value of each newly issued share in the share capital of the recipient company(ies) is less than the value of each share in the dividing company. The total amount of cash or promissory notes involved in the transaction cannot exceed 10% of the aggregate nominal value of the newly issued share capital.[805] In making payments in cash to third party minority shareholders, the good faith requirements (see § 6.3.3), in this context meaning the requirement of equal treatment of shareholders, should be applied to the fullest extent possible (see § 11.3.3.1).

No shares in the capital of a recipient company will be received for shares in the capital of a dividing company that are held by or on behalf of such recipient or dividing company.[806] Furthermore, the shareholders of the dividing company will not become shareholders of all the recipient companies: (i) in the case of the recipient companies being incorporated at the time of the division and the dividing company receiving all their shares; (ii) in the

801. Art. 2:334a(4) BW.
802. Art. 2:334c(1) BW.
803. Art. 2:334a(2)-(3) BW.
804. Art. 2:334e(1) BW.
805. Art. 2:334x(2) BW.
806. Art. 2:334e(2) BW.

case of a 'qualified division'; or (iii) in the case of a triangular division (see § 11.4.1.2).[807]

The division deed (see § 11.4.4.4) may provide for a cancellation by a recipient company of shares in its own capital that it holds or will receive pursuant to the split-up, but not in excess of the total nominal value of the newly issued share capital. The detailed statutory provisions for a reduction of issued capital (see § 4.6) are not applicable here.[808]

In view of the modernisation of BV law per 1 October 2012, non-voting shares and non-profit-sharing shares can be issued by BVs. An NV cannot issue such shares; NV shares always carry voting and profit rights. In the event of a division between a BV and an NV, a holder of non-voting shares and non-profit-sharing shares may request compensation because it cannot receive such shares in the acquiring NV. In that case such shareholder receives cash (in return) instead of NV shares.[809] The amount of the compensation will be determined by one or more independent experts, taking into account (possible) relevant provisions in the articles of association of the BV or shareholder agreement regarding the pricing of shares. When such provisions are unambiguous, no experts have to be appointed.[810] A request for compensation must be filed by the shareholder in writing to the company, within one month after the company notified the shareholder of its right to ask for compensation. The civil law notary cannot execute the division deed before payment of the compensation, unless the companies involved in the division agreed that the acquiring company or companies will pay the compensation.[811]

11.4.4 Procedure

11.4.4.1 Division Plan

The division plan (*voorstel tot splitsing*) is a joint proposal by the management boards of the companies involved.[812] It forms the basis for the notarial deed that completes the division procedure. The plan must be signed by all managing directors and approved and signed by all supervisory directors, where applicable.[813] If a director fails to sign, a reasoned explanation of this is required.[814]

807. Art. 2:334e(3) BW.
808. Art. 2:334x(3) BW.
809. Art. 2:334ee1(1) BW.
810. Art. 2:334ee1(2) BW.
811. Art. 2:334ee1(3) BW.
812. Art. 2:334f(1) BW.
813. Art. 2:334f(3),(4) BW.
814. Art. 2:334f(3),(4) BW.

The division plan must describe in detail the proposed actions, including, as a minimum:[815]

(a) the legal form, name and statutory seat of the companies involved and the companies to be incorporated at the time of the division, where applicable;
(b) the articles of association of the recipient companies and the surviving company in their then existing form and in their form after the division or, if the recipient companies are newly established, the draft deed of incorporation;
(c) whether all the assets and liabilities of the dividing company will be transferred or only part thereof;
(d) a description on the basis of which it can be accurately determined which assets and liabilities of the dividing company will be transferred to each of the recipient companies and, if not all assets and liabilities of the dividing company will be transferred, which assets and liabilities will remain with the surviving company, as well as a pro forma profit and loss account of the recipient companies and the surviving company;
(e) the value of the assets and liabilities that each of the recipient companies will receive and of the assets and liabilities that will remain with the surviving company, as well as the value of the shares in the capital of the recipient companies that the surviving company will receive in the division;
(f) the rights or compensatory payments which are chargeable to the recipient companies and which are granted to persons who, other than as shareholders, have special rights *vis-à-vis* the dividing company, such as profit rights or share subscription rights, and their effective date;
(g) the benefits in connection with the division, conferred on the managing or supervisory directors of the companies involved or other persons involved in the division;
(h) the proposed composition of the management boards and the supervisory boards of the recipient companies and the surviving company, where applicable;
(i) the effective date from which financial information regarding the relevant parts of the assets and liabilities to be transferred shall be incorporated in the annual accounts of the recipient companies;
(j) the proposed measures in connection with the receipt by the shareholders of the dividing company of shares of the recipient companies;

815. Arts 2:334f(2) and (4), 2:334y BW.

(k) the proposed continuation or discontinuation of business activities;
(l) who must approve the division resolution;
(m) the proposed exchange ratio for the shares, and any cash consideration;
(n) the date from which, and extent to which, the shareholders of the dividing company will share in the profits of the recipient companies;
(o) the number of shares that will be cancelled (see § 11.4.3);
(p) the impact of the division on the amount of goodwill and the distributable reserves of the recipient companies and the surviving company;
(q) the consequences of the division for holders of non-voting or non-profit-sharing shares;
(r) the amount of compensation offered for a non-voting or non-profit-sharing share; and
(s) the total amount of compensation that can be requested as compensation by holders of non-voting shares and non-profit-sharing shares.

In the case of a qualified division, the division plan must state which shareholders will become shareholders in the respective recipient companies.[816]

11.4.4.2 Supporting Documents

The division plan must be supported by an explanatory memorandum prepared by the management boards of each company involved. This memorandum must describe the reasons for the division and must comment on the legal, economic and employment ramifications of the division.[817] It must also explain: the method or methods applied in determining the exchange ratio for the shares;[818] whether such method or methods are justified under the circumstances; the valuation resulting from each method applied, and, if more than one method has been applied, whether the relative weights attributed to the valuation methods applied may be considered generally acceptable; and whether there have been any specific difficulties in the valuation and the determination of the exchange ratio.[819] In the case of a qualified division the memorandum must also state the criteria for the allocation of the shareholders between the respective recipient companies.[820]

816. Art. 2:334cc(1) sub a BW.
817. Art. 2:334g(1) BW.
818. In the case where shares or depository receipts issued in respect of a dividing company are listed on a stock exchange, the exchange ratio may be made dependent on the price of the shares (or depository receipts) on that exchange on one or more dates preceding the division date and determined in the division plan (Art. 2:334x(1) BW).
819. Art. 2:334z BW.
820. Art. 2:334cc(1) sub b BW.

If more than six months of a company's financial year have elapsed by the time the division plan is filed at the commercial register (see § 12.1.1), its management board must prepare either annual accounts or an interim statement of assets and liabilities as of a date which is not earlier than the first day of the third month preceding the month of filing.[821]

Each company must retain an auditor to examine the division plan and certify whether in his opinion the exchange ratio for the shares is reasonable, and the auditor must also give an opinion on the statements made in the explanatory memorandum with respect to the valuation method or methods.[822] These requirements regarding the examination and opinion of the auditor can be waived, but only with the consent of all the shareholders of the companies involved.[823] In the case of a demerger, the auditor must also certify that the value of the assets and liabilities that shall remain with the surviving company, together with the value of the shares in the capital of the recipient companies to be received pursuant to the demerger, is as a minimum equal to the issued and called up part of the capital, increased by the reserves that the company must have by law or the articles immediately following the demerger and plus the total amount of compensation that will be paid to holders of non-voting shares or non-profit-sharing shares of a BV that merges into another entity than a BV (see § 11.4.3).[824] The auditors must have access to the books and records of all the parties to the division.[825] In the case of a qualified division the auditor must also certify that the allocation of the shareholders of the dividing company between the respective recipient companies is reasonable, unless each shareholder consents to waive this requirement.[826]

Each company involved must file with the commercial register (see § 12.1.1): the division plan; the annual accounts for the three preceding years together with the relevant auditor's opinion; the annual reports for the three preceding years; and any interim statements or annual accounts not yet adopted.[827] Filing can be done electronically. These documents, together with the explanatory memorandum, as well as any advice or recommendations by the works council and the trade unions, where applicable, must also be deposited at each company's head office for inspection by shareholders and others who have a special right *vis-à-vis* the company.[828] A notice that the

821. Art. 2:334g(2) BW. This provision does not apply to listed companies that comply with the obligations of Art. 5:25d Wft to publish half-yearly results; see Art. 2:334g(3) BW.
822. Arts. 2:334aa(1), (3) BW.
823. Art. 2:334aa(7) BW.
824. Art. 2:334aa(2) BW.
825. Art. 2:334aa(5) BW.
826. Arts. 2:334cc(1) sub c, (2) BW.
827. Art. 2:334h(1) BW.
828. Arts. 2:334h(2),(4) BW.

filings have been made must be published in a daily newspaper with national circulation.[829]

11.4.4.3 Decision-making

As a general rule, a division resolution must be taken by the shareholders' meeting.[830] No resolution can be taken on the division within the one-month period following the notification in a national newspaper (see § 11.4.4.2 (for timing, see § 11.4.4.4)).[831] A division resolution is similar to a resolution to amend the articles (see § 11.2), except that if less than one half of the issued capital is represented at the shareholders' meeting, a qualified majority of two thirds of the votes is required.[832] A division resolution for a qualified division can only be taken by a majority of three quarters of the votes cast in a meeting where at least 95% of the issued capital is represented.[833]

A recipient company may authorise the division by resolution of its management board, provided that this procedure is not opposed by shareholders representing 5% or more of its issued capital, and provided the articles so permit and the intention to do so has been stated in the notice of deposit referred to above under § 11.4.4.2. The same applies to a demerging company, in two situations: (i) if all recipient companies are incorporated at the time of the demerger and the demerging company will become their sole shareholder;[834] and (ii) when the recipient companies hold all shares of the demerging company.[835]

11.4.4.4 Timing

The works council, where applicable, and, if the Merger Code apply, the trade unions, have the right to be consulted well in advance of the decision-making (see § 11.3.1.3).[836]

The division is completed by the execution of a deed before a Dutch civil law notary, effective the following day.[837] The deed cannot be executed until any creditor opposition (see § 11.4.6) has been withdrawn or upon a court order

829. Art. 2:334h(3) BW.
830. Art. 2:334m(1) BW. The shareholders' meeting does not have the power to amend the division plan.
831. Art. 2:334m(2) BW.
832. Arts 2:334m(3), 2:334ee(1) BW.
833. Art. 2:334cc(1) sub d BW.
834. Art. 2:334ff BW. Although not specifically mentioned in Art. 2:107a BW, a resolution of the management board regarding the demerger may fall under the scope of this article.
835. Art. 2:334ff(4) BW.
836. Their recommendations must be deposited for shareholder inspection (see § 11.4.4.2).
837. Art. 2:334n(1) BW. The description of assets and liabilities referred to in § 11.4.4.1 is attached to the deed (Art. 2:334n(2) BW).

setting aside such opposition has become enforceable.[838] The notarial deed must be executed within six months of the notice of deposit (see § 11.4.4.2) or, in case this is not possible as a result of creditor opposition, within one month following the withdrawal or setting aside of such creditor opposition.[839] The civil law notary is responsible for compliance with the mandatory statutory requirements and the requirements of the articles, and must render an opinion that all the requirements have been satisfied.[840] Within an eight-day period following the execution of the division deed, each of the recipient companies and the surviving company, where applicable, must file a certified copy of the division deed with the competent commercial registers (see § 12.1.1).[841]

11.4.5 Short-Form Demerger

A short-form demerger, with simplified procedures, is available for demergers in which all recipient companies are incorporated at the time of the demerger, and the demerging company will become their sole shareholder pursuant to the demerger.[842]

Another short-form demerger is possible when all recipient companies are incorporated at the time of the demerger, and the shares of the recipient companies will be attributed to the shareholders of the demerging company in the same proportion as their current shareholdings in the demerging company ('proportional demerger').[843]

The simplified procedures for a short-form division entail exemptions for: (i) the items in the division plan mentioned above in § 11.4.4.1 (m) to (s); (ii) the approval of the division plan by the supervisory directors; (iii) the valuation statements in the explanatory memorandum; (iv) the auditors' reports, and, in the case of the proportional demerger described above, (v) the auditor's statement regarding the value of the contribution to the recipient company.[844]

---

838. Art. 2:334l(3) BW.
839. Art. 2:334n(1) BW.
840. Art. 2:334n(2) BW.
841. Art. 2:334n(3) BW. With respect to the company that has disappeared as a result of a division, this obligation lies on each of the recipient companies.
842. Art. 2:334hh(1) BW.
843. Art. 2:334hh(2) BW.
844. Arts. 2:334hh(1), (2) BW.

11.4.6 Third Party Protection

To a large extent third parties derive protection from the detailed procedural rules for a division. However, the law contains specific additional provisions with respect to third party protection.

Firstly, contractual relations (to which the dividing company is a party) can only be transferred in their entirety.[845] However, if a contractual relation is inherent to assets or liabilities that will be transferred to different recipient companies, the contractual relation may be divided between the recipient companies pro rata to its connection with the assets and liabilities that each recipient company will receive.[846]

Secondly, upon request of a creditor of one of the parties to the division, at least one of the companies involved must provide security for, or otherwise guarantee, the payment of the creditors' claim. This is not required if the payment of the creditor's claim is sufficiently secured or if the financial condition of the debtor after the division does not provide less security for the payment of the claim.[847] During a one-month period following the notice of deposit by the companies involved (see § 11.4.4.2), a party to a contract with any of them may, by filing a petition with the District Court, oppose the division proposal on the ground that it infringes the allocation rules with respect to that party's contractual relation or that the requested security or guarantee was not given.[848]

Thirdly, pledgees and beneficiaries of a life interest (right of usufruct) in shares of the dividing company will, as a general rule, receive a similar right in shares of the recipient companies.[849] Alternatively, a person who, other than as a shareholder, has a special right *vis-à-vis* a dividing company, such as profit rights or share subscription rights, must either receive; (i) rights in the recipient companies that, together with the rights *vis-à-vis* the surviving company (where applicable), are equivalent to his rights prior to the division, or; (ii) compensation.[850]

---

845. Art. 2:334j(1) BW.
846. Art. 2:334j(2) BW. The same principle applies to contractual relations that are partly connected to assets and liabilities that will remain with the surviving company (Art. 2:334j(3) BW).
847. Art. 2:334k BW.
848. Art. 2:334l(1) BW. Prior to its ruling, the court may enable the companies involved to amend their division plan (and publish the same in accordance with the publication requirements discussed above in § 11.4.4.2) or to give a security or guarantee (Art. 2:334l(2) BW).
849. Art. 2:334o(1) BW. In the case of a surviving company, the existing pledge or usufruct will remain in place.
850. Art. 2:334p(1) BW.

Fourthly, parties to contracts with a party to the division may, under certain conditions, have their contracts amended or rescinded by court order and damages may be awarded.[851]

Fifthly, the law contains detailed rules for the situation in which the description of the allocation of assets and liabilities is not clear. In a case where all the assets and liabilities of the dividing company have been transferred and the description is not clear, the recipient companies are deemed jointly entitled to the assets and jointly and severally liable for the debts. With respect to the assets, the entitlement of each recipient company is proportional to the value of its part of the assets, and liabilities received.[852] If all the assets and liabilities have been transferred and the description is not clear, the entitlement to the assets is deemed to be with the surviving company.[853]

Finally, the law provides that the recipient companies and the surviving company are jointly liable for the performance of the obligations of the surviving company at the time of the demerger.[854] For indivisible obligations this liability is several.[855] For divisible obligations either the recipient company or the surviving company, depending on whom the obligation was transferred to, is liable for the whole.[856] For other companies than the recipient company or the surviving company that received or kept the obligation, liability for divisible obligations is limited to the value of the assets and liabilities received or retained in the division.[857]

11.5 Adoption of a Different Legal Form

An NV can be converted (*omgezet*) into a BV, and a BV into an NV by a decision of the general meeting of shareholders to convert and to amend the articles.[858] The amendment must incorporate all the statutory provisions specifically required for the newly adopted corporate form. The conversion does not in any way affect the identity or continued existence of the company[859] (the company is not dissolved) and it continues to have the same assets and liabilities, tax status, managing directors, and, where applicable, supervisory directors. Associations, co-operatives, mutuals and foundations can also be

851. Art. 2:334r(1),(3) BW.
852. Arts. 2:334s(2), (4) BW.
853. Art. 2:334s(3) BW.
854. Art. 2:334t(1) BW.
855. Art. 2:334t(2) BW.
856. Art. 2:334t(3) BW.
857. Art. 2:334t(3) BW. These other companies are required to perform these obligations only upon failure of the recipient company or the surviving company to do so (Art. 2:334t(4) BW).
858. Arts. 2:18(1), (2) and 2:72(1)/183(1) BW.
859. Court of Appeal Amsterdam 17 Jul. 1980, NJ 1981, 214 (*Moussatorfabriek Bos Huizen/Vos*).

converted into NVs or BVs, and vice versa. For the conversion of a foundation to another legal entity, the conversion of another legal entity to a foundation, and the conversion of an NV or BV to an association, the conversion is subject to court approval.[860] Such approval will *inter alia* be withheld if the interests of holders of non-voting shares and non-profit-sharing shares are not sufficiently taken care of.[861]

For a conversion of a BV to an NV, the law requires an opinion from a Dutch registered accountant that confirms that the equity on a date within the five-month period preceding the conversion date was equal to or in excess of the issued and called up capital.[862] A similar provision exists for all other types of conversions of a legal entity in an NV.[863]

With regard to a conversion of a BV into another legal form, the law contains special provisions regarding the position of holders of non-voting and non-profit-sharing shares. In short, these provide for compensation (in cash) of a holder of such shares who does not consent to the conversion.[864]

11.6 Sale of Assets; Dissolution; Winding Up

11.6.1 Sale of Assets

A sale of all, or substantially all, of the company's assets may preclude the company from continuing the business it has been operating. With respect to NVs there is a statutory provision covering this specific event, which prescribes that a management board resolution to transfer the entire or substantially all of the enterprise requires the approval of the general meeting of shareholders.[865] Also with respect to BVs, for which no specific provision of law to this extent exists, certain legal commentators consider this a matter outside the realm of powers of the management board and consider it an action equivalent to dissolution of the company, which requires a shareholders' resolution.[866]

The question as to whether the transfer conflicts with the company's purposes has limited importance in practice, as an action on the basis of ultra vires (see § 3.5) can only be instituted by the company itself. However, any minority shareholder of the seller may challenge the sale of the seller's business to an acquiror on the basis of an alleged violation of the good faith requirements (see § 6.3.3). Such claim is more likely to be successful if the

860. Art. 2:18(4) BW.
861. Art. 2:181(6) BW.
862. Art. 2:72(1)(b) BW.
863. Art. 2:72(2)(b) BW.
864. Art. 2:181 BW.
865. Art. 2:107a BW.
866. Asser/Maeijer, Van Solinge & Nieuwe Weme 2-II* 2009/231 and 324-325.

majority shareholder has a special relationship with the acquiror that would benefit from a sale on terms other than at arm's length. To avoid legal disputes, it may be advisable to have the business to be transferred appraised by an independent expert.

11.6.2 Dissolution

11.6.2.1 Voluntary Dissolution

Shareholders may adopt a resolution to dissolve the company,[867] with the result that the liquidation proceeds, if any, will be distributed to shareholders in accordance with the articles of association. Certain shareholders, usually owners of preference shares, may have preferential rights to these distributions. Unless the articles require a qualified majority, any affirmative vote of the shareholders' meeting is sufficient to bring the company into a state of dissolution. The action is irreversible,[868] although there is case law[869] stating that if the resolution has not yet been implemented (e.g., the liquidation phase has not already started) it is possible to withdraw, with the intervention of the court, the resolution to dissolve.

There are no special statutory notice or quorum requirements in order to dissolve a company. For an NV or BV that is not a 'large' company, no authorisation by the management board or the supervisory board is required. To put a proposal to dissolve a 'large' company on the agenda of the shareholders' meeting, the management board needs the prior approval of the supervisory board.[870]

11.6.2.2 Involuntary Dissolution

The law does not require a company to be dissolved once it becomes insolvent.[871] However, any creditor, or the company, may file for bankruptcy once the company fails to pay two or more of its creditors.[872] Unless the articles provide otherwise, the management board requires an affirmative resolution of the shareholders, authorising it them file for bankruptcy (in the case of a liquidation).[873] This shareholders' resolution is also required when the

867. Art. 2:19(1)(a) BW.
868. Supreme Court 26 May 2000, LJN: AA5956 (*Machines BV/KvK Haaglanden*).
869. District Court of The Hague, 30 Jan. 2007, JOR 2007, 66 (*KvK Rotterdam/PMDC Europe BV*).
870. Art. 2:164(1)(h)/274(1)(h) BW.
871. In the event the equity of an NV falls below 50% of its issued capital, the management board must convene a shareholders' meeting to discuss appropriate steps (Art. 2:108a BW).
872. Art. 1(1) Bankruptcy Act (*Faillissementswet*).
873. Art. 2:136/246 BW.

company has the status of a 'large' company (see § 8.2.1.2), in which case the prior approval of the supervisory board must also be obtained.[874] For the liability of managing directors and supervisory directors in the event of bankruptcy, see Chapter 9. Bankruptcy (in the event of liquidation) has the effect of dissolving the company.

A court may also order the dissolution of a company in an action brought by the public prosecutor in the event that the company has an illegal purpose,[875] and also by an action of an interested party, if, inter alia: its articles do not comply with the statutory requirements; or the company is grossly violating either its articles;[876] or (for an NV) the critical rules concerning the preservation of capital or the rules concerning the minimum capital (see § 4.3);[877] or if the company is no longer in a financial position to conduct business in accordance with its purposes; or is no longer in business.[878] This latter provision is of particular importance in view of dissolving 'dormant' companies. The public prosecutor will notify the competent Chamber of Commerce of its intention to bring an action for dissolution of the company.[879] This provision is intended to co-ordinate actions by the public prosecutor and the Chamber of Commerce, which has been given the power to dissolve dormant companies by an administrative decision in order to combat fraud and clean-up the commercial register.

The Chamber of Commerce (see § 12.1.1) must dissolve a company, co-operative or mutual upon the occurrence of two or more of the following conditions:[880]

(a) the legal entity has not paid its filing fees for one year or more after registration;
(b) the legal entity has not registered any managing directors for one year or more, or the managing director is deceased, could not be reached for one year or more at the address registered with the commercial register, nor at the register of his municipality, or his address was not registered at all with the commercial register for one year or more;
(c) the legal entity has not published its annual accounts in accordance with the law; or
(d) the legal entity has not complied with the obligation to file a return for corporate income tax for one year or more.

874. Art. 2:164(1)(i)/274(1)(i) BW.
875. Art. 2:20(2) BW.
876. Art. 2:21(1) BW.
877. Art. 2:74(2) BW.
878. Art. 2:74(1)/185(1) BW.
879. Art. 2:74(1)/185(1) BW.
880. Art. 2:19a(1) BW.

For registered associations or foundations that do not conduct a registered business enterprise (see §§ 2.5.1.7 and 2.5.2), the non-payment of the respective filing fees in combination with one of the events mentioned above under (b) will trigger an action for dissolution by the Chamber of Commerce.[881] The Chamber of Commerce must notify the legal entity and its registered managing directors of its intention to take the dissolution action, including the grounds for such action and will publish this notification in the Government Gazette (*Staatscourant*). If the legal entity has not properly registered any managing directors for a period of one year or more, as outlined under (b) above, the Chamber of Commerce will also publish this event in the Government Gazette.[882] Unless the grounds for dissolution have been remedied in a timely manner, the Chamber of Commerce will dissolve the legal entity by administrative decision after a period of eight weeks following the date of notification.[883] The administrative decision can be appealed against at the Trade and Industry Appeals Tribunal (*College van Beroep voor het bedrijfsleven*).[884]

The public prosecutor, or an interested party, may also petition the court to order dissolution if the company was formed in violation of the rules concerning the formation of companies[885] or to order nullification of a purported company if business was conducted in the name of a company that was never formed.[886] The Enterprise Court can also order the company to be dissolved if an investigation into the affairs of the company (in respect of enquiry proceedings) shows mismanagement and the court deems dissolution the most appropriate solution (see § 10.2).[887]

11.6.3 Winding Up

The resolution to dissolve the company does not bring the existence of such company to an end. However, the nature of the company in liquidation changes. The object of the company in liquidation is from then onwards to wind up its affairs (*vereffening*). Upon dissolution other than in the context of bankruptcy, the corporate affairs must be wound up by a liquidator (*vereffenaar*). In the case of a voluntary dissolution, the articles will usually empower the shareholders' meeting to appoint the liquidator in charge of the winding-up process (see § 11.6.2.1). If no liquidator is appointed or designated, the managing

881. Art. 2:19a(2) BW.
882. Art. 2:19a(3) BW.
883. Art. 2:19a(4) BW. The administrative decision will be notified to the legal entity and its registered managing directors, if any (Art. 2:19a(5) BW).
884. Art. 2:19a(8) BW.
885. Art. 2:21(1)(a) BW.
886. Arts. 2:4(1), (3) BW.
887. Art. 2:356(f) BW.

directors will serve as liquidators of the estate of the dissolved company.[888] If no liquidators can be appointed or designated on the basis of the above, the Chamber of Commerce will serve as the liquidator.[889] The estate of a company dissolved by court order (see § 11.6.2.2) will be wound up by one or more liquidators appointed by the court.[890] If the company is dissolved by court order, the liquidator will be designated in the order.

After discharging all liabilities of the company, or making adequate provisions for discharge, the company may distribute the remainder of its assets to its shareholders,[891] in accordance with the articles of the company. In the event of disputed creditors or claims, and unidentifiable shareholders, the liquidator may, after a certain period of time, deposit funds with the court that are adequate to meet these claims to the extent they are entitled to share in the distribution.[892]

The liquidator must give an account of the liquidation and, if there are more than two persons entitled to the liquidation surplus, also prepare a plan of distribution. Both the account and the plan of distribution must be filed at both the offices of the company and the commercial register (see § 12.1.1). The liquidator must announce the filings in newspapers and, if required by the court, in the Government Gazette (*Staatscourant*).[893] Any creditor or person entitled to the liquidation surplus may oppose the plan of distribution by submitting objections to the District Court within two months after the announcement is made in the newspaper and the Government Gazette.[894] No distribution to persons entitled to the liquidation surplus can be made without the consent of the District Court during the two-month period after filing; only in the period before the beginning of the two-month period can the liquidation surplus be distributed (in whole or in part) in advance without said consent.[895]

After the two-month opposition period has elapsed, the liquidator may make the final distributions to the parties entitled to them. At that precise moment, when no assets or benefits are known to the liquidator, the company ceases to exist. This event must be filed with the commercial register, together with notification of the identity of the keeper of the books of the company. These books must be stored for a period of seven years.

Liquidation of Dutch companies may require the assistance of tax counsel. The shares of a Dutch company continue in existence until the company

888. Art. 2:23(1) BW.
889. Art. 2:19a(7) BW.
890. Art. 2:23(1) BW.
891. Art. 2:23b(1) BW.
892. Art. 2:23b(8) BW.
893. Art. 2:23b(4) BW. A violation of these provisions is a criminal offence, see Art. 1(4) WED.
894. Art. 2:23b(5) BW.
895. Art. 2:23b(6) BW.

as a legal entity ceases to exist, i.e. until the moment that no assets of the company are any longer known.

If after the date the company ceases to exist a creditor or a person potentially entitled to the liquidation surplus appears, or an asset belonging to the liquidated company becomes known, any interested party may request the court to reopen the liquidation.[896] The requesting party must demonstrate an apparent claim or interest. Case law gives an example in which this procedure was used by a victim of asbestos-related illness, who was successful in his claim to reopen the liquidation of the company which, as his former employer, was liable for damages to him. The victim claimed that the company had insurance coverage which could be used to compensate him.[897]

The revival of the company will only be for the purpose of settling the claim, after which the company will again cease to exist.

The fact that the company ceases to exist at the moment no assets are known to the liquidator has resulted in a legal constraint that is often called a 'turbo liquidation'.[898] If this company has no assets or liabilities at the moment that the shareholders' meeting adopts the resolution to dissolve the company, the company immediately ceases to exist. There will be no liquidation procedure and no opposition period. Creditors should not be prejudiced. Because no opposition period was observed, the courts may be more easily persuaded to reopen the liquidation. If the liquidator notes that the debts would exceed the assets of the company, he must file for bankruptcy.[899]

11.7 Transfer of Seat

11.7.1 Extraordinary Events

Under Netherlands law, the statutory seat of a company must be in the Netherlands in order for it to be recognised as a Dutch company.[900] Normally, the transfer of the seat of a Dutch company to another country is not possible under Netherlands law without dissolution of this company in the Netherlands and incorporation of a new company in the other country. However, upon the occurrence of certain extraordinary events, such as war, immediate danger of war, revolution and similar situations, a transfer of seat is possible to other

896. Art. 2:23c BW.
897. Supreme Court 31 Oct. 1997, NJ 1998, 258 (*Andeweg*).
898. Art. 2:19(5) BW.
899. Art. 2:23a(4) BW.
900. Art. 2:66(3)/177(3) BW.

parts of the Kingdom of the Netherlands,[901] or to other countries.[902] For a transfer of seat, the anticipated transfer must also be in 'the interests of the company' (see § 1.2).[903]

11.7.2 Transfer of Seat in Other Situations

Currently, there is no legislation in the Netherlands regarding transfer of seat in circumstances other than the extraordinary events described in § 11.7.1. However, a cross-border statutory merger between an NV or a BV and an equivalent company in another EU member state can have a similar effect as a transfer of seat. A BV that intends to transfer its seat to Germany could merge with a German GmbH as a result of which all assets and liabilities of the BV will be transferred under universal succession of title to the German GmbH; the BV being transformed into a GmbH.

According to case law of the CJEU, the freedom of establishment includes to a certain extent the freedom to transfer the seat of a legal entity (without dissolution) to another member state of the EU, but only if the laws of that member state allow such transfer.[904] From the 'Vale'-decision of the CJEU, it may (presumably) be concluded that when national legislation exists which enables companies established under national law to convert to another company form, but does not allow foreign companies to convert into a national company, this infringes the freedom of establishment.[905] It is expected that, due to this case law, in the near future corporate law the Netherlands will explicitly provide for provisions that allow and regulate a transfer of seat to other countries within the EU.

---

901. Art. 1(2) Act on Voluntary Transfer of Seat (*Rijkswet vrijwillige zetelverplaatsing van rechtspersonen*), Stb. 1967,161.
902. Stb. 2000, 283.
903. Art. 6(1)a Act on Voluntary Transfer of Seat.
904. CJEU 16 Dec. 2008, JOR 2009, 35 (*Cartesio*).
905. CJEU 12 Jul. 2012, JOR 2012, 285 (*Vale*).

Chapter 12
Commercial Register

12.1 The Commercial Register

12.1.1 General

The Netherlands is divided into districts, each having its own Chamber of Commerce, non-governmental agencies established under the Wet KvK 1997.

Each Chamber of Commerce maintains an online commercial register. All Dutch and foreign-owned business organisations, companies, European legal entities with their statutory seat in the Netherlands, general and limited partnerships, and other legal entities meeting the requirements set out in the HrW 2007[906] must register and disclose an extensive amount of information. Companies, mutual associations, co-operatives, certain associations and foundations that conduct a business (see § 2.1.2 and Chapter 3) and limited partnerships, whose fully liable partners are foreign companies must also file their annual accounts.[907] The criteria vary, depending on the legal form in which the business is conducted or the agent is operating, but essentially all business forms, agents and representatives are subject to the registration requirements once they have an address in the Netherlands. The legal and commercial effects of these disclosures are significant. Third parties acting in good faith may rely on the filed statements, even if the filings are erroneous or filed without proper corporate authority. The commercial effect is that disclosure makes it possible to analyse the financial strength of public and non-public companies, including competitors, and that for almost every business operation, basic corporate information is freely accessible to outsiders.

12.1.2 Where to File

As a general rule, under the HrW 2007, a single filing in the district in which a legal person or company has its official seat or its principal place of business

906. Arts 5-8 HrW.
907. Arts 2:394(1), 2:360 BW.

suffices.[908] Formal foreign companies (see § 2.2.1) with no actual seat in the Netherlands must also file with the commercial register.[909]

The information filed, with the exception of some personal information on certain persons concerned,[910] may be viewed at nominal cost by any person, without any requirement that a particular interest be demonstrated.[911] Copies of the filings and extracts from the filings of certain corporate information can also be obtained at nominal cost.[912]

12.1.3 Registration Number on Letterhead

Each business organisation must state its registration number on its headed stationery, invoices and order forms, as well as any offering and tender documents.[913]

12.1.4 Duty to Register

Each managing director, owner of a business enterprise and person responsible for the Dutch business or branch of a foreign organisation[914] is under a statutory duty to make filings within one week of the occurrence of any event that triggers the filing requirement.[915]

The Chamber of Commerce may in certain circumstances refuse or amend certain registrations concerning a business enterprise.[916]

Any interested person can lodge an administrative appeal against certain registrations. Compliance with the registration requirements is enforced by the Chamber of Commerce, and a violation of the provisions of the HrW 2007 is an economic offence.[917]

12.2 Information to be Disclosed

Disclosures are made in the form of registrations and filings with the competent commercial register.

---

908. Art. 18(6) HrW 2007.
909. Art. 2 Wfbv.
910. That information can be viewed by a lawyer, civil-law notary, bailiff and other persons set out in Art. 51 HrB 2008.
911. Art. 21 HrW 2007, Art. 51 HrB 2008.
912. Art. 22 HrW 2007.
913. Art. 27 HrW 2007. A violation of this provision is a criminal offence, see Art. 1(4) WED.
914. Art. 18 HrW 2007.
915. Art. 20 HrW 2007.
916. Arts 32-39 HrW 2007, Art. 5 HrB 2008. The Chamber of Commerce must notify the person having the primary responsibility for filing such amendments (Art. 34 (3) HrW 2007).
917. Art. 1(4) WED.

The information that must be registered and filed differs for the various legal forms in which a business enterprise can be conducted, and agents, distributors and other legal representatives are likewise subject to their own requirements:

(a) personal data for each managing director and supervisory director, including the date on which these positions were obtained and whether the managing directors are solely or jointly authorised to represent the company (see § 8.2.5.3);
(b) personal data for persons other than managing directors who have been granted the authority to represent the company, as well as the terms of such powers (see § 8.2.5.4);
(c) only for the NV: the authorised capital, as well as the amount of the issued capital and the paid up part thereof, divided by type of shares, where applicable;
(d) only for the NV: in the case of issued shares that have not been fully paid up: personal data for the holders of such shares, including the number of shares held by each such holder and the amounts contributed to such shares;
(e) only for the BV: the issued capital and the paid up part thereof;
(f) personal data for the holder of all shares in the capital of the company, disregarding the shares held by the company itself or any of its subsidiaries;
(g) in the case of an investment company with variable capital (see § 3.1.3), changes in the registered capital must be filed at least once a year; and
(h) where applicable, that the articles of the company are in conformity with the articles for a 'large' company.

12.3 Legal Effect

Disclosures in the commercial register create a high degree of certainty about what third parties will be presumed to know.[918] Registration of certain facts with the commercial register give a certain protection to both the company and to parties who have entered, or want to enter, into a contractual relationship with the company. This statutory presumption is nevertheless subject to limitations. Information required to be disclosed may not be asserted against third parties who were not aware of it until this information is actually disclosed

918. Art. 2:6(4) BW.

in accordance with the HrW 2007.[919] The company or owner of a business organisation cannot validly argue that a third party should not have relied on disclosed information that proves to be erroneous or incomplete.[920]

Under certain circumstances, the company may not claim the protection of the registration with the commercial register regarding the way the company can be legally bound and by whom, *inter alia*:

(a) if it would be contrary to the general good faith principles to provide legal protection to the company on the basis of its registration with the commercial register in view of the misunderstandings about the prevailing acts that were caused by the company; and
(b) if a third party may assume the authority of the acting person to bind the company on the basis of the job or position of the acting person under the specific circumstances of the case and the appearance of such authorisation (i.e. apparent authority).[921]

12.4 Filing Fees

The Chambers of Commerce are largely self-supporting as a result of which the commercial registers are dependent on registration fees from the parties making the filings, fees from third parties requesting information and annual registration levies.[922] The annual registration levies differ for each Chamber of Commerce, but remain within limits determined by government decree.[923]

919. Art. 25(1) HrW 2007, Arts 2:6(2), 3:61(3) BW.
920. Art. 25(3) HrW 2007, Art. 2:6(3) BW.
921. Supreme Court 23 Oct. 1998, NJ 1999, 582 (*Nacap/Kurstjens*).
922. Arts 32-43 Wet KvK 1997.
923. Financial Commercial Register Decree (*Financieel Besluit Handelsregister*), Stb. 2008, 241.

Chapter 13
Works Councils

13.1 General

Netherlands law does not entitle employees to representation on the management board of an enterprise (no *Mittbestimmung*), nor does it entitle employees to determine the allocation of profits.

The most important body through which labour participation is exercised at an enterprise level is the works council, which possesses the powers vested in it by the *Wet op de ondernemingsraden* (Works Council Act) (WOR). The works council is an integral part of corporate governance, and its mandatory involvement in decision-making processes makes it part of Dutch corporate law. A works council is mandatory for each enterprise in the Netherlands, which has 50 or more employees,[924] regardless of its legal form or nationality.

The Dutch legislature has implemented the Directive for the European Works Council (see § 13.3). A company with a community-scale dimension may, instead of forming a European works council, comply with this directive by instituting certain information and consultation procedures, negotiated between that company and a so-called special negotiating body. Compared with the powers of the Dutch works council, the powers of a statutory European works council are restricted.

13.2 Works Councils

13.2.1 Scope

13.2.1.1 General

The 'entrepreneur', defined as the natural or legal person that maintains the qualifying business enterprise, must set up a works council.[925] For an incorporated business enterprise, the entrepreneur for the purposes of the WOR is the company, represented by its management. For convenience, whenever a

924. Art. 2(1) WOR.
925. Art. 1(1)(d) WOR.

reference under the WOR is made to 'entrepreneur', references in this chapter will be to 'management' or the 'company'.

The WOR defines 'enterprise' as every organisation operating as an independent organisation in which work is performed on the basis of an employment agreement or an appointment as civil servant (for this purpose, including persons employed by any governmental instrumentality on a contractual basis).[926] Consequently, governmental agencies and non-profit organisations must also apply the WOR. Further references to 'enterprise' mean that this term is confined to business enterprises only.

13.2.1.2 Applicability for Foreign Companies

A Dutch enterprise may be owned by a Dutch company, or a foreign company through its Dutch office. In conformity with the Dutch rules for the conflicts of law, only enterprises located in the Netherlands fall within the scope of the WOR. The activities of a Dutch enterprise outside the Netherlands may be taken into account for the applicability of the WOR only if they are managed directly by the Dutch organisation and are considered activities inherently connected with the Dutch labour organisation.[927]

13.2.2 Joint, Group and Central Works Councils

If a company or a group of affiliated companies owns two or more enterprises employing 50 employees or more, it must set up a joint works council for all or several of these enterprises if this would advance the proper implementation of the WOR.[928] Alternatively, the management of an enterprise with 50 employees or more must set up a separate works council for any substantial part of that enterprise if it would advance the proper implementation of the WOR within its enterprise.[929]

A company or group which has established two or more works councils must establish a central works council for the enterprises involved, if this would advance the proper implementation of the WOR. In the case of more than two works councils within the same divisional structure of a group, a group works council must be established for this division if this would advance

926. Art. 1(1)(c) WOR.
927. However, the works council of a Dutch enterprise has the right to render advice on proposed management actions relating to the establishment, takeover or relinquishment of control over a foreign enterprise, or to important modifications in the co-operation with or participation in such foreign enterprise, if it can reasonably be anticipated that the proposed action will have significant implications for the Dutch enterprise (Art. 25(1)(b) WOR, see § 13.2.4.3).
928. Art. 3(1),(2) WOR.
929. Art. 3(1),(2) WOR.

the proper implementation of the WOR.[930] The central or group works council only handles matters which are of common interest to the enterprises for which they are established, irrespective of any powers of the individual works councils in these matters.[931] Any powers of the individual works councils with regard to matters of common interest are by operation of law vested in the central or group works councils, with the group works councils in turn being subordinate to the central works council.[932]

This distribution of works councils' powers at different levels of the corporate hierarchy has in the past led to various conflicts between them.[933]

13.2.3 Organisation

13.2.3.1 Composition, Committees and Experts

The works council consists of elected employees only, with a minimum of three members where there are fewer than 50 employees, and a maximum of 25 members where there are 7,000 or more employees.[934]

The works council may establish standing committees to address matters involving such groups of employees or issues as it may designate, committees for separate locations of the enterprise, and committees to prepare certain issues for its consideration.[935]

The works council may invite one or more experts to attend a meeting.[936]

930. Art. 3(1),(2) WOR.
931. Art. 35(1) WOR.
932. Art. 35(2) WOR.
933. For example, in the case of an anticipated acquisition, the central works council of the seller may be inclined to give positive advice (see § 13.2.4.3) on the ground that the acquisition would be beneficial to the group of enterprises as a whole, while the works council of a certain enterprise may try to oppose the acquisition on the grounds that this would be disadvantageous to that enterprise (Enterprise Court 30 Aug 1984, NJ 1985, 475). For the delineation of powers between works councils, group works councils and central works councils, see Enterprise Court 10 May 1990, NJ 1992, 126 (*HSA*), Enterprise Court 10 Jul. 1997, NJ 1997, 669 (*De Groepsondernemingsraad NS Reizigers/NS Reizigers*), Enterprise Court 16 Mar. 2000, JAR 2000, 80 (*Philips Lighting*).
934. Art. 6(1) WOR.
935. Art. 15 WOR.
936. Art. 16 WOR.

13.2.3.2 Election

The members of the works council are elected by, and must be employees of, the enterprise.[937] They are elected from a list of candidates, which may be submitted by:[938]

(a) a trade union which is active in the relevant enterprise or type of industry and has among its members employees in the enterprise qualified to vote; or
(b) the lesser of 30 persons or one third of the number of employees qualified to vote, who are not members of a trade union that has submitted a list of candidates as described under (a) above.

13.2.3.3 Job Protection

Except for 'urgent cause', an employee who is a member of the works council, or who has a special relationship with the works council cannot be dismissed without the involvement of the cantonal division of the District Court.[939] The Court shall ensure that the reason for the dismissal shall not relate to membership of the works council.

13.2.3.4 Secrecy

The members of the works council, as well as its committees or experts retained (see § 13.2.3.1), are under a strict obligation of secrecy.[940] This obligation survives the termination of membership of the works council.

13.2.4 Powers of the Works Council

13.2.4.1 Information

The works council and its committees are entitled to receive from management all information reasonably required for the performance of their duties, including financial and business information and information on social policies. The information must be in writing if so requested.[941] At the beginning

---

937. Art. 6(1) WOR. The members of the works council are elected by employees of at least six months' standing (Art. 6(2) WOR). Membership is open only to employees with at least one year's standing (Art. 6(3) WOR).
938. Art. 9(2) WOR.
939. Arts 7:670 (4), 7:670 (a), 7:670 (b), 7:685(1) BW.
940. Art. 20(1) WOR.
941. Art. 31(1) WOR.

of each term of office of the works council and as soon as possible after any change, the company must provide information about the corporate form, the contents of the articles of association and the names and addresses of the members of the supervisory and management boards. If the entrepreneur is a group company, the works council must be informed of the identities of the companies comprising that group, the allocation of control and the names and addresses of those who, as a result of such allocation, may exercise direct control over the company. With respect to financial data, the works council of a group company must (inter alia) be given such written information as will enable it to determine the extent to which the company for which it was established has contributed to the aggregate result of the group to which the company belongs.

13.2.4.2 Consultation Process

Consultations between the management and the works council take place at consultation meetings held within two weeks following a request from either management or the works council.[942] The general business of the enterprise must be discussed at least twice per calendar year.[943] At these meetings, management must inform the works council about operations and results of the company over the intervening period and about any actions proposed with respect to matters requiring prior consultation with, or the consent of, the works council (see §§ 13.2.4.3 and 13.2.4.4). The parties shall actively try to agree at what stage and in which manner the works council shall be engaged in the decision-making process with respect to such matters.[944]

13.2.4.3 Matters Requiring Prior Consultation

Management must give the works council the opportunity to give advice on any proposed action[945] involving:[946]

(a) the transfer of control over the enterprise or any part of it;
(b) the establishment, take-over or relinquishment of control over another enterprise, or the formation, substantial modification or discontinua-

942. Art. 23(1) WOR. Management is represented by the person who either alone or jointly with others in an enterprise, directly exercises the highest authority in the management of the work (Arts 1(1)(e), 23(4) WOR).
943. Art. 24(1) WOR.
944. Art. 24(1) WOR.
945. The WOR specifically refers to 'proposed decisions' of management. The term 'decisions', in fact, includes actions, whether or not formalised, for which management is responsible.
946. Art. 25(1) WOR.

tion of any long-term co-operation with other enterprises, including the formation, substantial modification or discontinuation of a substantial financial participation by or on behalf of such enterprise;
(c) the discontinuation of the activities of the enterprise or of a major part of these activities;
(d) a substantial change in the activities of the enterprise;
(e) a substantial change in the organisation of the enterprise or in the allocation of responsibility within the enterprise;
(f) a change of the location at which the enterprise carries on its activities;
(g) the recruitment or subcontracting of groups of workers;
(h) any major capital investment made by the enterprise;
(i) the seeking of substantial credit by the enterprise;
(j) the granting of substantial credit and provision of security for substantial debts of another company, unless within the ordinary course of business of the enterprise;
(k) the introduction or modification of a major technological facility;
(l) major initiatives by the enterprise regarding care for the environment, including introducing or modifying any policy and any organisational or administrative facility relating to the environment;
(m) the adoption of provisions for self-insurance referred to in Art. 40(1) Wfsv; and
(n) the retention of, and the terms of reference for, any outside expert to provide advice on any of the matters above.

In addition, management and the works council may, with agreement to that effect (see § 13.2.6), expand the list of matters that require the advice of the works council, and the provisions of the works council will apply accordingly to these additional matters.[947]

The substantiality test depends, inter alia, on the size and nature of the enterprise.[948] The provisions under (b) and (n) above, insofar as the latter relate to any matter referred to under (b) above, are not applicable if the other enterprise is or is to be established abroad, and if it cannot be reasonably expected that the proposed management action will lead to changes under paragraphs (c) to (f) above with regard to an enterprise in the Netherlands.[949]

947. Art. 32(2) WOR.
948. A change in the activities of the enterprise that does not entail important and direct consequences may nevertheless be considered 'substantial' for this purpose because of its long-term structural consequences (Enterprise Court 19 Feb. 1981, NJ 1982, 244), Enterprise Court 15 May 1997, JAR 1997, 141 (*De Ondernemingsraad Gerechtelijk Diensten Arondissement Middelburg/De Staat der Nederlanden*).
949. Art. 25(1) WOR.

Any request for advice must be made in writing and at a time that such advice can have a significant influence on the proposed action.[950]

In practice, the decision as to when the works council's advice should be requested is not always an easy one. In the case of an anticipated acquisition or joint venture, advice must be sought prior to initialling or signing a binding letter of intent. However, advice should not be requested too early either, as would be the case if the proposed action is not sufficiently clear and its consequences cannot be sufficiently assessed.[951]

The request for the works council's advice must be accompanied by a detailed summary of the reasons for the proposed action, the anticipated consequences for the employees of the enterprise and the proposed measures to be taken in relation to the proposed action.[952]

The works council may not give its advice until there has been at least one consultation meeting on the subject.[953] The works council must give its advice within a 'reasonable' time, depending, inter alia, on the complexity of the matter, the urgency involved and the speed with which the information has been provided by the company.

Only after the works council has given its advice may management take the proposed action. The works council must be notified of this promptly in writing. If the works council's advice is not followed or is only partially followed, the works council must be informed as to the reason why.[954] If the advice is not or only partly followed, the implementation of the action must be suspended for one full month following notice.[955] During this one-month period, the works council is entitled to appeal against the action (see § 13.2.5).

Management must also seek the advice of the works council prior to any action involving the appointment or removal of a managing director of the enterprise.[956] However, the works council is not entitled to appeal against a decision by the entrepreneur to appoint or remove a managing director contrary to the works council's advice.

---

950. Arts 25(2), 30(2) WOR.
951. Court of Appeal Amsterdam 25 Apr. 1991, NJ 1992, 271 (*PTT Telecom*).
952. Art. 25(3) WOR.
953. Art. 25(4) WOR.
954. Art. 25(5) WOR.
955. Art. 25(6) WOR. Non-compliance with this suspension requirement is a criminal offence, see Art. 1(4) WED.
956. Art. 30(1) WOR. With respect to the proposed appointment or removal of a managing director, the entrepreneur must provide the works council with the reasons for the decision and, in the event of an appointment, with information on the basis on which the works council can form an opinion about the person involved and about his future position within the enterprise (Art. 30(3) WOR).

13.2.4.4 Matters Requiring Prior Consent

There are a number of matters that cannot be undertaken by management without the prior consent of the works council. These include the introduction, modification or repeal of:[957]

(a) arrangements involving pension funds, profit-sharing plans or savings plans;
(b) rules pertaining to working hours or vacation policy;
(c) remuneration or job classification systems;
(d) rules pertaining to safety, health or welfare in connection with work or absence through illness;
(e) rules pertaining to hire, dismissal or promotion policies;
(f) rules pertaining to employee training;
(g) rules pertaining to employee performance review;
(h) rules pertaining to industrial social work;
(i) rules pertaining to work consultation;
(j) rules pertaining to the handling of complaints;
(k) rules pertaining to the registration, use and protection of personal data of the enterprise's employees; and
(l) rules pertaining to the facilities aimed at or suitable for observation or control of presence, behaviour or performance of the employees.

However, the works council is not required to approve matters if, and to the extent that, those matters which would ordinarily require the consent of the works council have already been covered in appropriate detail by a collective bargaining agreement.[958]

13.2.5 Appeal and Risks of Non-Compliance

13.2.5.1 Appeal Regarding Consultation Matters

If management has decided to pursue an action involving one of the matters requiring formal consultation of a works council (see § 13.2.4.3) that is contrary to the advice given by that works council, or if facts or circumstances become known which, had they been known to the works council at the time its advice was given, might have led to a different result, the works council

957. Art. 27(1) WOR.
958. Art. 27(3) WOR.

may appeal to the Enterprise Court within one month following management's written notice of the action.[959]

During this one-month period management must suspend the implementation of the proposed action.[960]

The only available ground for appeal is that management 'could not reasonably have reached the decision had it weighed the interests involved'.[961] Because of this limited scope of appeal, appeals are not easily granted on substantive issues. Procedural inadequacies will, however, almost invariably lead to the conclusion that the interests have been improperly weighed and procedural issues (e.g. disputes on whether sufficient information was provided or whether sufficient consultation took place on alternative solutions put forward by the works council) are subject to full review by the Enterprise Court. If the Enterprise Court sustains any claim it may, *inter alia*, give an order requiring the company to repeal the action, in whole or in part, and to reverse any specific effects of that action, with due respect to the acquired rights of third parties.[962]

13.2.5.2 Non-Compliance with Consent Requirement

Any decision or management action with respect to any consent matters (see § 13.2.4.4) without the prior approval of the works council shall be null and void by operation of law. This nullity is, however, subject to a formal statement to that effect being issued by the works council within one month from the date the decision was communicated or (in the absence of such communication) any action by management showing the implementation of that decision.[963]

13.2.6 Agreements with the Works Council

Management and the works council may conclude agreements, generally known as *convenanten*, for a variety of purposes. However, such agreements may not limit or restrict the statutory powers of the works council pursuant to the WOR. Many such agreements have been concluded in the restructuring of enterprises or in the merger or joint venture context. Other examples include agreements for the desired 'profile' of the supervisory board (in terms of skills and background, etc.) in 'large' companies.

---

959. Art. 26(1) WOR.
960. Art. 26(2) WOR. Works councils often commence preliminary court proceedings to prevent an action from becoming irreversible, particularly due to the statutory provisions requiring that the rights of third parties be respected.
961. Art. 26(4) WOR.
962. Art. 26(5) WOR.
963. Art. 27(5) WOR.

In the restructuring of enterprises, one common type of agreement is geared to the situation in which an international group with its parent-holding company in the Netherlands intends to hive down its Dutch activities to a Dutch sub-holding company. In Dutch and international corporate practice, it is often felt that works councils of a specific country should not be in a position to be involved in matters which do not specifically relate to that country. Thus, it is almost standard practice in the Netherlands to resolve this issue by 'pushing down' the works council to the national level only.

The Dutch Supreme Court ruled that the provisions of the WOR similarly apply to additional powers of the works council pursuant to an agreement with management.[964] The WOR states that a works council may be granted additional powers either: (i) as provided for in a collective bargaining agreement;[965] or (ii) by means of an agreement between the enterprise and the works council.[966] In the event that the agreement provides for additional matters requiring prior consultation with, or consent by, the works council, the respective actions for non-compliance are similarly applicable (see § 13.2.5).[967]

13.2.7 Employee Participation in Small Enterprises

13.2.7.1 Enterprises with Fewer than 50 but at least 10 Employees

The management of an enterprise with 10 or more, but fewer than 50 employees, and for which no works council has been established, is required, as a minimum, to set up bi-annual meetings with its employees.[968]

Management must give the employees an opportunity to give advice on any proposed action that may lead to: (i) the loss of jobs; or (ii) an important change in the nature of work, the working conditions, or the circumstances under which the work is performed for one quarter or more of the employees.[969]

If management takes action contrary to the advice of its employees, it is not required to suspend the implementation of the action. Moreover, the employees may not appeal against any such management action.

The WOR provides for the optional adoption of a body for 'employee representation' (*personeelsvertegenwoordiging*), consisting of a minimum

964. Supreme Court 17 Mar. 1993, NJ 1993, 366 (*Smit Vlootbeheer*).
965. Art. 32(1) WOR.
966. Art. 32(2) WOR.
967. Art. 32(4) WOR. The statutory basis for agreements between the enterprise and the works council is similarly applicable to agreements between the enterprise and the employee representation (see § 13.2.7).
968. Art. 35b WOR.
969. Art. 35b(5) WOR.

number of three people.[970] However, at the request of the majority of the employees, management must institute such body.[971] The employee representation body must consent to any introduction, modification or repeal of rules pertaining to: (a) working hours or vacation policy; and (b) safety, health or welfare in connection with work or absence through illness.[972]

The WOR provides for a statutory basis for the granting of additional powers to the employee representation body.[973]

13.2.7.2 Enterprises with Fewer than 10 Employees

The management of an enterprise with fewer than 10 employees and for which no works council has been established may institute an employee representation body as discussed above under § 13.2.7.1. This body must consent to any introduction, modification or repeal of rules pertaining to working hours or vacation policy.[974]

The WOR provides for a statutory basis for the granting of additional powers to any employee representation body.[975]

13.3 European Works Councils

13.3.1 General

The Dutch legislature has opted to implement the directive for the European works councils by means of a separate statute the *Wet op de Europese ondernemingsraden* (European Works Councils Act) (WEOR), in an effort to emphasise that under existing legislation Dutch works councils (see § 13.2) will not be considered subordinate to European works councils.[976] Instead, the powers of the Dutch works councils are expanded by additional powers, inter alia, to appoint and remove both the Dutch members to the special negotiating body and the members of the mandatory European works council.

For a good understanding of the WEOR, a distinction must be made between:

---

970. Art. 35c WOR.
971. Art. 35c(2) WOR.
972. Arts 27(1), 35c(3) WOR.
973. Arts 32, 35c(3) WOR.
974. Arts 27(1), 35d(2) WOR.
975. Arts 32, 35d(2) WOR.
976. The Dutch legislator adopted in November 2011 an amended version of the WEOR, implementing the EU Recast Directive for the establishment of European Works Councils of 6 May 2009, No. 2009/38, O.J. EUR. COMM. (No. L122) 28 (2009). This amendment of the WEOR closely follows the content of the recast directive and will not lead to material changes to the existing rules.

(a) a statutory European works council, formed in the absence of an agreed arrangement;
(b) an agreed European works council; and
(c) any other agreed procedure, concluded pursuant to an agreed arrangement.

13.3.2 Scope

13.3.2.1 General

As a general rule, the obligations stipulated in the WEOR apply only to the extent no other pre-existing agreements are in place which serve a similar purpose.

The substantive provisions of the WEOR apply to Dutch community-scale enterprises and Dutch community-scale groups of enterprises.

A community-scale enterprise or community-scale group of enterprises is considered 'Dutch' for purposes of the WEOR if:[977]

(a) the community-scale enterprise or the 'controlling' enterprise (within a community-scale group) has its domicile or seat in the Netherlands; or
(b) in the situation that the community-scale enterprise or the 'controlling' enterprise has its domicile or seat outside any of the Member States, a branch or group enterprise for which the management has been appointed or is considered the 'central management' for purposes of the WEOR has its residence or seat in the Netherlands.[978]

The law which applies to a certain enterprise determines whether that enterprise qualifies as a 'controlling' enterprise.[979]

A Dutch enterprise is considered the 'controlling' enterprise within a community-scale group if it can exercise control, directly or indirectly, over another enterprise within a community-scale group and is not itself an enterprise which is controlled by another enterprise. Control is deemed to exist if such enterprise either alone or jointly with any other enterprises controlled by it:

977. Art. 6 WEOR.
978. If the branch or group enterprise has the largest number of employees compared to the number of employees in other Member States.
979. Art. 2(6) WEOR. If that law is not the law of a Member State, this is determined by the law which applies to the group enterprise whose management represents the 'controlling' enterprise for the purposes of the WEOR.

(a) appoints more than one half of the members of the administrative, managing or supervisory body of the other enterprise; or
(b) exercises more than one half of the voting rights in the shareholders' meeting (assuming all votes were cast); or
(c) provides more than one half of the issued capital of the other enterprise.[980]

An enterprise has a community-scale dimension for the purposes of the WEOR if, for the two preceding years, it had 150 or more employees in each of two Member States, and, in the aggregate, 1,000 employees or more in all Member States (Dutch community-scale enterprise).[981]

A group of enterprises has a community-scale dimension for the purposes of the WEOR if it consists of a controlling enterprise and one or more group enterprises of which two or more are established in different Member States and, for the two preceding years, at least one enterprise had on average at least 150 employees in one Member State and another enterprise had on average at least 150 employees in another Member State and group enterprises had, in the aggregate, 1,000 or more employees in all Member States (Dutch community-scale group).[982]

The law of each Member State determines whether an individual is considered to be an 'employee'. For people working in the Netherlands, the WEOR defines 'employees' as people working in a community-scale Enterprise or community-scale group on the basis of an employment agreement.[983]

The obligations of the WEOR to institute a European works council or an agreed procedure rest upon the central management of the Dutch community-scale enterprise or Dutch community-scale group, as defined above.

For a Dutch community-scale group, central management is defined as the central management of the controlling undertaking.[984]

980. Art. 2(1)-(2) WEOR. If more than one group enterprise meets one or more of these tests, the enterprise which meets the test under (a) is deemed to be the 'controlling' enterprise, and the right to appoint managing directors shall prevail. If no enterprise meets the test under (a), the test under (b) shall prevail over the test under (c), without prejudice to the right to establish that yet another enterprise should be considered to be the 'controlling' enterprise (Art. 2(7) WEOR).
981. Art. 1(1)(c) WEOR.
982. Art. 1(1)(d) WEOR.
983. Art. 3(1) WEOR. Individuals employed under Netherlands law other than civil servants, under a contract or otherwise, are deemed to have an employment agreement, with the exception of temporary employees, contractors and independent consultants.
984. Art. 1(1)(f) WEOR.

For a Dutch community-scale enterprise having its residence or seat outside the Member States, the central management for the purposes of the WEOR is deemed to be:[985]

(a) a person appointed by the community-scale enterprise who is charged with the actual management of (one of) its enterprise(s) within the Netherlands, or, in the absence of such designation;
(b) the person or persons who are charged with the actual management of the branch in the Netherlands.[986]

For a Dutch community-scale group whose controlling enterprise has its residence or seat outside the Member States, the central management for the purposes of the WEOR is deemed to be:[987]

(a) the management of a group enterprise having its residence or seat in the Netherlands and designated as such by the controlling enterprise; or, in the absence of such designation
(b) the management of such group enterprise in the Netherlands considered as such by the WEOR as a result of the fact that it employs the largest number of employees compared to the number of employees in other Member States.

The central management of a Dutch community-scale enterprise or Dutch Community-scale group may decide to form a special negotiating body (see § 13.3.3) in order to negotiate on the formation of a European works council or procedure for providing information to and consulting with its employees concerning transnational matters (agreed arrangements).[988] However, central management must form a special negotiating body upon the written request of 100 employees or more (or of their representatives,[989]) provided these employees represent two or more enterprises or branches in two or more different Member States.[990]

Central management is required to establish a European works council with the powers accruing to it by operation of the WEOR (a mandatory

985. Art. 1(2) WEOR.
986. This branch must have the largest number of employees compared to the number of employees in other Member States in order for the community-scale enterprise to qualify as 'Dutch'.
987. Art. 1(3) WEOR.
988. Art. 8(1) WEOR.
989. For employees working in the Netherlands, the relevant works councils are considered to be their representatives for this purpose (Art. 3(2) WEOR).
990. Art. 8(2) WEOR.

European works council formed under Netherlands law (statutory European works council) in the event:[991]

(a) central management has demonstrated its unwillingness to negotiate with a special negotiating body within a six-month period following a request thereto as referred to above; or
(b) central management and the special negotiating body have not concluded an agreed arrangement within the three-year period[992] following such request thereto, or, if central management had indeed formed a special negotiating body, within the three-year period following its formation.[993]

The powers of the statutory European works council (see § 13.3.4) are a benchmark for any agreed arrangement. Central management must ensure proper compliance with statutory European works councils, agreed arrangements and, as the case may be, any pre-existing agreements.[994]

13.3.2.2 Grandfathering Clause

Any Dutch community-scale enterprise or Dutch community-scale group that, prior to 5 February 1997, had concluded an agreement pertaining to the provision of information to and consultation with employees is exempt from the WEOR, provided such agreement was concluded with a party that the Dutch community-scale enterprise or Dutch community-scale group could have reasonably considered to be the representative of its employees.[995] A few large Dutch corporate groups have concluded such an agreement.

13.3.3 Special Negotiating Body

The Dutch members of a special negotiating body are elected employees only. They shall be appointed, or their appointment shall be withdrawn, by the

991. Art. 15 WEOR.
992. The WEOR does not provide for a maximum period for the actual formation of a European works council or an agreed arrangement.
993. Unless that special negotiating body had decided not to open or to discontinue negotiations (Arts 15, 11(2) WEOR).
994. Arts 11(8), 15, 24(2) WEOR.
995. Art. 24(1) WEOR. In order to remain exempt from the provisions of the WEOR, such agreements must provide, or be amended to provide, within the five-year period following the effective date of the WEOR, that the employees (or their representatives) of enterprises or branches which will become part of the Dutch community-scale enterprise or the Dutch community-scale group within such five-year period will be involved in the renewal or amendment of such agreements or will be represented in the agreed information and consultation procedure.

Dutch works councils of the branches or enterprises in the Netherlands.[996] The special negotiating body must be constituted in such a way that per Member State in which the Dutch community-scale enterprise or Dutch community-scale group has employees, one member shall be appointed for each 10%, or a part thereof, of the employees employed in such Member State, as a percentage of the overall number of employees.[997]

13.3.4 Statutory European Works Councils

13.3.4.1 General

The statutory European works council consists of elected employees only. The Dutch members of the statutory European works council shall be appointed, or their appointment shall be withdrawn, by the Dutch works council of the branches or enterprises in the Netherlands.[998] Their appointment shall be for a term of four years.[999] The statutory European works council must be constituted in such a way that per Member State in which such Dutch community-scale enterprise or Dutch community-scale group has employees, one member shall be appointed for each 10% or a part thereof, of the employees employed in such Member State, as a percentage of the overall number of employees.[1000]

13.3.4.2 Powers

13.3.4.2.1 General Limitation

The powers of a statutory European works council are limited to information and consultation on issues which are of importance for the whole Dutch community-scale enterprise or Dutch community-scale group or for at least two branches or enterprises of the group in different Member States. These powers are moreover limited to matters concerning all branches or enterprises of the group or concerning at least two branches or enterprises in different Member States.[1001]

996. Art. 10(1) WEOR. In the event that no Dutch works council has been established, the Dutch members of the special negotiating body shall be elected by the employees in the Netherlands (Art. 10(5) WEOR).
997. Art. 9(1) WEOR.
998. Arts 17(1), 10(1) WEOR. In the event that no Dutch works council has been established, the Dutch members of the statutory European works council shall be elected by the employees in the Netherlands (Arts 17(1), 10(5) WEOR).
999. Art. 17(1) WEOR.
1000. Art. 16(1) WEOR.
1001. Art. 1(1)(e) WEOR.

13.3.4.2.2 Annual Consultation Meetings

Central management is required, at least once every calendar year, to inform the statutory European works council in writing and consult with it concerning the general business and anticipated prospects of the Dutch community-scale enterprise or the Dutch community-scale group. The information and consultations with respect to such Dutch community-scale enterprise or Dutch community-scale group must in particular address:[1002]

(a) the structure of the enterprise or group;
(b) the financial and economic situation of the enterprise or group;
(c) the anticipated developments in activities, production and sales;
(d) capital expenditure;
(e) substantial changes in its organisation;
(f) the introduction of new work or production methods;
(g) its care for the environment;
(h) any merger;
(i) any relocation;
(j) any reductions in the number of or closures of enterprises, branches or important parts of the enterprise or group; and
(k) the currently existing status quo of developments in the workforce and any mass lay-offs.

13.3.4.2.3 Special Consultation Meetings

The central management of a Dutch community-scale enterprise or Dutch community-scale group must inform the statutory European works council of all the circumstances and proposed actions which could significantly affect the interests of the employees of two or more branches or enterprises located in different Member States, in particular regarding relocations or closures of branches or any mass lay-offs.[1003]

Upon the request of the statutory European works council, central management (or a more appropriate level of management having its own decision-making power as the case may be), is required to meet with the statutory European works council for consultation regarding the circumstances or proposed management actions under discussion on the basis of a written report prepared by management. This meeting must take place sufficiently early so that the provision of information and consultation is still meaningful.[1004]

1002. Art. 19(1) WEOR.
1003. Art. 19(2) WEOR.
1004. Art. 1(1)(g), (h) WEOR.

The statutory European works council is entitled to render non-binding recommendations with respect to the report within a reasonable time period following the special consultation meeting.[1005]

13.3.4.2.4 Withholding Information on the Grounds of Secrecy

Provided it can reasonably be anticipated that the disclosure of certain information would either seriously prejudice or harm the Dutch community-scale enterprise or Dutch community-scale group, central management is exempt from the obligation to provide such information to the statutory European works council.[1006] Moreover, central management, upon reasonable grounds, is entitled to require that the information that it is to provide be treated as confidential.[1007]

13.3.5 Minimum Requirements for Agreed Arrangements

Subject to certain minimum requirements, the WEOR offers central management and the special negotiating body ample freedom to tailor any agreed arrangement, resulting either in an agreed European works council or an agreed procedure, to their respective needs.[1008]

Central management and the special negotiating body may agree that for parts of the Dutch community-scale enterprise or Dutch community-scale group separate agreed European works councils shall be established or separate agreed procedures shall apply. Alternatively, they may agree that for one or more parts of the Dutch community-scale enterprise or the Dutch community-scale group, one or more agreed European works councils shall be formed and that one or more agreed procedures shall apply to different parts.[1009]

However, any agreed arrangement must contain provisions regarding the term of the agreed arrangement, the manner of negotiating a new agreed arrangement and the manner in which the agreed arrangement is to be amended to reflect any changes in the structure or size of the Dutch community-scale enterprise or Dutch community-scale group or in the numbers of employees in the Member States.[1010]

1005. Art. 1(1)(h) WEOR.
1006. Art. 19(6) WEOR.
1007. Art. 19(6) WEOR.
1008. Art. 11 WEOR.
1009. Art. 11(5) WEOR.
1010. Art. 11(6) WEOR. If the agreed arrangement does not provide that the employees (or their representatives) of enterprises or branches which are to become part of the Dutch community-scale enterprise or the Dutch community-scale group following its conclusion will be involved in the renewal or amendment of such agreed arrangement within a two-year period, or will be represented in the agreed European works council or involved in an agreed procedure, central

13.3.6 Job Protection and Secrecy

Except for 'urgent cause', an employee working in the Netherlands who is a member of a special negotiating body or a statutory works council, or who was a member of either during the preceding two-year period, cannot be dismissed without the approval of the cantonal division of the District Court. The Court shall ensure that the reason for the proposed dismissal does not relate to membership of the special negotiating body or the statutory works council.[1011]

Members of the special negotiating body and the statutory works council are under a strict obligation of secrecy.[1012] The same job protection and secrecy rules apply with respect to members of an agreed European works council or employees involved in an agreed procedure.[1013]

13.3.7 Interaction with the WOR

Employees and their representatives have less powers under the WEOR than under the WOR. Statutory European works councils can deliver non-binding recommendations only. Central management may disregard such recommendations and is not required to suspend any actions following a negative recommendation, as is the case where a matter requires the formal advice of a Dutch works council (see § 13.2.4.3).

The WEOR does not restrict the powers of Dutch works councils.

13.3.8 Enforcement of Compliance with the WEOR

Each interested party[1014] is entitled to request that the Enterprise Court enforces the WEOR, with the exception of matters relating to the job protection and secrecy rules for members of a special negotiating body, a statutory European works council, an agreed European works council and the employees involved in an agreed procedure.[1015] A special negotiating body, its members and a European works council, established by virtue of the WEOR, cannot be ordered to pay the procedural costs of such an action.

---

management must, upon the request of 100 or more or such employees (or their representatives), form a new special negotiating body (Art. 11(6) WEOR).

1011. Arts 7:670(4), 7:670a BW.

1012. Art. 4(4)-(6) WEOR.

1013. Art. 4(1) WEOR.

1014. The Minister for Social Affairs and Employment has indicated that for this purpose 'interested parties' include the special negotiating body and the statutory European works council, as well as representatives of employees in other procedures for informing and consultation of employees (MvT TK 24641, No. 3, p. 23). The relevant trade unions would therefore also qualify as 'interested parties'.

1015. Art. 5 WEOR.

List of Abbreviations

AFM	*Stichting Autoriteit Financiële Markten* (Netherlands Authority for the Financial Markets)
BV	*Besloten vennootschap met beperkte aansprakelijkheid* (Dutch private limited liability company)
BVIE	*Benelux Verdrag inzake de Intellectuele Eigendom* (Benelux Convention on Intellectual Property)
BW	*Burgerlijk Wetboek* (Civil Code)
CCP	Code of Civil Procedure (see also Rv)
CGC	(Dutch) Corporate Governance Code
CJEU	Court of Justice of the European Union
EEIG	European Economic Interest Grouping
EK	*Eerste Kamer* (Upper House)
EU	European Union
Euroclear	Euroclear Nederland (Central Securities Depository of the Netherlands)
HrB 2008	*Handelsregisterbesluit 2008* (Commercial Register Decree)
HrW 2007	*Handelsregisterwet 2007* (Commercial Register Act)
HnW	*Handelsnaamwet* (Trade Names Act)
Inv. 1990	*Invorderingswet 1990* (Collection of State Taxes Act 1990)
MvA	*Memorie van Antwoord* (Memorandum of Reply)
MvT	*Memorie van Toelichting* (Explanatory Memorandum)

NMa	*Nederlandse Mededingsingsautoriteit* (Netherlands Competition Authority)
NV	*Naamloze vennootschap* (Dutch public limited liability company)
OJ. EUR.COMM.	Official Journal of the European Union
RO	*Wet op de rechterlijke organisatie* (Judicial Structure Act)
Rv	*Wetboek van Burgerlijke Rechtsvordering* (Code of Civil Procedure or CCP)
SCE	*Societas Cooperativa Europaea* (European Co-operative)
Stb.	*Staatsblad* (Official Statute Book)
SE	*Societas Europaea* (European Public Company)
Stcrt.	*Staatscourant* (Government Gazette)
TFEU	Treaty on the Functioning of the European Union as amended by the Treaty of Lisbon and in force since 1 December 2009
TK	*Tweede Kamer* (Lower House)
Trb.	*Tractatenblad* (Treaty Book)
WED	*Wet op de Economische Delicten* (Economic Offences Act)
WEOR	*Wet op de Europese ondernemingsraden* (European Works Councils Act)
Wet KvK 1997	*Wet op de Kamers van Koophandel en Fabrieken 1997* (Chambers of Commerce and Industry Act)
Wfbv	*Wet op de formeel buitenlandse vennootschappen* (Formal Foreign Entities Act)
Wfsv	*Wet financiering sociale verzekeringen* (Social Insurance (Funding) Act)
Wft	*Wet op het financieel toezicht* (Financial Supervision Act)
Wge	*Weg giraal effectenverkeer* (Securities Giro Act)

Wna	*Wet op het notarisambt* (Notaries Act)
WOR	*Wet op de ondernemingsraden* (Works Council Act)
Wtfv	*Wet toezicht financiële verslaglegging* (Act on the Supervision of Financial Reporting)
WvK	*Wetboek van Koophandel* (Commercial Code)

Legal Journals

JAR	*Jurisprudentie Arbeidsrecht* (Case law)
JOR	*Jurisprudentie Onderneming & Recht* (Case law)
LJN	*Landelijk Jurisprudentie Nummer* (number given to all judicial decisions published in the Netherlands, most of them to be found on <www.rechtspraak.nl>), in the course of 2013 to be substituted by the ECLI (European Case Law Identifier)
NJ	*Nederlandse Jurisprudentie* (Case law)

List of References

Asser/Van Der Grinten/Kortmann 2-I 2004
S.C.J.J. Kortmann, Mr. C. Assers Handleiding tot de beoefening van het Nederlands Burgerlijk Recht. 2. Vertegenwoordiging en rechtspersoon. Deel I, De vertegenwoordiging, Kluwer, Deventer, 2004

Asser/Maeijer & Van Olffen 7-VII 2010*
M. van Olffen, Mr. C. Assers Handleiding tot de beoefening van het Nederlands Burgerlijk Recht. 7. Bijzondere overeenkomsten. Deel VII. Personenvennootschappen, Kluwer, Deventer, 2010

Asser/Maeijer, Van Solinge & Nieuwe Weme 2-II 2009*
G. van Solinge & M.P. Nieuwe Weme (m.m.v. R.G.J. Nowak), Mr. C. Assers Handleiding tot de beoefening van het Nederlands Burgerlijk Recht. 2. Rechtspersonenrecht. Deel II. De naamloze en besloten vennootschap, Kluwer, Deventer, 2009

Asser/Rensen 2-III 2012*
G.J.C. Rensen (m.m.v. J.M. Blanco Fernández), Mr. C. Assers Handleiding tot de beoefening van het Nederlands Burgerlijk Recht. 2. Rechtspersonenrecht. Deel III. Overige rechtspersonen. Vereniging, coöperatie, onderlinge waarborgmaatschappij, stichting, kerkgenootschap en Europese rechtsvormen, Kluwer, Deventer, 2012

Grapperhaus & Verburg 2009
F.J. Grapperhaus & L.C. Verburg, Employment Law and Works Councils of the Netherlands, Kluwer Law International, The Hague, 2009

Jennen & Van de Vijver 2010
B. Jennen & N. van de Vijver, Banking and Securities Regulation in the Netherlands, Kluwer Law International, The Hague, 2010

Van Hooijdonk & Eijsvoogel 2012
Marieke Van Hooijdonk & Peter Eijsvoogel, Litigation in The Netherlands, Kluwer Law International, The Hague, 2012

Offices of Allen & Overy

See www.allenovery.com for more information on Allen & Overy and its international offices.

Abu Dhabi
5th Floor
Al Mamoura Building B
Muroor Road
Abu Dhabi
United Arab Emirates
Tel.: (+971 2) 418 0400

Amsterdam
Apollolaan 15
1077 AB Amsterdam
The Netherlands
Tel.: (+31 20) 674 1000

Antwerp
Uitbreidingstraat 80
B-2600 Antwerp
Belgium
Tel.: (+32 3) 287 7222

Athens
2 Navarchou Nikodimou
Athens 10557
Greece
Tel.: (+30 21) 0325 6030

Bangkok
22nd Floor,
Sindhorn Building III
130-132 Wireless Road
Bangkok 10330
Thailand
Tel.: (+662 2) 63 7600

Beijing
46th Floor China World Tower
No. 1 Jian Guo Men Wai Avenue
Beijing
100004
China
Tel.: (+86 10) 6535 4188

Belfast
Allen & Overy (SSF) Ltd
68 Donegall Quay
BT1 3NL Belfast
United Kingdom
Tel.: (+44 28) 90 607500

Bratislava
Eurovea Central 1
Pribinova 4
Bratislava
81109
Slovakia
Tel.: (+421 2) 5920 2400

Brussels
Avenue de Tervueren 268 A
B-1150 Brussels
Belgium
Tel.: (+32 2) 780 2222

Bucharest
Radu Tărăcilă Pădurari Retevoescu SCA in association with Allen & Overy LLP
60 Dacia Boulevard
020061 Bucharest
Romania
Tel.: (+40 31) 405 7777

Budapest
Madách Trade Center
Madách Imre utca 13-14
H-1075 Budapest
Hungary
Tel.: (+36 1) 483 2200

Casablanca
Naciri & Associés Allen & Overy
Twin Center - Tour A, 7th floor
Corner of Boulevard Zerktouni and Massira Al Khadra
Casablanca
Morocco
Tel.: (+ 212 520) 478 000

Doha
Allen & Overy LLP
23rd Floor, Tornado Tower
Al Funduq Street
West Bay
Doha
Qatar
Tel.: (+ 974 44) 19 4444

Dubai
Level 2
Gate Village Building No. 8
Dubai International Financial Centre
Dubai
United Arab Emirates
Tel.: (+971 4) 426 7100

Frankfurt
Haus am OpernTurm
Bockenheimer Landstraße 2
60306 Frankfurt am Main
Germany
Tel.: (+49 69) 2648 5000

Hamburg
Kehrwieder 12
20457 Hamburg
Germany
Tel.: (+49 40) 82 22 12 0

Hanoi
5th Floor, Pacific Place
83B Ly Thuong Kiet
Hoan Kiem District
Hanoi
Vietnam
Tel.: (+84 4) 6270 5388

Hong Kong
9th Floor
Three Exchange Square
Central
Hong Kong
Tel.: (+852 2) 974 7000

Istanbul
Allen & Overy Danismanlik
Hizmetleri Avukatlik Ortakligi
Buyukdere Çad. No:185,
Kanyon Ofis Binası, Kat:6, Ofis No:
1018-1022
Levent/ Sisli, 34394 Istanbul
Turkey
Tel.: (+ 90 212) 371 2907

Jakarta
Ginting & Reksodiputro in association with Allen & Overy LLP
The Energy Building, 15th Floor
Sudirman Central Business District
Jl Jend Sudirman Kav 52-53
Jakarta
12190
Indonesia
Tel.: (+62 21) 2995 1700

London
One Bishops Square
E1 6AD London
United Kingdom
Tel.: (+44 20) 3088 0000

Luxemburg
33 avenue J.F. Kennedy
L-1855
Luxembourg
Tel.: (+352) 4444 551

Madrid
Pedro de Valdivia 10
28006 Madrid
Spain
Tel.: (+34 91) 782 9800

Milan
Via Manzoni, 4
20121 Milan
Italy
Tel.: (+39 02) 290 491

Moscow
Dmitrovsky pereulok 9
Moscow
107031
Russia
Tel.: (+7 495) 725 7900

New York
1221 Avenue of the Americas
New York, NY 10020
United States of America
Tel.: (+1 212) 610 6300

Paris
52 avenue Hoche
CS 90005
75008 Paris
France
Tel.: (+33 1) 4006 5400

Prague
V Celnici 4
5th Floor
110 00 Prague
Czech Republic
Tel.: (+420 2) 2210 7111

Rome
Corso Vittorio Emanuele II, 284
00186 Rome
Italy
Tel.: (+39 06) 684 271

São Paulo
Allen & Overy LLP - Consultores em Direito
Estrangeiro / Direito Norte-Americano
Rua das Olimpíadas, 100 - 10°andar
Vila Olímpia
CEP 04551-000 São Paulo
Brazil
Tel.: (+55 11) 3848 8750

Shanghai
15F, Phase II, Shanghai IFC
8 Century Avenue
Pudong
Shanghai
200120
China
Tel.: (+86 21) 2036 7000

Singapore
50 Collyer Quay
#09-01 OUE Bayfront
Singapore
049321
Singapore
Tel.: (+65 6) 671 6000

Sydney
Level 25
85 Castlereagh Street
Sydney
NSW 2000
Australia
Tel.: (+61 2) 9373 7700

Tokyo
Allen & Overy Gaikokuho Kyodo
Jigyo Horitsu Jimusho
38F Roppongi Hills Mori Tower
6-10-1 Roppongi, Minato-ku
106-6138 Tokyo
Japan
Tel.: (+81 3) 6438 5200

Warsaw
Rondo ONZ 1
34 floor
Warsaw 00124
Poland
Tel.: (+48 22) 820 6100

Washington, D.C.
1301 K Street NW
9th Floor, East Tower
Washington, D.C.
20005
United States
Tel.: (+1 202) 683 3800

DUTCH BUSINESS LAW SERIES

1. Ferdinand B.J. Grapperhaus and Leonard G. Verburg, *Employment Law and Works Councils of the Netherlands*, 2009 (ISBN 978-90-411-2858-4)

2. Bas Jennen and Niels van de Vijver, *Banking and Securities Regulation in the Netherlands*, 2010 (ISBN 978-90-411-2863-8)

3. Marieke van Hooijdonk and Peter Eijsvoogel, *Litigation in the Netherlands: Civil Procedure, Arbitration and Administrative Litigation*, 2012 (ISBN 978-90-411-4143-9)

4. Maarten H. Muller, *Corporate Law in the Netherlands*, 2013 (ISBN 978-90-411-2864-5)

www.ingramcontent.com/pod-product-compliance
Lightning Source LLC
Chambersburg PA
CBHW071243230926
51849CB00001B/207
9789041128645